W9-BHG-258

A

GLOSSARY OF REFERENCE

ON

SUBJECTS CONNECTED WITH THE FAR EAST

A

GLOSSARY OF REFERENCE

ON

SUBJECTS CONNECTED WITH THE FAR EAST

BY

HERBERT A. GILES, M.A., LL.D. (Aberd.)

*Professor of Chinese in the University of Cambridge
and late H.B.M. Consul at Ningpo*

THIRD EDITION

LONDON
CURZON PRESS

ROWMAN & LITTLEFIELD
TOTOWA, N. J.

First published 1878
Second edition 1886
Third edition 1900
Reprinted 1974

Curzon Press Ltd · London and Dublin

and

Rowman & Littlefield · Totowa · N. J.

ISBN

UK 0 7007 0041 2
US 0 87471 510 5

Printed in Great Britain
by Kingprint Ltd · Richmond · Surrey

EXTRACT FROM PREFACE TO FIRST EDITION.

The following curious passage occurs in an able article on *The Anglo-Indian Tongue* published in Blackwood's Magazine for May 1877:—

> No man can ever expect to be appreciated in Anglo-Indian society until he has caught up its shibboleth, no matter how great his other accomplishments may be..... In Madras the native domestics speak English of purity and idiom which rival in eccentricity the famous *pidgin* English of the treaty ports in China; and the masters mechanically adopt the language of their servants. Thus an Englishman wishing to assure himself that an order has been duly executed, asks, "Is that done gone finished, Appoo?" and Appoo replies in the same elegant phraseology, "Yes, sare, all done gone finished whole."

Now it is partly as a key to the shibboleth of Anglo-Chinese society that this *Glossary* has been designed, though to judge by the opening lines of the same article, which the writer tells us would be perfectly intelligible in a Calcutta drawing-room, there is no comparison between the phraseological difficulties in the way of new arrivals in the Far East and those to be encountered by the "griffin" who wishes to be appreciated in Anglo-Indian society. These lines run thus:

> I'm dikk'ed to death! The khansamah has got chhutti, and the whole bangla is ulta-pulta. The khidmatghars loot everything, and the masalchi is breaking all the surwa-basans; and when I give a hukhm to cut their tallabs, they get magra and ask their jawabs. And then the maistries are putting up jill-mills, and making such a gol-mol ("pompon bobbery" in Japanese Pidgin-English,) that I say darwaza band to everybody. But when all is tik, I hope you will tiff with us.
>
> The translation of this is:—I'm bothered to death! The butler has got leave, and the whole house is turned upside down. The table-servants steal everything, and the scullion is breaking all the soup-plates; and when I order their wages to be cut, they all grow sulky and give warning. And then the carpenters are putting up venetians, and making such an uproar, that I am obliged to say "not at home" to everybody. But when all is put to rights, I hope you will lunch with us.

A GLOSSARY OF REFERENCE

ABACUS *or* SWAN-P'AN: 算 盤 —calculating tray. A wooden frame in which are fixed a number of beads strung upon parallel wires. It is used by the Chinese for all kinds of arithmetical calculations. The system is one of decimals, and the beads are divided into two sections; the lower containing five beads, each representing 1 or unit, and the upper only two, but each representing 5. Thus, to write down 1, one of the beads on the lower half of the frame is pushed up to the division between the sections, and so on up to four; five is written by bringing down a bead from the top section to the other side of the division; nine by pushing four up from below and bringing down a five from above; and ten by pushing up one of the lower beads on the nearest left-hand wire to that on which the calculator first chose to represent his units, and so on. Very intricate calculations can be performed by an expert on the *swan-p'an*, and quite as rapidly as with pen and ink, but with the signal disadvantage of not being able to work backwards in search of a fault, each step disappearing as the work proceeds.

Abacus is from the Hebrew word *abak* (dust), tables covered with dust having been used in early ages among the Jews for purposes of writing and calculation. The abacus which replaced these originally contained six wires with ten beads on each.

ABHIDHARMA : 論. The philosophical section of Buddhist literature. See *Tripitaka.*

ACCAD *or* AKKADIA. The south-eastern division of ancient Babylonia, mentioned as a city in Genesis x. 10. Its people appear to have been the originators of Babylonish civilisation and of the earliest form of cuneiform writing, which was vertical. They were also called "the black-haired;" and from these and a few other points of contact the late T. de la Couperie jumped to the conclusion that Accad was the cradle of the Chinese race. The following is a specimen of his arguments. He identifies the monarch Nakhunte of Elamite history with the legendary Chinese Emperor Nai Huang Ti. But *Nai* was a mistaken reading published by the late W. F. Mayers in his chronological tables. We are told in K'ang Hsi's lexicon that the character in question should be read *Hsiung.*

ACTOR. See *Theatre.*

ACUPUNCTURE : 鍼法. Has been known and practised in China for the past 2,000 years.

AGAR-AGAR : 海菜. The Malay term for a kind of sea-weed *(Fucus saccharinus)*, used in China to express edible sea-weed generally.

AIMAK : 愛瑪克. A Mongolian "tribe" 部.

AINOS *or* AINUS : 鰕夷—crab barbarians. The name of a tribe of aborigines, also called Jebis, extending from Japan to Kamschatka. "They pass their time in running up huts "of leaves, planting vegetables, stitching skins and pieces "of bark for clothing, and catching salmon, which they "salt in huge quantities."

The above two characters are used by the Chinese, interchangeably with 毛人 "hairy people," (Jap. *mosin*) for the people of Yesso, who were believed to burrow in the ground like crabs. The inhabitants of the island of Saghalien are similarly called 北蝦夷 —northern crab barbarians.

"The original inhabitants, the Aino, are now only to be "seen in the northern island of Yezo." *Adams*.

Their numerals are: —

1—Schnape		6—U-an
2—Tupaisch		7—Aruan
3—Lepaisch		8—Topaishi
4—Mede		9—Schnapaishi
5—Aschkei		10—Wambi

"Aino, literally *man*, is the name by which the Ainos "designate themselves." *B. H. Chamberlain*.

Aino is also said to be a corruption of *inu* 犬 a dog.

ALCHEMY: 煉金法術. Has been practised in China for many centuries. Dr. Martin (*China Review*, vol. VII, p. 242) would have us believe that "alchemy is indigenous "to China, and coeval with the dawn of letters." His proofs however are drawn from works admittedly spurious, and in one case (page 254, note 2) he quotes in connection with alchemy a poem which refers only to the elixir of life. Altogether it would appear that alchemy was unknown in China before the 2nd cent. A.D., and its existence even then is probably due to Greek influence.

ALEURITES: 石栗—stone chestnuts. The fruit of the *A. triloba*, a handsome tree belonging to the *N. O. Euphorbiaceae*, and a native of Polynesia, southern Asia, and some of the Malay islands. Is grown in the south of

China, and the word frequently appears in the Hongkong market list. The seeds are said to be aphrodisiac, and yield an oil used for burning.

ALMARI. A wardrobe. Commonly used in India ; also in Hongkong and the Straits. From the Latin *armarium* through the Portuguese *almario*.

ALMOND EYES : 杏 眼. This is a common metaphor in Chinese, and is not, as is usually supposed, the exclusive product of the English language.

A-LUM. The famous Hongkong baker whose bread was poisoned with arsenic by some person never discovered, in the hope of destroying all the foreign residents in the Colony : January 1857.

AMAH : 阿 媽. A nurse; from the Portuguese *ama*. Used in India of *wet nurses* only. In the north of China *ma-ma* is frequently heard, meaning either mother or nurse, and may be compared with the Sanskrit *amma* which has the same signification.

Ayah, also from the Portuguese *aia*, is not common in China.

AMAINU. Japanese name for the stone lions at the gates of temples and elsewhere.

AMBAN : 昂 拜. A Manchu word, signifying *governor*. Frequently applied by European writers to the political representatives of China in Mongolia and Turkestan.

AMBER : 琥 珀. Believed by the Chinese to be resin, which after lying in the earth for a thousand years is changed into 茯 苓 China Root *(q.v.)*, which in turn changes into amber. It is mentioned in the history of the Han dynasty as coming from 罽 賓 Kophene or the modern Cabulistan and Ta-ch'in *(q.v.)* or Syria. Others say it is made from burning bees-wax, while the *Pên-ts'ao* explains it as 虎魄 the soul of the tiger which goes into the earth at death.

AMHERST'S EMBASSY, LORD. A mission dispatched from England to China in 1816, during the reign of the Emperor Chia Ch'ing, with a view to putting trade upon a more satisfactory basis. Among the Ambassador's suite were Sir G. Staunton, Dr. Morrison, and Sir John Davis. Lord Amherst, however, refused to perform the *kotow*, and returned from Peking without having seen the Emperor. Bonaparte said that he thought "the English ministers "had acted wrong in not having ordered Lord Amherst "to comply with the custom of the place he was sent "to, or that they ought not to have sent him at all.... "It is my opinion that whatever is the custom of a nation "and is practised by the first characters of that nation "towards their chief, cannot degrade strangers who perform "the same." *W. Forsyth.*

AMIDA BUDDHA. See *Ometo Fu.*

AMOK *or* AMUCK. A term used by Malays to signify an ungovernable state of mind, in which a desire to murder is predominant. It has been supposed to be a kind of monomania induced by disorder of the digestive organs, but is frequently indulged in to gratify revenge. A crowd will sometimes (as when Mr. Birch was killed) raise a cry of "Amok, amok!" = "Ta, ta!" *(q.v.)* in China.

"An Amok took place last night, by a Malay, which "resulted in the loss of his own life and the wounding of "16 persons. The Chinese in the Campong *(q.v.)* came "forward, and this appeared to excite him to a violent "degree. He ran amok among them, and wounded a "number before he could be seized." *Straits Times.*

AMOOR *or* AMUR: 黑龍江 —black dragon river. Amoor = great river.

AMOY: 厦門 —gate or harbour of Hsia. Also known to the Chinese as 鷺島 —Egret Island—from the large number of white egrets which annually frequent this locality. It was one of the five ports opened by Nanking Treaty of 1842, but visited by the Portuguese as early as 1544, and later on by the English until 1730, when trade there was forbidden to all nations except the Spanish, though as a matter of fact it continued much as usual. Our word is from the local pronunciation of the first two characters. See *Ku-lang Su.*

AMUY: 亞妹. Younger sister. Cantonese amahs frequently give the above as their *name*, whence results the edifying spectacle of a European mistress calling her Chinese nurse "sister." As a rule, foreigners in China who do not understand the language will do well to avoid names, and address their servants as "boy," "coolie," or "amah," as the case may be. In one well-known instance a Chinese valet said his name was Tek-koh, and his master forthwith proceeded to call him so, *i.e.*—brother Tek.

ANÆSTHETICS: 迷蒙藥. Said to have been first used in the form of hashish by a famous surgeon named 華佗 Hua T'o who died A.D. 220.

ANALECTS: 論語. A name chosen by Dr. Legge for his translation of the third of the Four Books *(q.v.)*, containing the *Discourses* of Confucius with his disciples and others. The Confucian Gospels. They were compiled, according to Chinese accounts, by the actual disciples of Confucius; but Dr. Legge shews that it was more probably by *their* disciples towards the end of the fifth or beginning of the fourth century B.C.

"The Book of Proverbs is not a whit better than the "maxims of Confucius, so far as we know them." Inman's *Ancient Faiths*, II. 761.

E. G. — "Love one another." "Return good for good; "for evil, justice." "What you would not others should do "unto you, do not unto them."

"Let loyalty and truth be paramount with you. Have "no friends not equal to yourself. If you have faults, shrink "not from correcting them."

"Man is born to be upright. If he be not so, and yet "live, he is lucky to have escaped."

"In mourning, it is better to be sincere than to be "punctilious." See *Confucius*.

ANCESTRAL WORSHIP. A Chinese religious ceremony performed on stated occasions before tablets inscribed with the names of deceased ancestors, and consisting of prayers, prostrations, and offerings of food and paper-money to the spirits of the dead. The early Jesuit fathers *(q.v.)* tolerated this harmless custom among the first converts to Christianity; but the jealous rivalry of other orders brought about a direct prohibition from Clement XI. against the established practice, a move which only resulted in the ultimate collapse of Roman Catholic influence in China and the subsequent persecution of all Catholic missionaries.

Abusive language is commonly used amongst the Chinese in jest; but the line is drawn at a man's progenitors, whose persons or memories, as the case may be, are always held strictly sacred. It is only in serious brawls, when words have already given place to blows, that mutual vilification of ancestors is heard, though relatives of the same generation may be freely abused without fear of disastrous consequences.

ANDIJANI, THE. A term which has occasionally been applied in the *Peking Gazette* to the late Yakub Khan or Yakoob Beg (阿古伯), once designated Ameer of Kashgar, from Andijan 安集延 the town in Kokand whence he and many of his followers came. He has also been styled 安酋 "the An[dijani] chieftain."

ANDON. The oil lamp of the Japanese, enclosed in a square or circular frame covered with paper.

AN-HUI: 安徽—"Peace and Beauty." One of the Eighteen Provinces. So called from the first characters in the names of its two largest cities, 安慶府 An-ch'ing Fu the capital, and 徽州府 Hui-chou Fu. Old name 皖·

ANNA. The sixteenth part of a rupee. Eurasians *(q.v.)* are often spoken of as so many annas in the rupee, referring to the proportion of "dark" blood in their veins. Thus, "four annas in the rupee" would be the equivalent of *Quadroon.*

ARGOLS. Cakes of dried camels' dung, used in Mongolia for fuel.

ARHAN *or* ARHAT: 阿羅漢—"deserving and worthy." The term applied by Chinese Buddhists to the 500 disciples of Shâkyamuni Buddha. Same as *Lo-han.*

The Eighteen Arhans, so often seen in Chinese temples, are regarded as the personal disciples of Buddha. Sixteen of these were Hindus, and two Chinese have been added.

ARIMAS. Japanese equivalent of "have got."

ARIMASEN. Japanese equivalent of "no got."

ARMS: 兵器. Bows and arrows, swords, and spears, have been employed in China from time immemorial. In later ages cross-bows drawn and discharged by machinery, huge ballistae, etc., were much used. Then came rude matchlocks (see *Jingal*), and cannon which the *Jesuits (q.v.)* taught the Chinese to cast, which state of things lasted until after the war of 1860—1861. In ancient times, buff jerkins and armour were worn by combatants.

ARMY, THE CHINESE. Looks well on paper, consisting, according to statute, of about 330,000 infantry in garrison, 200,000 infantry, and 90,000 cavalry, besides about 250,000 Manchus arranged under the Eight Banners *(q.v.)*. Many of these warriors, however, appear only on the pay-sheets, and have no real existence.

"ARROW" CASE, THE. On Oct. 8, 1856, a party of Chinese under an officer boarded a lorcha, called the *Arrow*, in the Canton river. They took off twelve sailors on a charge of piracy, leaving two of their own men on the lorcha. The *Arrow* was declared by its owners to be a British vessel. Our Consul at Canton, Mr. (afterwards Sir Harry) Parkes, demanded from Yeh, the Chinese Viceroy, the return of the men. Yeh contended, however, that the lorcha was not an English but a Chinese vessel—a Chinese pirate, venturing occasionally for her own purposes to fly the flag of England which she had no right whatever to hoist. The *Arrow* had somehow obtained British registration, but it had expired about ten days before the occurrence in the Canton river. As a matter of fact, the *Arrow* was not an English vessel, but only a Chinese vessel which had obtained by false pretences the temporary possession of a British flag. Sir J. Bowring sent to the Chinese authorities, and demanded the surrender of all the men taken from the *Arrow*. He insisted that an apology should be offered for their arrest, and a formal pledge given that no such act should ever be committed again.... Yeh sent back the men.... and he even undertook to promise that for the future great care should be taken that no British ship should be visited improperly by Chinese officers. But he could not offer an apology. Accordingly Sir J. Bowring immediately made war on China, and Canton was bombarded by the fleet which Admiral Sir Michael Seymour commanded.

ASANKYA. A Buddhist number, extending to 141 places of figures.

ATHALIK GHAZI. "Champion Father,"—a title conferred in 1874 by the Ameer of Bokhara upon the celebrated Yakoob Beg.

ATTAP. The dried leaf of the nipah palm, doubled over a small stick of bamboo, and thus used in the Malay peninsula for roofing houses.

AWABI. A kind of shell-fish found in Japanese and Korean waters.

BABA. A local name for Chinese born in the Straits Settlements, and for the children of foreigners. Used in India as a respectful form of address towards a man of the lower or middle classes. From the Turki *bābā* father. See *Sinkeh*.

BABOO. The Bengali equivalent of "Mr."

BABY TOWER: 骨 塔. Brick receptacles for *dead* children of both sexes, below the age which qualifies for burial in the usual way. The Chinese have been falsely accused of depositing living children in these Towers. See *Infanticide*.

BADGES, MANDARIN: 補 子. Large pieces of embroidery worn on official robes, the different grades of civil officials being distinguished by various birds, those of military officials by animals.

BAIL. Is personal, not pecuniary, in China. That is, if the bailee absconds, the bailor has to take his place.

BAJU. The upper portion of the Malay dress.

BAKA: 馬 鹿—horse deer. A Japanese term of abuse —*Fool!*

BAKIN, KIOKUTEI. A.D. 1767—1848. The famous Japanese novelist, author of about 300 works, many of which are very voluminous.

BALACHONG. A relish made of pickled fish. From the Malay *bâlachan.*

BAMBOO: 竹. Originally *mambu*, as known to the early Portuguese settlers in India, and possibly a Canarese word. Hence is said to be derived the word "bamboozle," the allusion being to a certain treacherous kind of swimming-belt made of bamboo.

The bamboo is the common instrument for flogging criminals in China, and consists of a strip of split bamboo planed down smooth. Strictly speaking, there are two kinds, the *heavy* and the *light*; the former, however, is now hardly if ever used. Until the reign of K'ang Hsi, all strokes were given across the back; but that Emperor removed the *locus operandi* lower down, for fear of injuring the liver or the lungs—a curious fact when taken in conjunction with the statement by the late Dr. Ayres, Colonial Surgeon at Hongkong, that flogging Chinese on the back is apt to bring about congestion of the lungs or other pulmonary complaints.

In point of utility to man the bamboo is probably unrivalled. It is employed in the manufacture of almost every conceivable object of household furniture or domestic use, and is frequently spoken of as "the friend of China." Its varieties are numerous. The thorny bamboo 棘 竹 grows to nearly 50 feet in height, with a diameter of from 2 to 3 feet. The speckled bamboo 斑 竹 is prettily mottled;—it shaded the grave of the famous Shun (see

Yao), and was thus marked by the tears of his two disconsolate widows. A variety with a square stem grows in the Fuhkien province.

A *bamboo* is the slang term for a wine-glassful of sherry and vermouth in equal proportions.

BAMBOO BOOKS, THE: 竹書紀. A collection of ancient writings inscribed in the Lesser Seal character on slips of bamboo, and said to have been discovered A.D. 279. Among the rest was a copy of the Book of Changes *(q.v.)*. Bamboo tablets were commonly used in China before the invention of paper.

BAMBOO CHOW-CHOW. "Stick food." The pidgin-English term for a thrashing, an idiom not altogether unknown either in English or in the elegant book-language of China: —不然脛股當有椎喫 "If you don't, you'll *have a taste* of the stick." A Mahommedan who is bastinadoed is said to be made to "eat stick."

BAMBOO GROVE: 竹林. A famous club, founded in the 3rd century A.D. and consisting of seven members 七賢 of strong Bacchanalian tendencies. The most famous of them was Liu Ling, who expressed a wish to be buried near a pottery, in order that his body might re-appear on earth under the form of wine-cups.

BAMBOO OYSTERS. A small and delicately-flavoured species of oyster found at the port of Foochow. Large bamboos are cut down and planted deeply in the water, the ends being first fired to prevent decay; and upon these stakes the oysters collect in large quantities. Hence the name.

BAMBOO SHOOTS: 笋. Are given by the Chinese to suckling mothers to increase the flow of milk. Europeans eat them served like asparagus.

BANANA. See *Plantain*.

BANGLE. A bracelet or anklet. From the Hindi word *bangree* or *bangrī* a bracelet of glass.

BANIAN *or* BANYAN 榕樹. (1) The *ficus wightiana*, Wall., common in China. (2) The name by which Hindi traders are known abroad, *e.g.* at Muscat and Zanzibar. In this sense a corruption of Baniya or Vāniya, the name of a trading caste in India with which sailors were early brought into contact. In common with most other respectable castes, its members abstain from flesh. Hence the old term "Banyan days" at sea, *sc.* Mondays, Wednesdays, and Fridays, when no meat was served out.

BANIAN CITY, THE: 榕城. A fancy name for Foochow, from the number of banian trees which grow there.

BANNERS, THE EIGHT: 八旗. The eight divisions under which the Manchus are marshalled, first established in 1814 to supersede the division of the Manchu army under three nationalities. The banners are red, yellow, white, and blue; four being plain (正), and four bordered (鑲) with a margin of another colour. Hence Manchus are often spoken of as Bannermen. There are also eight Mongol and eight Chinese "banners," the latter being descendants of those natives who assisted in consolidating the Manchu dynasty. See *Army.*

BARBARIANS. The common Chinese designation for all foreigners. By Treaty of Tientsin, 1858, it was agreed that thenceforward one of the worst characters 夷 *i* should "not be applied to the government or subjects of her "Britannic Majesty, in any Chinese official document issued "by the Chinese authorities either in the capital or in "the provinces." *Art. LI.*

The use of this term has now almost disappeared amongst the people as well; but only to be replaced by such synonymous words as 番 *fan* and 彝 *i*, by 毛子 *mao tzǔ (q.v.)*, by 鬼子 *kuei-tzǔ* "devils," etc. etc. The character 番 *fan*, which is quite as disrespectful as the Treaty-tabooed 夷 *i*[1], may still be seen in use all over Hongkong, and is often publicly placarded before the shops of Chinese tradesmen, washermen and others. Another term is "red-haired barbarians" 紅毛番, explained in the History of the Ming dynasty 明史 to be a common name for the Dutch 和蘭. But the most curious title of all is that frequently bestowed by the people of Swatow and its neighbourhood upon the various foreign Consular officers residing there. They are called "Jesus mandarins" 耶穌官, shewing, in this instance at any rate, how intimately the masses of China connect the presence of foreigners among them with other objects than that of legitimate trade alone.

Of the term 洋人 *yang jen* "men from beyond the sea," now generally accepted on all sides as the best equivalent for "foreigners," it is only necessary to say that, as far as mere phraseology goes, these words by no means place us on an equality with 中國人 "the men of the Middle Kingdom," though infinitely superior to 外國人 "outside nation men," an expression which has a force peculiarly its own. 西國人 "men of the western nation" is the least objectionable of all, now generally understood to include citizens of the United States; and if 泰 is prefixed, the term becomes as respectful as the most exacting can require.

BARBARIAN EYE: 夷目. An opprobrious epithet applied

---

[1] It is worthy of note that Tso Tsung-t'ang, in his last memorial on coast defence, spoke of foreigners collectively as 外夷.

by the Chinese authorities to Lord Napier, on his arrival at Canton as Superintendent of Trade, 1834. The word "eye" here simply means "head." Cf. 吏目 the head constable.

BARBER BOAT. A small kind of paddle boat, something like a canoe and occasionally called a *dugout*, is known to foreigners under this name at Canton. The Chinese call them simply sampans, in common with the more usual form that passes under that designation. The word "barber" has no particular *raison d'être*, except that formerly the barbers who attended the shipping at Whampoa during the palmy days of that now deserted port, were in the habit of using the kind of boat that still goes by this name.

BARGAIN-CHOPS. Are scrip used by opium merchants and issued to persons buying the drug "to arrive" on time. A deposit of money is given in return, and the transaction becomes favourable or unfavourable to the holder of the scrip according to the difference (more or less) between the price named on the scrip and the actual market rate on the date fixed for delivery of the drug. For instance, if in the interval opium goes up in price, the holder has to pay to the issuer of the scrip the difference between the original rate and the market rate on the day named for delivery of the purchase, and *vice versâ*. But there is very frequently no opium whatever present in the transaction, the drug being merely used as an imaginary basis for this kind of gambling; though the buyer has always the right to demand delivery of his consignment, and by doing so is not unusually able to place the speculative seller in a very awkward position.

"If history repeats itself, why will not the days of

"*bargain-chops* do likewise?" *The China Mail:* 27 Oct., 1877.

BARRIERS: 子口. Lesser or subordinate Customs' stations, placed along the inland trade-routes for the collection of duties on passing goods.

BASCHPA. See *Mongol.*

BATS: Five bats (五 蝠 *wu fu*) are frequently seen painted on Chinese plates. They stand for the Five Blessings (五 福 *wu fu*) longevity, wealth, *mens sana in corpore sano,* love of virtue, and a peaceful end—the character for *bat* being identical in sound with that for *blessing.*

BATTA. A Hindi word, correctly written *bhātā,* meaning an extra allowance to troops on service.

BAT'URU: 巴圖魯. A Manchu word meaning "brave." Instituted as a kind of order by the Emperor Shun Chih 順法 for rewarding military prowess; but only bestowed on such officers as have been previously decorated with the peacock's feather.

BAYAN: 佰顏. The famous Mongol general whose prowess so greatly assisted Kublai Khan in his conquest of China. The name is sometimes written 百眼 *pai yen* or *poh yen*—"hundred eyes," from the extreme vigilance for which he was noted. Marco Polo speaks of him as "a "Baron whose name was Bayan Chingsan, which is as "much as to say 'Bayan, hundred eyes'," and Col. Yule adds, "Bayan (signifying *great* or *noble*) is a name of "very old renown among the Nomade nations."

BAZAAR. From the Persian *bāzār* a market, in which sense it is commonly employed in China.

BEAN-CAKE: 荳餅 *or* 荳石. The refuse of the bean after all the oil has been expressed. Largely exported from Newchwang and Chefoo to Swatow for manuring the sugar plantations in that neighbourhood.

BEAN-CURD: 荳 腐. A thick jelly made from beans, and much eaten in the north of China. Yamên runners *(q.v.)* are sometimes called "bean-curd officials" 荳 腐 官.

BEASTIE *or* BHEESTY. A water-carrier; *lit.* "angel." Corruption of the Persian *bihishti*, from *bihist* "Paradise." This is one of the honorific titles by which servants in India speak of or to one another. The tailor is called *Khalifa* "Commander of the faithful;" the sweeper is called *Mehtar* "Prince (of the w.c.)" etc.

BEG: 佰 克. A title, equivalent to chieftain, in use among the Chinese Mahommedans of Turkestan, etc. With this term Sung-yün (1823) has identified 比 *pi*, the rulers of the Cossack tribes.

BEGGARS: 化 子 *or* 乞 丐. An organised fraternity, acting under the orders of a head beggar for each particular area. Shops which pay a fixed periodical sum to the Beggars' Guild, exhibit in their shops the legend 大 吉 利 市 Great joy and plenty of trade. These characters are usually written on a gourd, the emblem of beggardom. Other shops are liable to visitations during business hours from beggars with gongs, dead animals, or even snakes, who remain until bought off.

BEGGAR KING, THE. A name given to the founder of the Ming dynasty, A.D. 1368, in reference to his lowly origin.

BEGUM. A Persian word meaning *Queen* or *Princess.*

BEILÊH: 貝 勒. The Manchu title bestowed on the sons of the Imperial Princes of China. Often preceded by the word 勖 *zealous.*

BEITSZE: 貝 子. The Manchu title bestowed on the sons of a beilêh.

BENKEI. The Hercules of Japan.

BENTŌ BAKŌ. A Japanese luncheon box.

BERI BERI. See *Kakke*.

BETEL-NUT : 檳榔 *pin lang*—an imitation of the Malay word *pinang*. The leaf of the *sirih* or betelpepper smeared with chunam, or lime, and tobacco, and the nut of the areca palm, chewed together by the Chinese and other eastern nations.

BETTO. A Japanese horse-boy or groom.

BEZOAR : 牛黃. A valuable substance found in the stomachs of ruminant animals. Used by the Chinese as a paint and a drug.

BHAR. A Malay weight = about 3½ cwt.

BICHO-DA-MAR *or* BÊCHE-DE-MER : 海參. A large kind of sea-slug much relished by the Chinese. Found in the Pacific and Indian Archipelagos.

BIKSHU *or* BHIKSHU : 比丘 (*fem.* bikshuni 比丘尼). A wandering Buddhist mendicant, generally credited with the power of performing miracles. From *bhiksha* to beg.

BILLAL. The Mussulman assistant preacher or parson of a Malay village. See *Khateeb*.

BILLS OF EXCHANGE : 匯 (or 會) 票. Came into use under the Emperor 憲宗 Hsien Tsung of the T'ang dynasty, A.D. 806—820, and were then known as 飛錢 flying money.

BIOGRAPHY. Has occupied a prominent place in Chinese literature from the earliest ages. The various dynastic histories since the time of Christ contain biographies of all the eminent personages who figure in their pages. The biographies of Emperors are written up daily during the life of each monarch, who is not allowed to know what will be published about him after death.

BIRDS'-NESTS : 燕窩. The gelatinous nests of a swallow

(Hirundo esculenta) found in the Malay archipelago, from which is made the celebrated "birds'-nest soup." The nests are formed of a kind of seaweed.

BITESHI *or* BITGHESHI: 筆 帖 式. A Manchu word meaning scholar or clerk, the sound of which is imitated by the above three Chinese characters. Those Manchus who have passed the examination for *biteshi* are employed as scribes in the public offices at Peking. Similar to the Chinese *shu-pan (q.v.)*, *bit-hê* being the Manchu word for a book.

BLACK CROWS. The followers of a Turkic chieftain who assisted the Emperor Hsi Tsung of the T'ang dynasty to defeat the rebel Huang Ch'ao (A.D. 884) were so called from their black uniform.

BLACK FLAGS: 黑 旗. Part of a band of desperadoes who passed across the south-western frontier of China after the T'ai-p'ing rebellion. After having ravaged the provinces to the north of Tongking there was a split in the camp. The other portion essayed, under the style of the Yellow Flags, to found an independent principality at the head of the river Claire. The Black Flags, commanded by an able chieftain named 劉 永 福 Liu Yung-fu, took up a position at Lao-kai and offered their services to the Annamite government. Liu subsequently fought for China against the Japanese in Formosa, 1894, but with very indifferent success.

BLACK-HAIRED PEOPLE: 黎 民. A name for the Chinese people (see *Accad*), because of their black hair. This is the explanation given in K'ang Hsi's dictionary, but its accuracy has been questioned by some European scholars. Occurs in the *Great Learning (q.v.)* ch. x, 14: 保 我 子 孫 黎 民 "preserve my sons and grandsons,

"and *black-haired* people." The name 黔首 "black heads"
was given to the Chinese by 始皇帝 Shih Huang Ti, some
200 years before the Christian era.

BLOCKADE, THE HONGKONG. The establishment, by
the Chinese Superintendent of Customs at Canton, of a
system for the protection of his revenue from the great loss
entailed thereon by the smuggling of dutiable goods into
China in junks by native merchants from the neighbouring
island of Hongkong. Customs' stations were accordingly
placed at 佛頭洲，長洲, and 汲水門; and when
once a suspected junk was well outside the Hongkong
port limits, she was chased and seized by one of the
revenue cruisers employed, and if detected in smuggling,
vessel and cargo were confiscated.

BLUE (more correctly "blue and white"). A kind of Chinese
porcelain which is much prized in Europe and has an
especial charm for collectors from the fact that it cannot
be reproduced. Blue and white, *i.e.*, blue painting on a
white ground is to be found of all periods, some of it
dating from the time of the Mings. The merit of the
most ancient consists principally in the texture of the
porcelain and excellence of the designs. That blue and
white, however, which is most highly prized in Europe
is of a much later period, viz., K'ang Hsi and Ch'ien
Lung *(q.v.)*; and in this the ground is of translucent blue,
the design being in white. It is said that this particular
blue, which is certainly very beautiful, was produced with
pounded lapis lazuli, and certain it is that the best of it
has a decided resemblance in colour to that stone. The
Hawthorn pattern is of the greatest value in England, and
a good pot of this sort has a market value of, say £500.

BLUE-CAP MAHOMMEDANS, THE: 藍帽回子. A

name applied to the Jews, most of whom came to China from Persia.

BO TREE, THE : 菩 提 樹, i.e. the Bôdhidruma or Tree of Knowledge (*ficus religiosa* Willd.); also known as the 思 惟 樹 or Tree of Meditation. The original Bo tree grew near Gaya in Bengal, and was so called after the seven years of penance which Shâkyamuni spent under its shade before he became a Buddha. A slip of it was taken and planted in the sacred city of Amarapoora, in Burmah, B.C. 288. This is said to be in existence still. Sir J. E. Tennet refers to historic documents in which it is mentioned at different dates, as A.D. 182, 223, and so on to the present day. There is another flourishing specimen in the Buddhist temple at Pt. de Galles, also said to have come from the parent tree at Gaya.

BOARDS, THE SIX : 六 部. The Government offices at Peking, nearly equivalent to our Admiralty, Treasury, etc. They are—

1. 吏 部—*Li pu*, Board of Civil Office, which manages the civil service of the empire, so called since 3rd cent. A.D.

2. 戶 部—*Hu pu*, Board of Revenue, which collects duties and taxes, and superintends fiscal arrangements generally, so called since 7th cent. A.D.

3. 禮 部—*Li pu*, Board of Rites, which directs the ceremonial observances, literary distinctions, etc. etc., so called since 10th cent. A.D.

4. 兵 部—*Ping pu*, Board of War, so called since 7th cent. A.D.

5. 刑 部—*Hsing pu*, Board of Punishments, which is entrusted with the due administration of the laws, so called since 7th cent. A.D.

6. 工部—*Kung pu*, Board of Works, so called since 7th cent. A.D.

The Six Boards were known under the 晉 Chin dynasty as the 六曹, and under the 隋 Sui dynasty their names were (1) 銓 (2) 版 (3) 祠 (4) 武 (5) 憲 (6) 起, the order in which they are enumerated being also the order of their relative importance. In addition to these names, which are still in literary use, No. 2 is known as 農部 *Nung pu* or 民部 *Min pu*, No. 4 as 犀部 *Hsi pu*, No. 5 as 比部 *Pi pu* or 西曹 *Hsi ts'ao*, and No. 6 as 水部 *Shui pu*.

BOBBERY. From the Cantonese 吧蔽 *a noise.* Commonly used in pidgin-English; e.g. "What for you bobbery my?" i.e., scold or abuse.

The term *bobbery* is a corruption of the Hindi *Bāp re* "O father!"

BÔDHISATVA: 苦提薩埵 or more frequently 菩薩 P'u-sa=one whose essence has become intelligence. A being that has only once more to pass through human existence before it attains to Buddhaship. One who has fulfilled all the conditions necessary to the attainment of Buddhahood (and its consequent Nirvâna), but from charity continues voluntarily subject to re-incorporation for the benefit of mankind. Of the Bôdhisatva there are three degrees:—he who attains quickly, less quickly, and least quickly.

BOGUE, THE: 虎門—"Tiger's Gate," otherwise called Bocca Tigris. The principal embouchure of the Canton river, near which may still be seen traces of the celebrated forts captured 26 Feb. 1842 by the British forces under Commodore Sir Gordon Bremer. *Bogue* is a corruption of the Portuguese rendering—*boca tigre*—of the Chinese term.

BOHEA: 武彝. Two ranges of hills in the province of Fuhkien, from which the celebrated tea *(q.v.)* is procured. Formerly, all tea was called *bohea*, which is an imitation of the sounds of the above two characters.

> To part her time 'twixt reading and *bohea*,
> To muse and spill her solitary tea.
> *Pope.*

> As some frail cup of China's fairest mould,
> The tumults of the boiling *bohea* braves,
> And holds secure the coffee's sable waves.
> *Tickell.*

> For if my pure libations exceed three,
> I feel my heart become so sympathetic,
>   That I must have recourse to black *Bohea*:
> 'Tis pity wine should be so deleterious,
> For tea and coffee leave us much more serious.
> *Byron.*

BOMBAY DUCK. The bummelo or *harpodon nehereus*, a small fish found on the coasts of India and in the Archipelago, which, after being dried and salted, is toasted and eaten hot with curry, etc. The Hongkong name is 乾魚肚 "dried fish bellies," but of the European term we are unable to give any explanation. Bombay Englishmen are spoken of as "Ducks." See *Ditcher.*

BONJI: 梵字. The sacred characters of the Buddhist scriptures. [Japanese.]

BONZE: (1) From the Japanese 梵僧 *bonso* a Buddhist priest, generally used contemptuously.

(2) From 梵字 *bonji*, the name of the writing of the Buddhist scriptures, which was afterwards applied to the persons who made use of it, viz. Buddhist priests.

(3) From 浮屠 *bodzu*, these characters being used to express the word "Buddha."

BOUSY: 烟屑. A Hindustani word, meaning *saw-dust*. Used for packing balls of opium in chests.

BOY. The common term in China for a servant, such as a house-boy, office-boy, etc. It has been suggested that this is a mere corruption of the Hindustani "bhaiee," which means a servant; but it seems almost equally probable that the English word has been adopted in the sense of the French *garçon*.

"Ajeeb then said to the eunuch, Boy, I long for a "little diversion." ["The term *boy* is not used here to "imply that the eunuch was a youth; but in the sense in "which it is often employed by us; as synonymous with "*servant*."] Lane's *Arabian Nights*.

BRAHMANISM. The ancient Hindu religion, or religion of caste, against the thrall of which Buddhism was a protest. Its chief doctrine was that by severe penances and torture of the body a man may acquire perfect wisdom.

BRAVES: 勇. Chinese soldiers. So called because they wear the above character which means "brave" upon their backs. "Braves" are strictly speaking irregular levies, called into existence and disbanded as occasion may require; but among foreigners the word has come to be used in the general sense given above.

BRICK TEA: 茶磚. A common kind of tea prepared in the tea districts of Central China by softening refuse leaves, twigs, and dust with boiling water, and then pressing the compound into large slabs like bricks. Subdivided into (1) Large Green, (2) Small Green, and (3) Black. Is consumed in great quantities in Siberia and Mongolia, where it is also used as a medium of exchange.

"The Mongol tests the soundness of tea by placing a "brick on his head, and pulling the extremities downwards "with both hands; if the brick does not break or give, "it is sound; if it breaks or bends it is comparatively "worthless."—*C. M. Grant.*

BRIDGES: 橋梁. The earliest mention of a bridge in China will be found in the *Canon of Poetry*, and refers to a bridge of boats. Stone bridges, and even suspension bridges, have been in use for many centuries. A fine specimen of the former is to be seen at Foochow. It was built about 800 years ago, is about $1/4$ of a mile long and 14 ft. wide. The Polam bridge, some 20 miles from Amoy, is built of huge blocks of stone, the longest being 70 ft. by 6 ft. wide and 7 ft. in depth.

BRINJAL: 茄子. A kind of egg-plant (*solanum melongena,* L.) found all over China. The name is derived from the Portuguese *bringella.* Known in Bengal as *bangun* or *baingun.*

BU: 分. A Japanese silver coin equal to about 1/4d, now no longer in circulation. 4 *bu* were equal to 1 *riō* or tael.

BUBBLING WELL: 海眼—eye of the sea. A well about 3 miles from Shanghai, near the 靜安 Ching-an temple, the water of which is mere drainage, the "bubbling" being caused by the passage of carburetted hydrogen.

An ornamental wall has been built around the well, bearing the following inscriptions: 天下第六泉 "The "sixth of the springs under heaven"—(the other five being in various parts of the empire); and 旺經處 "The "spot where the *sûtras* were listened to,"—in reference to a certain priest who lived hard by and recited the Buddhist liturgies so eloquently that the very frogs sat up to hear him.

BUDDHA: 佛陀 or 淨度 or 佛啚. Literally, one who knows or is awake; hence, the enlightened, or he who has perfect wisdom. Every intelligent being who has thrown off the bondage of sense, perception, and self, and knows the utter unreality of all phenomena, and is ready to enter into Nirvâna. The first person of the Buddhist Trinity.

The great founder of Buddhism, Prince Siddartha, known as Shâkyamuni Gâutama Buddha, was born B.C. 624 at Kapilavastu on the borders of Nepaul, and died in his 80th year. He was the son of a king; but renounced the pomps and vanities of this wicked world to devote himself to the great task of overthrowing Brahmanism, the religion of caste.

BUDDHA, THE LAUGHING. A name for Maitrêya Buddha *(q.v.)*.

BUDDHA, LIVING: 活佛. A popular name for the Hutukhtu *(q.v.)*. Also applied to very worthy persons.

BUDDHA, THE SLEEPING: 臥佛. A recumbent figure of Buddha, found in certain temples known as Sleeping Buddha temples.

BUDDHA'S FINGERS: 佛手. A kind of citron, almost all rind, found on the 櫞 tree. One end of it terminates like a hand, with fingers. Used by the Chinese for scenting rooms, at religious sacrifices, etc.

BUDDHA SHELLS: 佛公壳. Mussel-shells found in Siam, containing one or more figures of a sitting Buddha, in relief; and regarded by the simple as material evidences of the truth of the Buddhist faith. The figures however, are produced by human agency. Pious priests watch for half-open mussels, and slip into their shells thin clay images of the World-honoured One, over which the mussel in process of time deposits a thick layer of nacre, with the result described above.

BUDDHISM: 釋 (or 佛) 教. According to Buddhism there

is no Creator, no being that is self-existent and eternal. Any being whatever may be a candidate for the Buddhaship; but it is only by the uniform pursuit of this object throughout innumerable ages that it can be obtained. The power that controls the universe is *karma*, literally "action," consisting of merit and demerit. There is no immaterial spirit, but at the death of any being the aggregate of his merit and demerit is transferred to some other being, which new being is caused by the karma of the previous being, and receives from that karma all the circumstances of its existence. The cause of the continuance of existence is *ignorance*. Hence, merit and demerit, consciousness, desire, reproduction, disease, and death. Thus there is a regular succession of birth and death; the moral cause of which is desire, the instrumental is karma. It is therefore the great object of all who would be released from the sorrows of rebirth, to destroy the moral cause. This may be accomplished by a course of discipline, leading into one of the Four Paths and thence to Nirvâna *(q.v.)*. See *Precious Ones, Three.*

The earliest appearance of Buddhism in China was during the reign of the First Emperor, B.C. 259—210, when certain Shamans, 室利房 Shih-li-fang and others, who came to proselytise, were seized and put in prison. They escaped however through the aid of 金人 an angel who appeared to them in the middle of the night and opened their prison doors. Later, in A.D. 61, the reigning Emperor is said to have had a dream, in consequence of which he sent a mission to India and obtained the services of Kashyapmatanga and Gobharana, who translated the Sûtra of Forty-two Sections. Buddhism was introduced into Japan about A.D. 550.

The Buddhism of China, Japan, Mongolia, Tibet, and Nepaul, is known as Northern Buddhism, being the system developed after contact with the northern tribes settled on the Indus. Southern Buddhism is common to Ceylon, Burmah, and Siam, and represents the primitive form of the faith as it came from the hands of its founder and his immediate successors.

BUDMASHES. From *bad* "bad" and *maásh* "living." A Persian and Arabic compound term for rowdies or professional bullies, occasionally used in China.

" . . . a local outbreak in the district of P'u-ch'êng, where a band of budmashes under the leadership of a man heretofore. . ."—*N. C. Herald, 25th Oct., 1877.*

BUGIS, THE. A race of people from the southern part of the island of Celebes, now found as colonists in Perak. They are distinct from the Malays in point of language and in intelligence, though very similar in appearance.

BUKIT. A Malay word meaning hill or mountain, commonly occurring in names of places.

BUND. The common term in China for a quay, such as those along the banks of the Seine in Paris, less the parapet. The part alone of the *bund* at Shanghai which fronts the British Settlement is some 3,500 feet in length by sixty-five in breadth. Is the same Persian word which appears in *Cummerbund (q.v.)*, and is common all over India.

BUNDER. Any startling story or rumour which turns out to be untrue. From *bund (q.v.)*. French, *canard*. A volume of "Bunders" was published some years ago in Shanghai, containing several amusing skits upon local celebrities, its forthcoming appearance being heralded by an "express" *(q.v.)*—THE BUNDERS ARE COMING!

The ponies for hire on the bund at Tientsin are also called *bunders*.

Bunder (Pers. *bandar*) is used in Hindustani for a "port." Cf. the Bombay terms "bunder boat" and "Apollo Bunder."

BUNGALOW. From the Hindi *bungala*. Strictly speaking a one-storeyed, thatched house, generally surrounded by a verandah. Also said to be derived from Bengal.

BURIAT MONGOLS: 布里雅特. A tribe of Mongols subject to Russia.

BURLINGAME MISSION. A Chinese Embassy to foreign States in 1869, under the leadership of 滿安臣 Mr. Anson Burlingame, then American Minister at Peking, as chief Ambassador, with Mr. McLeavy Brown, then of H.M. Consular Service, as Secretary of Legation and interpreter to the mission; the other important members being two associate Chinese Envoys, Sun and Chih, both men of a certain rank and position. This embassy is commonly supposed to have been sent to Europe and America to bring to the notice of governments China's right, as an independent power, to manage her internal affairs without undue interference from outside. It was then that Mr. Burlingame spoke of China as longing only to cement friendly relations with foreign countries, and declared, in a now celebrated phrase, that within some few short years we should be gratified by the sight of "a shining "cross on every hill" in the Middle Kingdom. But Mr. Burlingame himself knew nothing of the Chinese language; hence probably the allusion in Inman's *Ancient Faiths* (I. 257),—"as completely as we should disbelieve a man, "who, calling himself ambassador plenipotentiary from China "to Britain, brings credentials written in English, and only "speaks our mother tongue."

BURNING OF THE BOOKS. The First Emperor of the
Ch'in (秦) dynasty issued instructions, at the suggestion
of his prime minister, that all records of previous dynasties
and all copies of all existing books, with the exception of
such as treated of medicine, divination, and husbandry,
should be forthwith burned. The advice was given partly
out of flattery to the Emperor from whose reign literature
would take a fresh start, and partly with a view of
strengthening the recently-established dynasty of Ch'in.
At any rate it was immediately put into force as law,
about B.C. 212; and subsequently several hundred scholars
were buried alive for their disobedience in concealing
forbidden volumes. Thus perished many valuable works,
and it was only by accident ·that the prohibited portions
of the Chinese Classics, hidden away by devoted enthusiasts,
were subsequently discovered and preserved for future ages.

A second Burning of the Books was perpetrated by
元帝 the Emperor Yüan of the 梁 Liang dynasty, A.D.
552—555, who is said to have destroyed one hundred
and forty thousand volumes of ancient and modern works.

BUSS. Stop! Can do! etc. Used in the Straits and in India.
From the Persian *bas*.

BUTTONS: 頂子 or 頂戴. The knobs adopted by the
Manchu dynasty to indicate rank and worn at the top
of the official hat. They are:—

1. Transparent red button—ruby; for half dress, coral.

2. Opaque red button—coral; for full dress "flowered
"coral."

3. Transparent blue button—sapphire.

4. Opaque   do.   do. —lapis lazuli.

5. Transparent white do. —crystal.

6. Opaque   do. do. —stone.

7. Plain gold   button.

8. Worked gold   do.

9.   do.   do.

These are of two classes, viz: 正 *principal* and 從 *subordinate*. The distinction lies in the latter being engraved with the character for "old age" (see *Show*), the former being plain. No. 9 has *two* of these characters, and is the button which every one who has taken his first or bachelor's degree is forthwith entitled to wear.

CAMBALUC. See *Khambalu*.

CAMBODIA. A once powerful and highly civilised state, known as the kingdom of Khmer, which now forms part of the French Protectorate in Cochin-China. Many colossal ruins of great antiquity are still to be seen there; but the country was historically unknown previous to the 13th century. The ruins of Angcor are of gigantic proportions, and seem as though reared by the hands of a giant race long since extinct.

CAMELS: 駱駝. The two-humped Bactrian camel is the chief burden-carrier between the north of China and Mongolia, and long strings of these animals may be seen daily in the streets of Peking.

CAMOENS' GARDEN. The celebrated spot at Macao which is said to have been a favourite resort of the great Portuguese poet of that name, author of the Lusiad. Odes in the poet's honour have been composed by Sir J. E. Davis and others, and are now to be seen engraved on tablets outside the grotto. The following are specimen verses :—

Hic in remotis sol ubi rupibus
Frondes per altas mollius incidit
Fervebat in pulchram camœnam
Ingenium Camoentis ardens.

Davis.

Gem of the orient earth and open sea,
Macao!......that in thy lap and on thy breast
Hast gathered beauties all the loveliest
Which the sun smiles on in his majesty.

Bowring.

Patané! lieu charmant et si cher au poète,
Je n'oublirai jamais ton illustre retraite,
Ici Camoens au bruit du flot retentissant
Mêla l'accord plaintif de son luth gémissant.

Anonymous.

And one in Chinese:

才德超人因妒被難

"Surpassing others in genius and virtue, because of jealousy he suffered evil."

奇詩大典立碑傳世

"To commemorate his marvellous poetry and his noble character, this stone is now put up."

CAMPO, THE. The foreign settlement at Ningpo is so called, the term being a corruption of 江北 *Kong po* (local pronunciation) north of river, *i.e.* the north bank of the river on which the foreign houses stand.

CAMPOI: 揀焙—carefully fired, *or* selected for firing. A selected variety of Congou tea. From the Cantonese pronunciation of the above two characters.

CAMPONG. A Malay word meaning *enclosure*. Generally used for a *village*.

CANDAREEN: 分. The hundredth part of an ounce of pure silver. From the Malayan *Kenderi*, which is one-eighth of a *wang* and is represented in weight by a bean of the *Abrus precatorius*.

CANDLES: 蠟燭. Were first used in China in the 4th cent. A.D.

CANFU: 澉浦. The old port of Hangchow, visited by two Arabian travellers in the 9th century, and by Marco Polo in 1290, but now washed away or submerged. An attempt however has been made to discredit this identification in favour of *Canton*, through the Chinese Kuang-*chow Fu*.

CANGO. See *Kago*.

CANGUE. The heavy square wooden collar—*necktie* 木風領, as the Chinese humorously call it—worn by criminals for such offences as petty larceny, etc. Its maximum weight is regulated by law, as also the limit of time for which it may be imposed. It is generally taken off at night; but during the day the wearer must be fed by friends, not being able to reach his mouth himself.

From the Portuguese *canga*, yoke.

CANTON. A corruption of Kuang-tung 廣東, from the Portuguese method of writing it—*kamton*. The capital city of the province of Kuang-tung, said to date back to the fourth century B.C. First visited by the British in 1637, but not formally opened to trade until 1842, under the Treaty of Nanking. The Portuguese had arrived a century earlier (1517); they were followed by the Dutch, but by the end of the 17th century the trade was almost entirely in the hands of British merchants. Canton was captured by the allied forces of England and France in December 1857, and was held for about four years. The city wall dates from the 11th century, and has a circuit of somewhat over six miles.

CAPITALS OF CHINA under the various dynasties.

Ch'in,	B.C.	249,	at 咸陽	Hsien-yang	in Shensi.
W. Han,	„	200,	„ 長安	Ch'ang-an	„ „
E. Han,	A.D.	25,	„ 洛陽	Lo-yang	„ Honan.

3

Chin,   A.D. 280, at 洛陽 Lo-yang   in Honan.

E. Chin, „   317, „ 建業 Chien-yeh „ Kiangsu.

Sui,   „   582, „ 長安 Ch'ang-an „ Shensi.

T'ang,   „   904, „ 洛陽 Lo-yang   „ Honan.

Sung, „ { 960, 汴梁 Pien-liang „ „

          { 1129, „ 臨安 Lin-an   „ Chehkiang.

Yüan, „ 1280, 燕京 Yen-ching „ Chihli.

Ming, „ { 1368, „ 南京 Nan-ching „ Kiangsu.

          { 1403, „ 北京 Pei-ching   „ Chihli.

[Since 1403 the capital has been Peking, in spite of the change of dynasty.]

CAPITAN: 甲必丹. Malay corruption of the word "captain," the sounds of which are imitated by the Chinese.

CAPOOR CUTCHERY: 三賴 or 三奈 or 三棯 or 番棯. A root found in Fuhkien and Ssŭch'uan, and powdered for making plasters. The Indian name means "root of camphor."

CARAMBOLA: 五歛子, vulgarly known as 楊 (or 羊) 桃. The curious polyagonal "Canton gooseberry" is so called.

CARDS, PLAYING: 紙牌. Are of various kinds, with many varieties in the method of playing. In Peking, the ordinary pack consists of 160 cards. They are about $2^1/_2 \times {}^3/_4$ inches in size, and have black backs so as not to show the dirt. The date of their invention is not known.

CARDS, VISITING: 名片. As used in China by men only, are oblong pieces of red paper, about 5 inches in length, inscribed with the name and surname of the owner. On the back, there is often an inscription in small characters, stating that the card is only for ceremonial purposes, meaning that it may not be used as a receipt for letters or money, or in evidence of any business transaction. Han-lin scholars of not less than three years' standing are permitted as a mark of distinction to use larger-sized cards, inscribed with proportionately larger characters written down the middle of the paper; but of late years it has been customary for the high authorities to use these in their intercourse with foreign officials.

During the period of 27 months' mourning for a parent, either the colour of the card is changed to light-brown, or the characters 在苫 "with a clod (for a pillow)," or 制 "statute," are added to the name. Similarly, during the year's mourning for a grandfather or a brother, 期 (read *chi*) is used; and during the lesser period of 5 and 3 months, the character 功; but in these cases the colour is not changed. When visiting at houses where festivity is the order of the day, the mourner, in deference to his friends' feelings, substitutes 從吉 = "with you in your joy," for the characters above mentioned.

The form of visiting-card used between officials of the same or similar rank is called a 兄弟帖; as handed by an inferior to a superior, a 手本. This latter is in effect a petition, stating the rank and titles of the petitioner. Red paper was first used under the Ming dynasty, when the famous eunuch 劉瑾 Liu Chin (*d.* A.D. 1510) was at the head of the government; before that time the paper was white.

Women, instead of putting the surnames of the husband on their visiting-cards, use the name of the family district. Thus 歸潁州何氏端拜 "Mrs. Ying-chou, *née* Ho, presents her compliments" would be understood by everybody to mean Mrs. 陳 Ch'ên, Ying-chou being the original home of the Ch'ên family.

CASH: 錢. Fancy names 青蚨, 孔方, 阿堵, etc. From

caixa, the Portuguese name for the tin coin found at Malacca in 1511 and brought there from the Malabar coast. Cf. Sanskrit *kārsha*. [哈沙 is said to be a Manchu term for *cash*.] Now used of the only coin cast in China, one thousand of which were originally equal to one tael or Chinese ounce of silver. Each cash has a square hole in the middle for convenience in carrying a large quantity; hence the expression "strings of cash." Hence, too, the *jeu-de-mots* that a man should resemble a cash and be 志 (*or* 智) 圓行方 *round in disposition square in action*, or, by reading the first character 質 —then, *round in shape, convenient for use.*

Rare specimens are frequently worn as charms by children and even by adults.

Copper cash seem to have been first coined in B.C. 136, previous to which time 貝 pearl-oyster shells (old form resembling an open shell) were used like cowries. Some authorities date the coinage of cash as far back as the Emperor 景 Ching of the Chou dynasty, B.C. 544.

CAT, THE : 貓 *miao*. Cats, which are not mentioned in the Bible, are referred to in the *Odes (q.v.).* The character is said to be so written because rats injure cereal sprouts (*miao* 苗) and cats catch rats! Dead cats are not buried, but hung on trees. A cat washing its face portends the arrival of a stranger. Its nose is always cold, except on the day of the summer solstice. Kittens have great difficulty in surviving the 5th day of the 5th moon. Directions are often given in almanacs for telling the time by cats' eyes, which have been observed to change between morning and night.

CATALOGUE OF THE IMPERIAL LIBRARY : 四庫全書總目. A descriptive Catalogue of the books in the Imperial collection at Peking, published in 1782 by order of the Emperor Ch'ien Lung. The works are arranged under four heads as Classics, History, Philosophy, and Belles Lettres, in 200 sections.

CATECHU. See *Cutch.*

CATHAY. China. Said to be a Persian corruption of 契丹, *i.e.* the Kitans who ruled northern China from A.D. 1118 to 1235 under the name of the 金朝 Golden Dynasty, and were so called from their tattooing. Marco Polo always speaks of China as Kitai, and Tennyson writes—"Better fifty years of Europe than a cycle of "Cathay." In reference to which it has, however, been somewhat waggishly remarked that a Chinese cycle consists of only 60 years.

CATTY: 觔 *or* 斤. The Chinese pound=1$\frac{1}{3}$ *lb.* avoirdupois, is so called. Catty, or *kati*, is a Malayan word for the Chinese pound. N.B. Although the decimal system otherwise prevails throughout the Chinese weights and measures, the catty or *lb.* is, as with us, divided into 16 parts.

CAVAN *or* CABAN. A grain measure used in the Philippine Islands=3.47 cubic feet.

CELESTIAL EMPIRE. A common name for China, taken probably from the phrase 天朝 Heavenly Dynasty, which has been for many centuries in use amongst the Chinese themselves. Under the Han dynasty, China was often called 天漢 "Heavenly Han;" and generally speaking, the epithet is a favourite one with the Chinese.

CENSOR: 御史 *or* 都老爺. A member of the Censorate 都察院, which is a body of men stationed at Peking under two presidents, one Chinese and the other Manchu, the officers of which are sent to various parts of the empire as Imperial inspectors. They are privileged to censure the Emperor for any act which they consider illegal, extravagant or unjust, without risk of losing their lives, though they are sometimes degraded for unpalatable advice. Also called "the ears and eyes" of the Emperor 耳目官·

CENSUS, THE. Is an old-established institution in China, but is taken in a very irregular manner both as to time and method. House-tickets are served out to the head of every household in each ward, and he is responsible for the return of all inmates, including lodgers; but as there is no fixed day on which these tickets are returnable, the results are approximate rather than exact. The population of China has been recorded as follows:—

By Père Amiot   in 1743＝150,265,475.
  „ Lord Macartney, „ 1792＝333,000,000.
  „ Official Census   „ 1813＝360,279,897.
  „ Sacharoff   „ 1842＝413,686,994.

CENT. The hundredth part of a dollar. From the Latin *centum* a hundred. Written 先時 or 仙 at Hongkong; 占 at Amoy; 寸 at Foochow; at Shanghai 分·

CENTIPEDES: 蜈蚣. Are common in most parts of China, and especially in the south-western provinces. They are much used in medicine, the "juice" of a centipede being said to be good for thrush. Chickens eat them readily; hence probably the popular notion that the saliva of a fowl is a cure for centipede bites.

CHA-NO-YU or Hot Water Tea. An elaborate ceremonial in connection with tea-drinking among political or literary friends, practised in Japan at least since the early part of the 15th cent., according to fixed rules and "in purity, "peacefulness, reverence, and abstraction."

CHAAM FA: 蠶花. Cocoons produced from eggs which

have been kept over from the preceding year. They are thin, and worth much less than others.

CHAA-SZE: 茶師—tea expert. A tea-taster; or more irreverently, a *tea-gobber*, from the habit of spitting out the tea tasted, instead of swallowing it.

CHAI MUI: 猜枚 *or* 拇戰. A game played by two persons at a Chinese dinner-party or on any other festive occasion. The players look each other steadily in the face, and simultaneously extend one hand showing all, some, or none, of the five fingers stretched out, at the same time crying out what each thinks will be the sum total of the two sets of fingers thus exhibited. When either succeeds in guessing aright, his opponent has to swallow a cup of wine as a forfeit. Many fanciful formulas, varying in different parts of the Empire, have been substituted for the mere numerals which would sound harsh to a Chinese ear. The following is an example of one of these:—

一心 . .	*one heart.*
二好 . .	*two friends.*
三元 . .	*three firsts.*[a]
四季 . .	*four seasons.*
五子 . .	*five sons.*[b]
六合 . .	*six cardinals.*[c]
七巧 . .	*seven changeables.*[d]
八仙 . .	*eight genii.*[e]
九長 . .	*nine long.*[f]
十全 . .	*ten complete.*
對手 . .	*hands opposite;*

the latter being used when one player holds out his closed fist and expects his adversary to do the same.

"Every Person shall be liable to a penalty not exceeding

"Ten Dollars who shall utter Shouts or Cries or make
"other Noises while playing the Game known as *Chai*
"*Mui*, between the Hours of 11 P.M. and 6 A.M., within
"any District or Place not permitted by some Regulation
"of the Governor in Council."—*Hongkong Ordinance*,
No. 2 of 1872.

　　a. First on the list at the three great public examinations.
　　b. Alluding to the five sons of Tou Yen-shan who all
　　　　took high degrees.
　　c. The six cardinal points;—north, south, east, west,
　　　　above, and below.
　　d. The seven pieces of the Chinese puzzle.
　　e. The eight Immortals of the Taoist religion.
　　f. 九 *nine* here stands for 入 long, in the sense of a
　　　　long life.

CHAIRS (SEDAN): 轎子. The Emperor alone is entitled
　　to employ 16 bearers for carrying his chair; a prince of
　　the blood 8; the highest provincial authorities also 8, a
　　privilege of which, however, they never avail themselves
　　except on occasions of religious or state ceremonial; all
　　other officials down to a Prefect 4, including a District
　　Magistrate, if in office, but not if merely expectant; below
　　this grade 2. A bridal chair is red; that of all officials
　　down to and inclusive of the Commissioners of Justice,
　　Finance, and the Salt Gabelle (三司),—green; below
　　this, blue, with slight variations of detail. A Taot'ai's
　　chair would strictly speaking be blue; but he usually has
　　brevet rank as Commissioner of Justice, on the strength
　　of which he changes the colour to green. Foreign Consuls
　　in China use green chairs, as being the highest local
　　officials of their particular nationality, and by Treaty of
　　equal rank with Taot'ais. Chinese etiquette makes it

necessary to get out of a chair to speak with a passing acquaintance. When two or more officials travel together, the highest in rank takes the foremost chair; were they on horseback the same official would be the second of the file, a servant always riding in front to clear the way. Within the city of Peking, only princes of the blood and some of the highest officials are permitted to use chairs.

CHAM. A mediæval corruption of *Khan* (可 汗 or 汗); the title Great *Cham* of Tartary having been first applied to Genghis Khan *(q.v.)*. Dr. Johnson was spoken of by Smollett as that "grim Cham of literature." Has occasionally been written *Chane.*

CHAMBER OF HORRORS: 地獄 or 陰 間—purgatory. That section of every municipal temple (城 隍 廟) which contains models of sinners undergoing the various punishments of the Taoist-Buddhist purgatory. The term is a fanciful one, in imitation of the celebrated Chamber at Madame Tussaud's wax-work exhibition. For a full account of the ten courts into which it is divided, with a description of the tortures therein inflicted, see Appendix to *Strange Stories from a Chinese Studio.*

CHANDOO. (Malay.) Opium prepared for smoking.

CHANG: 丈. A Chinese measure=to 141 English inches.

CHANGES, BOOK OF: 易 經. Contains a fanciful system of philosophy deduced from the combinations of the Eight Diagrams *(q.v.)*. Possibly composed B.C. 1150 by 文 王 Wên Wang. Is one of the Five Classics *(q.v.)*, the text consisting of sixty-four short essays, enigmatically and symbolically expressed, on important themes, mostly of a moral, social, and political character, and based upon the same number of lineal figures, each made up of six lines, some of which are whole and the others divided.

The text is followed by commentaries, called the *Ten Wings*, probably of a later date and commonly ascribed to Confucius, who declared that were a hundred years added to his life he would devote fifty to a study of the *Yih-king*.

The following is a specimen:—

Text. The first line, divided, shows one moving his great toes.

The fifth line, undivided, shows one moving the flesh along the spine above the heart. There will be no occasion for repentance.

Wing. He moves his great toes;—his mind is set on what is beyond himself.

He moves the flesh along the spine above the heart; —his aim is trivial.

CHARACTERS, CHINESE: 字 since the reign of the First Emperor, 3rd cent. B.C.; before that time 名 or 文. They are symbols of ideas, abstract and concrete. They are neither agglutinative nor inflexional, but vary in grammatical value as verb, substantive, or adjective, with their position in the sentence. K'ang Hsi's *(q.v.)* lexicon includes more than 40,000 separate characters, the origin of which appears to have been this:—

A few simple shapes of visible objects were followed up by others more or less easy to be identified, until the impossibilities of a wholly pictorial language gave place to the phonetic system upon which the present characters are based. Thus, the ancient Chinese drew a rude picture to represent the sound by which they designated a horse, viz: 馬 *ma*. But with a very limited number of vocables it followed that the sound *ma*, with differences of intonation, did duty in the spoken language for other ideas, as *ma* mother, *ma* agate, *ma* a locust, *ma* prawns, *ma* to curse, *ma* the head of a bed, etc. By the phonetic system, the Chinese wrote down each of the above as *ma* horse, and then added a distinguishing symbol on the left, now known as the *radical (q.v.)*. The new combinations formed would read thus: 媽 Woman-horse=mother; 瑪 jade-horse=agate; 螞 insect-horse=locust; 鰢 fish-horse=prawns; 嗎 mouth-horse=to curse; 榪 wood-horse=head of a bed. In many cases these composite characters became the phonetics of other sets of characters, distinguished in like manner by appropriate radicals; besides which there is a small class of so-called "ideographic" characters, where the sense of the component parts yields the sense of the whole; *e.g.*, 木 a tree, 林 a forest, and 森 dense, obscure; 佛 western-nation-man, *sc.* Buddha. See *Seal Character*.

CHARPOY. A bed. Term used in India and the Straits. From the Persian *chihār-pāī* four-footed.

CHAYA. A Japanese tea house.

CHEE-CHEES. Anglo-Indian term of contempt for Eurasians. From a native expression of disgust.

CHEFOO: 芝罘 or 之罘頭. A small headland on the coast of the Shantung province, which has given its name to the celebrated watering-place and sanitarium of China; though as the foreign settlement lies close to the hill and village of Yen-t'ai (烟臺—Smoke Terrace), this would be its more appropriate designation. Was occupied instead of 登州 Têng-chou, which was opened to trade by Treaty of Tientsin 1858 but possessed no suitable harbour.

CHEFOO AGREEMENT, THE. A still unratified settlement of the Yünnan outrage *(q.v.)* arranged at Chefoo between Sir Thomas Wade, K.C.B., and H.E. the Grand

Secretary, Li Hung-chang, in September 1867. Popularly known as the Chefoo *Convention*.

CHEHKIANG: 浙 or 浙江—crooked river. One of the Eighteen Provinces. So called from the *Chê* river which traverses its southern part. Capital city Hang-chou Fu 杭州府. Old name 越.

CHEIROMANCY. See *Palmistry*.

CHEMULPO: 濟物浦. A port in Korea opened to trade by Treaty of 26th November 1883.

CHESS. Has been known to the Chinese for many centuries under a form not very unlike our own game. The board has 64 squares, is played with 16 men on each side, the two at the corners having equal power, and the next two (called *horses*) having a move equivalent to that of our knight. The chief differences are that the Chinese adversaries are separated by a river, over which some pieces cannot pass, while the "King" is confined to a square of nine moves only; and that the pieces are placed upon the intersections of the lines forming the board, instead of on the squares.

CHETTIES. The usurers or money-lending section of the Klings *(q.v.)*.

CH'I. See *Doctrine of the Ch'i*.

CH'IEN: 錢. (1) A mace, or tenth part of a Chinese ounce. (2) *Cash*; money.

CH'IEN LUNG: 乾隆—enduring glory. The style of reign adopted by the great Emperor who ruled China from 1736 to 1796. Fourth of the present or Manchu dynasty. Received Lord Macartney's embassy 1794. Same as the Kien Long mentioned in De Quincey's magnificent essay —The Revolt of the Tartars—and elsewhere.

CH'IEN-LUNG: 錢龍—cash dragon. The harmless "hundred

"legs," so common in northern China; not to be confounded with the centipede 蜈蚣. Called "cash dragon" by the Chinese, because supposed to resemble a string of cash, and therefore regarded as rather an auspicious visitor.

CHIH-FU OR CHE-FOO: 知府—he who administers the *fu* or prefecture. The Prefect. [See *Fu.*] Has the general supervision of the civil business in his own prefecture.

CHIH-HSIEN, CHI-HEEN, *or* CHEHIEN: 知縣—he who administers the *hsien* or District. The District Magistrate. Familiarly called the "father and mother" of the people, (in common with Prefects), because of his close relations with them. Is responsible for the peace and order of his District. Has summary jurisdiction in civil and criminal cases; and as Coroner is bound to hold an inquest in all instances of death under unusual circumstances. Is directly subordinate to the Prefect [see *Chih-fu*]; sometimes to the Magistrate of an Independent Department. All transfers of land must be stamped with his seal.

CHIHLI: 直隸—direct rule. The most important of the *Eighteen Provinces.* So called because from this province (i.e. from Peking) emanates the supreme power which governs the empire. Capital city Pao-ting Fu 保定府. Old name 直.

CHIKAMATSU, MONZAYEMON. The Japanese Shakespeare, A.D. 1653—1724, said to have been a priest in early life. The selected edition of his works contains fifty-one plays, almost all of five acts; and he rivalled the fame of Lope da Vega by composing an entire play in a single night.

CH'I LIN. See *Kilin.*

CHIN-CHIN. A corruption of the Chinese salutation 請請 *ch'ing ch'ing,* which answers to our good-bye, presents compliments, etc. To "chin-chin Joss" is to perform religious worship of any kind. The Chinese, however, regard the expression as purely foreign, and are quite unaware that it is a mere imitation of their own term.

CHIN-SHIH: 進士—the entering scholar. Graduate of the third or doctor's degree, the examination for which is held once in every three years at Peking, whither intending candidates proceed from all parts of the empire. Only *chü-jen (q.v.)*, who have not already taken office, are allowed to compete. This degree was established in the year A.D. 606, under the reign of the first Emperor of the Sui dynasty.

CHIN-WANG-TAO or CH'IN-HUANG-TAO 秦皇島. A Treaty Port in the Gulf of Peichili, between the mouth of the Peiho and Shan-hai Kuan.

CHINA. The Chinese themselves have no term for their country which can be identified with this word. It may possibly be derived from the name of a dynasty—Ch'in or Ts'in 秦—which flourished B.C. 255—207, and became widely known in India, Persia, and other Asiatic countries, the final *a* being added by the Portuguese. Chinese Buddhists write the Indian name 支那 *Chih-na*; also 震旦 *Chên-tan*, the last syllable being intended for the Sanskrit *stan* a country. This word, in the sense of porcelain, was fashionably pronounced in England during the 18th cent. as chaney.

CHINA CLAY. A fine white potter's clay, known to the Chinese as *kao lin (q.v.)*, derived from the felspar of disintegrated granitic rocks and used in the manufacture of porcelain by the Chinese.

CHINA CONSUL, THE. The Magistrate of the Mixed Court *(q.v.)* at Shanghai is so called, being often addressed as "Consul" in open Court. He is actually so styled (領事) in the *Hu-pao* of 12 July 1884.

CHINA GRASS: 苧麻. The textile fibre of a hemp-producing plant (*Bœhmeria nivea,* Hook. and Arn.) from which grass-cloth is made.

CHINA ROOT: 土茯苓. A false tuber *(Pachyma cocos)* found growing like a fungus from the roots of fir trees. Used medicinally by the Chinese.

CHINA SODA. Pidgin-English for *alum.*

CHINA STRAWBERRY. Pidgin-English for the fruit of the *arbutus.*

CHINA'S SORROW. The Yellow River or Hoang Ho *(q.v.).* So named by the Emperor Tao Kuang because of the devastion caused by its oft-recurring floods. Has frequently been known to change its bed; especially in 1856, when instead of emptying itself into the Yellow Sea about lat. 34°, this huge river turned off at right angles near the city of K'ai-fêng Fu, the capital of Honan, and found its issue in the Gulf of Peichili, lat. 38°.

CHINESE GORDON. See *T'ai-p'ing.*

CHING: 經. (1) The Buddhist *sûtras.* (2) Taoist writings which have been "canonised." (3) The Sacred Books of China, of which only five are recognised as such under the present dynasty, namely:—

1—Book of Changes, 易經.
2— do. History, 書經.
3— do. Poetry, 詩經.
4— do. Rites, 禮記.
5—Spring & Autumn 春秋.

The character 經 means *text*; but "Canon," in the ecclesiastical sense of the term, is the best rendering.

CHINKIANG: 鎮江—guard the river. A treaty port, and prefectural city in the province of Kiangsu, near the junction of the Grand Canal and Yang-tsze. Opened by Tientsin Treaty 1858. Was captured by the British forces in 1842, and by the T'ai-p'ing rebels in 1853, from whom it was retaken in 1857. It is sometimes called 京口 Mouth of the Capital, in allusion to the tribute rice which was formerly sent viâ Chinkiang up the Grand Canal to Peking.

CHIT. From the Hindi word *chitthī* a letter, specially used of letters of recommendation given to servants. Used in China for all kinds of letters, notes, pencil scraps, I.O.U's, etc., etc.

CHIT-BOOK. The book which in China invariably accompanies letters or parcels sent, in order that the receiver may sign his initials against the entry relating to himself, as a proof to the sender of due delivery.

CHŌ: 町. A Japanese measure equal to 60 *ken (q.v.)* or 360 feet English. Also, land measure of 3,000 *tsubo (q.v.)*.

CHOGOLGAN. A league or association of Mongols.

CHON NOOKEE. See *Jon-nuké*.

CHOO HE *or* CHU-FU-TZŬ: 熹朱. The great critic, historian, poet, and commentator on the Chinese Classics, A.D. 1130—1200. His is the system of interpretation which obtains at the present day, its secret being nothing more than uniformity of exegesis. He refused to interpret the same combination in various ways merely to suit the supposed exigencies of the text. It is related that after death his coffin was seen suspended in the air, three feet from the ground, until at length his son-in-law approached, and kneeling down cried out "Master! the holy doctrine "of Confucius should be paramount—" (夫子當以聖 教爲重); implying that supernatural manifestations ill befitted a disciple of the materialistic Sage. The coffin then descended, and resumed its original position. See *Mirror of History.*

CHOP: 號 *or* 字 號. A mark, number, or brand. Hence a *chop* of tea means a certain number of chests of tea all bearing the same brand. A trade-mark or trade-name, imitation of which is not allowed in China, the rule being now extended to the trade-marks of foreign merchants. Anything is said to be *first chop* when it is of first-rate quality. "But oh, you should see her ladyship's behaviour "on her *first-chop* dinner-parties, when Lord and Lady "Longears come." *Thackeray.* Put your *chop* on it=put your seal or stamp on it. Also see *Bargain Chop, Security Chop*, etc.

Said to be derived from the Cantonese pronunciation of 劄 to puncture. But *chhápná* is the Hindi verb for "to stamp." Thus, *chápá khána* is "a printing-office."

CHOP. A hulk, in which in the old days foreigners used to reside.

"The Australian mail steamer *Brisbane*, which has "been anchored a little westward of the Police *Chop*, in "getting up her anchor last evening to leave the port, "found it foul of the chop moorings." Hongkong *Daily Press*, 9 Oct. 1877.

CHOP, THE GRAND: 紅 單 *or* 紅 牌. The port clearance granted by the Chinese Customs when all duties have been paid is so called, because formerly it was the most important of the *chops (q.v.)* known to foreigners. It is, literally, *red* chop, from the large vermilion official seal upon it; and this name is sometimes used by merchant captains and others.

CHOP-BOATS: 西 瓜 艑. Lighters or cargo-boats. Literally, "water-melon boats," from the resemblance of the roof

4

to half a water-melon. The last character is sometimes wrongly written 扁.

CHOP CHOP. The *pidgin* equivalent of "make haste." From the Cantonese pronunciation of 急急—*cup cup*, "quick, quick!"

CHOP-DOLLAR. A dollar chopped or stamped with a private mark as a guarantee of its genuineness. Many dollars are quite defaced by the repetition of this process; hence the phrase *chop dollar face* for a man deeply pitted with small-pox. A stand has recently been made in Hongkong against this practice which is confined to Chinese firms in the south of China only. Sometimes these dollars are chopped until the middle is broken out, leaving a large hole. They are then called "spectacle dollars."

CHOP-HOUSES. Customs' stations between Whampoa and Canton were formerly so called, from the chops or seals there used.

CHOP-STICKS: 快子—hasteners. Vulgarly written 筷子. In the book-language 箸 *or* 筋 "helpers." The bamboo or ivory sticks which take the place of knives and forks among the Chinese. The native term has been absurdly rendered "nimble lads," from a misconception of the value of the second character. It is said by 蔡葛山, a former Minister of State, to have been substituted for 箸, which has the same sound and tone as 住 to remain, and is accordingly an inauspicious word for travellers and others who would rather "hasten" home.

CHOSEN: 朝鮮. The Japanese-English transliteration of the two characters which form the Chinese official name of Korea *(q.v.)*.

CHOTA HAZRI. The "small breakfast," or the early tea

and toast. Recently extended to 12 o'clock breakfast, as commonly taken in China. Corrupted form of the Hindi *chhoti hāzri*.

CHOU HAN: 周漢. A native of Hunan, who has distinguished himself of late years by leading a violent crusade against foreign missionaries in China, coupled with the publication of much disgusting anti-foreign literature.

CHOW *or* CHOU: 周. A celebrated dynasty which lasted from B.C. 1122 to B.C. 255. The *Chow le* 禮周, or "Chow Ritual," an elaborate detail of the various officers of the Chow dynasty with their respective duties, is assigned to this period.

CHOW *or* CHOW-CHOW. Food of any kind. Pidgin term invented by Europeans probably in imitation of Chinese sounds. A *chow-chow* amah is a wet nurse. To "chow-chow Joss" is a phrase which illustrates both the adaptability and the undesirability of pidgin-English as a means of communication with the Chinese.

CHOW-CHOW. A preserve in syrup, made up of odds and ends of orange-peel, ginger, pumelo-rind, and leavings generally from the preparation of other preserves. Hence *chow-chow* pickle, which means nothing more than "miscellaneous" or "assorted."

CHOW-CHOW (of cargo). Miscellaneous, as opposed to staples. "He's a *chow-chow* man"=a dealer in all kinds of goods, such as matches, musical-boxes, photographs, etc., etc.

CHOW-CHOW WATER. Same as our nautical term *race*. An overfall of water produced by strong currents dangerous to small boats. Also used of eddying water. Origin of phrase unknown.

CHOW FAH. "Celestial Prince." The child of a king of

Siam by a wife who was herself the daughter of a king. Children by other mothers are *Phraong Chows*. Daughters of princes are *Maum Chows*.

CH'OW-FANG: 籌防—take measures for defence. The "defence tax." Originally known as *Hui-fang* 會防—join in defending. Was first imposed, in the shape of a voluntary capitation tax, for the recovery of the city of Soochow, taken by the T'aip'ing rebels May 1860; and subsequently continued, under its changed name, as a tax upon inland trade, chiefly in the neighbourhood of Shanghai.

CHOWRY: 塵尾 *or* 塵土拂. From a Hindi word meaning fly-brush. Specially applied to the Buddhistic emblem, which is generally a yak's tail and is commonly used in China as a fly-flapper 拂蠅. The chowry, under the Chin 普 dynasty, was the distinguishing mark of a great conversationist.

CHRONOLOGY, CHINESE. Begins, according to the historian Ssŭ-ma Ch'ien, with the Yellow Emperor, B.C. 2697; but B.C. 1,000 may be roughly fixed upon as the earliest date of which there remains any satisfactory record.

CHRYSANTHEMUM: 菊花. Has been a favourite flower in China for many centuries, though without any special significance. The Imperial badge of Japan was long regarded as a sixteen-petalled chrysanthemum; Mr. Haité, however, has recently shown that this so-called flower is really a device representing the sun.

CHRYSÉ. A term vaguely applied by Ptolemy to the border regions of Indo-China.

Col. Yule says "Chrysé is a literal version of the "Sanskrit Suvarnabhumi, or Golden Land, applied in "ancient India to Indo-Chinese regions."

CHU HSI. See *Choo He.*

CHUANG YÜAN: 狀元. The first on the list at the final contest for admission to the Han-lin Academy *(q.v.)* between candidates successful at the great triennial examination for the *chin-shih* or doctor's degree. This examination is called 殿試, because held within the palace at Peking; and the position of a *chuang yüan* may be compared with that of a Senior Wrangler, as being the first man of his year. It was instituted under the Empress who ruled China from A.D. 684 to 705, when the title of the first candidate was also 狀頭.

CHÜ-JÊN: 舉人—the raised man. A graduate of the second or master's degree, the examination for which is held triennially at all the provincial capitals. First created under the T'ang dynasty, during the reign of the Emperor 太宗 T'ai Tsung, A.D. 627—650. The name, however, goes back as far as the Han dynasty.

CH'UN CH'IU. See *Spring and Autumn Annals.*

CHUNAM. A Sanskrit word meaning *lime.* A mixture of lime, oil, and sand, used in China for paving yards, paths, racquet-courts, etc.

CHUSAN: 舟山—boat island. So called because it was thought to resemble a boat. Occupied by the British forces in 1842. Lies off the mouth of the Ningpo river. Towards the end of the 17th century the East India Company established a factory here, but met with no commercial success, and abandoned it only a few years afterwards.

CHUTNEY. A Hindi word (chatni), meaning a kind of pickle.

CLANS (Chinese): 族 *or* 宗族. Hamlets, villages, and sometimes even country towns, are inhabited by people of one common surname and ancestry, forming a tribe or clan.

CLASSICS, THE. A term which is applied by foreigners to what would be more appropriately called the *Sacred Books* of China (see *Four Books* and *Ching*). These were diligently sought out and recovered some few years after the Burning of the Books *(q.v.)*, and were formed into a Canon, the whole being engraved on 46 tablets of stone under the superintendence of a scholar and statesman named Ts'ai Yung about A.D. 172. See *Printing*.

CLEPSYDRA, THE: 更 漏. A water-clock or arrangement of several water-jars, the regulated leakage from which is shown upon a bamboo index. This method of keeping the time seems to have been known at a very early date; the term however does not occur in literature until about B.C. 100.

CLOISONNÉ. The French term for *enamel (q.v.)*; so called because of the *cloisons* or partitions of metal by which the colours are divided.

COCHIN CHINA. (1). This country was, under the Han Dynasty, subject to China, and constituted the 交 趾 (*or* 阯) 郡, which name, as pronounced in Canton—Kau-chi—seems to represent with sufficient accuracy the modern *Cochin*. See *Kiao-tchi*.

(2). From *Kowchin* 九 眞 a name for Annam and Cambodia.

COCK, THE. Is highly esteemed by the Chinese as possessing five excellent qualifications. He wears a hat (comb) like a civilian; he wears spurs like a soldier; he is brave in fight; he is chivalrous towards his hens; and he is faithful in announcing the dawn.

COCK-FIGHTING: 鬪 鷄. Was practised in China some five hundred years B.C.

COCOON: 蠶 繭. Has been derived from the Latin *coccum*,

a berry, through the Italian *coccone*; but is more probably a derivative of the French *coque*, shell.

Pierced cocoons, or those through which the insect has bored its way out, are called 繭壳.

CO-HONG. See *Hong Merchants*.

COIR: 椶. The fibre of cocoa-nut; also prepared from the bark of the hemp palm. Much used in China for ropes, brooms, mats, fly-brushes, etc.

COLANSOO. See *Ku-lang-su*.

COLAO: 閣老—cabinet elder. A Secretary of State under the Ming dynasty. Thus written by the Jesuit missionaries.

COLOURS :—

Yellow: the Imperial colour. Princes of the blood have yellow ropes for their sedan chairs (see *Girdle*). *Red*: the official colour of China under the Chou dynasty. The emblem of joy. The colour of ordinary visiting cards, mandarin seals, bride's dress, bridal chair, etc. *White*: emblem of mourning. White hats and white shoes are never worn except as mourning. *Blue*: At the death of an Emperor all official seals are stamped in this colour, and the paper of scrolls, etc., on doorposts is also changed to blue (or black and white). The ordinary colour of the chair *(q.v.)* of a mandarin below a certain rank. *Green*: The colour of the chair of a mandarin above a certain rank. *Light Brown*: colour of visiting cards when in mourning. After some time has elapsed, a small piece of paper of this colour, with the name inscribed, is pasted in the middle of the usual red card. *Mauve*: is used for the seals of the highest authorities. *Black*: is almost tabooed, as significant of evil. Black fans are used only by old people who are supposed to be beyond the reach of bad influences. Prisoners under the Han dynasty wore black clothes. Official underlings are called the "black band." Devils are always depicted with black faces. Dragon-boats *(q.v.)* are of all colours except black. Opium is called "black dirt," and "to be stained black" is to be addicted to the pipe.

COMMANDMENTS, THE TEN: 十戒 (Buddhist).

    1. Thou shalt not take life.

    2.   „   „   „   steal.

    3.   „   „   „   commit adultery.

    4.   „   „   „   lie.

    5.   „   „   „   drink wine.

    6.   „   „   „   recline on fine couches.

    7.   „   „   „   wear flowers or ribbons.

    8.   „   „   „   sing, dance, or witness plays.

    9.   „   „   „   wear jewels.

   10.   „   „   „   eat except at fixed hours.

    Lay Buddhists are, however, only bound to observe the first five of the above; the others are for the priests.

COMPASS, MARINER'S. Said to have been invented by Chou Kung (B.C. 1110), under the form of a "point-south-chariot," in order to guide on their return journey certain tribute-bearing envoys who had come to China from Tongking. This however is pure legend; and although the Chinese may have been acquainted with the properties of the magnet as early as the Christian era, there appears to be no authentic record of the use of the compass as nautical instrument by them previous to the 12th century of our era.

COMPOUND. The common term for a walled enclosure such as those in which stand the dwelling-house and offices of foreigners in China. The etymology of this word is unknown; it is said, however, to be a corruption of the Portuguese *campanha* derived from *campo* a plain. Compare the Malay *kampong*.

COMPRADORE: 買辦—negotiator of purchases. From the Portuguese *comprar* to buy. The name given to the Chinese agent through whose means foreign merchants in China effect their purchases and sales. Chinese store-keepers and ship-chandlers are also thus designated. The word *compradore* is often transliterated as follows: 江 北大 or 康白度 or 糠擺渡.

COMPRADORE'S ORDER. A draft payable by the compradore, in whose hands a sum of money is usually placed to meet the current expenses of a firm.

CONCORDANCE, THE. See *P'ei wên yün fu.*

CONFUCIAN PENCIL: 文筆塔. Stone columns and small pagodas in the form of the ordinary Chinese writing-brush or pencil are frequently erected to improve the Fêng-Shui *(q.v.)* of a locality. One of the former kind may be seen at Ningpo; the small pagodas of that shape are common all over the south of China. Two may be seen close to Whampoa.

CONFUCIAN TEMPLE: 文廟. To be found in every Prefecture, sub-Prefecture, District, and market-town throughout the empire. In it stand tablets of the Sage, his four evangelists 四配, twelve apostles 十二哲, and other disciples, besides numerous famous literary men of all ages who have contributed to a better understanding of the Confucian doctrines.

CONFUCIUS *or* CONFUTZEE *or* QUANGFOUTCHEE: 孔夫子—K'ung the Master. The Jesuit missionaries took the Chinese sounds of these three characters, K'ung fu tzŭ, and Latinised them into their present form.

The great ethical, not religious, teacher of China.

Flourished B.C. 551—479. [For specimens of his writings and sayings, see *Spring and Autumn* and *Analects*.] Like many others of the world's prophets, he was neglected in life to be honoured after death. Hereditary rank was bestowed by the Emperor Kao Tsu of the Han dynasty, B.C. 200, upon his senior descendant, and the family still continues to enjoy many privileges and immunities to this day. The personal name of Confucius was 丘 Ch'iu, a word which now is never uttered or written in full by devout Confucianists. 某 *mou* "a certain person" is substituted in speech, and in writing a stroke is left out. Confucius was placed by Comte in the second rank of teachers; but his name was wholly omitted from G. A. Sala's list of the Hundred Greatest Men, published a few years ago. Tennyson mentioned him in the 1st edition of *The Palace of Art*, as follows:

> Isaiah with fierce Ezekiel
> Swarth Moses by the Coptic sea,
> Plato, Petrarca, Livy, and Raphael,
> And Eastern Confutzee.

"Confucian literature," says the Rev. J. Chalmers, "is "so pure as not to offend even virgin chastity." The following quaint description of a man who for centuries has influenced hundreds of millions, is given in ch. x of the *Analects*, which makes it incumbent upon us to accept its details as exact:—

"Confucius, in his village home, looked simple and "sincere, as though he had nothing to say for himself. "But when in the ancestral temple or at Court, he spoke "minutely, though cautiously.

"He did not use deep purple or puce colour in the "trimmings of his dress. He required his sleeping-dress "to be half as long again as his body.

"He did not dislike to have his rice finely cleaned,
"nor to have his minced meat cut quite small. He did
"not eat meat which was not cut properly, nor if served
"without its proper sauce. Only in wine he laid down
"no limit, but he did not allow himself to be confused
"by it. He was never without ginger when he ate. He
"did not eat much. When eating, he would not talk.
"When in bed he would not speak. If his mat was not
"straight, he would not sit on it.

"When he saw any one in mourning, he would change
"countenance. When he was at an entertainment where
"there was an abundance of provisions set before him,
"he would change countenance and rise up. On a sudden
"clap of thunder, or a violent wind, he would change
"countenance."

Hence the following skit, from the pen of Bret Harte:—

Confucius—His Habits.—In walking the Master usually
put one foot before the other; when he rested it was
generally on both legs.

If in walking he came upon a stone, he would kick it
out of the way; if it were too heavy he would step over
or around it.

Happening once to kick a large stone, he changed
countenance.

The Superior Person wore his clothes in the ordinary
manner, never putting his shoes upon his head, nor his
cap upon his feet.

He always kept the skirts of his robe, before and
behind, evenly adjusted. He permitted not the unseemly
exposure of his undergarment of linen at any time.

When he met his visitors he rushed towards them with
his arms open like wings.

His Poetry.—The following was written in his sixty-fifth year, on leaving Loo:

> Oh, I fain would still look toward Loo,
> But this Kwei hill cuts off my view—
>   With an axe I will hew
>   This thicket all through
> That obscures the clear prospect of Loo.

In later years the following was composed by his disciple Shun:

> There once was a sage called Confu—
> Cius, whose remarks were not few:
>   He said, 'I will hew
>   'This blasted hill through.'
> While his friends remarked quietly, 'Do.'

His Ethics.—The Master said, 'One virtue goes a great 'way. In a jar of chow-chow, properly flavored with 'ginger, even a dead mouse is palatable.'

On Wau asking him if it were proper to put dead mice in chow-chow, he replied, 'It is the custom.'

When he heard that Chang had beheaded an entire province, he remarked, 'This is carrying things to an 'excess.'

On being asked his opinion of impalement, he replied that 'the end did not justify the means.'

Hop Kee asked him how to tell the superior man. The Master replied, 'How indeed!'

The Duke Shang asked him one day, 'What constitutes 'the State?' Confucius replied, 'The question is asinine.'

His Jokes.—One day being handed a two-foot rule, Confucius opened it the wrong way, whereupon it broke. The Master said quietly, that 'it was a poor rule that 'wouldn't work both ways.'

Observing that Wau Sing was much addicted to opium, the Master said; 'Filial regard is always beautiful.'

'Why?' asked his disciple. 'He loves his poppy,' replied the Master, changing countenance.

'Is that nankeen?' asked the great Mencius, as he carelessly examined the robe that enfolded the bosom of the fair Yau Sing. 'No,' replied the Master, calmly, 'that's Pekin.'

CONG FOU. See *Mesmerism*.

CONGEE: 粥 *or* 糜粥. A thickened decoction made of rice or millet boiled very soft. From the Hindi *kānji* "rice-gruel." Congee-house is sailor slang for "gaol."

CONGOU: 工夫 —labour. A kind of black tea, including several varieties, said to be thus named from the labour of preparing it. From the Amoy pronunciation of the above two characters.

CONSOO HOUSE. The public building belonging to the old hong-merchants *(q.v.)* at Canton. From the local pronunciation of 公司 *company*.

The *Consoo fund* was originally started to defray the debts of bankrupt Chinese hongs at Canton, dealing with foreigners under the old monopoly system. It was the proceeds of a tax of about 3 per cent. on all foreign exports and imports.

CONTRACTS: 合同. May be written or verbal. In the former case, the contract should be signed and *sealed* in the presence of witnesses. In the latter, it is necessary that bargain-money should have passed before the agreement can be held to be binding.

COOLIE. The menial of the east. Two etymologies have been given:—(1) *Kholees* or *Kolis*, the Hindi name of a degenerate race of Rajpoots in Guzerat. (2) A Tamil word *Kûli*, meaning wages. A third and more likely etymology is the Turkish word *kuli* a slave. The Chinese write the word in various ways without reference to its meaning; though we have seen 苦 *K'u*, "bitterness," and 力 *li*, "strength."

COOLIE CHINESE. A term used for the distorted Chinese employed by compradores, shroffs, and servants generally, with reference to their foreign masters and mistresses; e.g., the use of 末士 *mo-shih* for *Mr.* instead of the proper Chinese equivalent; 兵頭 *ping t'ao* "soldier boss" for H. E. the Governor of Hongkong; 江臣 *Kong-shăn* in imitation of the word "Consul," etc., etc.

COOLIE ORANGE: 橙. The *citrus aurantium* or common orange. Coolie here=common, just as *mandarin (q.v.)* often signifies *superior kind of* anything.

COPRAH. Hindi *Khoprā*. The dried kernel of the coco-nut, from which a valuable oil is expressed.

COPYRIGHT. Although no written copyright law exists in China, it is open to an author to prosecute any one who publishes his works, always provided that he carefully keeps the blocks under his own control and notifies the same on the title-page. And in 1896 it was announced at the Mixed Court, Shanghai, that foreigners producing works in China would be entitled to claim the same privilege. The phrase 翻刻必究="All rights reserved," is often seen upon title-pages of the better class of books.

CORAL: 珊瑚. Was known to the Chinese before the Christian era, and is mentioned as coming from Persia and Ceylon. Is used as a medicine, small quantities of powdered coral being administered in certain diseases of childhood.

COREA. See *Korea*.

CORIT: 奇必. A 丈 *chang* or measure of 10 Chinese feet.

CORMORANTS. See *Fishing*.

COTTON. Was introduced from Turkestan about the end of the 13th cent.

COURT DIALECT, THE. The dialect spoken in Peking and its neighbourhood. It has only 421 vocables, and four tones.

COURT OF CONSULS. A tribunal consisting of three Treaty Consuls chosen annually by the Consular Body, before which all suits against the Shanghai Municipal Council are heard and determined.

COVID. The Chinese foot measure of ten inches=14.1 inches English. [Portuguese *covado*, the Flemish ell.]

COWRY. A shell used as money, 200 being equal to one *ānā* or about three halfpence; but the value varies in different localities. The Hindi word is *kauri*. See *Pearl-Oyster*.

COXINGA. See *Koxinga*.

COYAN *or* KOIAN. Malay weight and measure of 40 piculs *(q.v.)*=about 2 tons.

CRACKLE: 逼 裂 文. A peculiar kind of chinaware covered with innumerable cracks; hence the name, which is the same both in English and Chinese.

CRICKETS, FIGHTING: 鬭 蟋 蟀. This is a common pastime in some parts of China. It appears to date from the 13th cent. A.D.

CRIMSON EYEBROWS: 赤 眉. A name given by Fan Ch'ung, leader of a band of insurgents against the rule of the usurper Wang Mang (A.D. 23), to his followers, who had painted their eyebrows red in token of their resolve to fight to the last drop of their blood.

CRORE. Corrupt form of the Hindi word *karor*=10,000,000.

CUDBEAR: 紫 粉. A red dye prepared from a kind of lichen found in France and Sweden, and an article of import into China. The name was invented by Dr. Cuthbert

Gordon, who obtained a patent for this powder, in order to connect it inseparably with his own.

CUE: 辮. The tail of hair worn by every Chinaman. Introduced into China by the present (Manchu) dynasty only about 250 years ago, and long resisted by the natives of the Amoy and Swatow districts, who, when finally compelled to adopt the distasteful fashion, concealed the badge of slavery beneath cotton turbans, the use of which has survived to the present day. It is said to have been originally adopted by the Manchus in imitation of a horse's tail, as a graceful tribute to the animal to which they owed so much.

CUMMERBUND. A sash worn round the waist instead of braces. From *kamar* the loins, and *band* a fastening. [Persian compound.]

CUMQUAT: 金橘—golden orange. A kind of small orange. The *citrus japonica*, Thbg. Found in the south of China, and so called in imitation of the Cantonese sounds. The Chinese term is used metaphorically in the sense of *darling*, much as *chou* "cabbage" in French.

CUMSHAW. A present of any kind. From the Amoy pronunciation of 感謝—grateful thanks. Often used by Chinese beggars to foreigners in the same sense as "baksheesh," which word is unknown to the phraseology of the Far East.

CURIO. Abbreviation for *curiosity*, as applied to bronzes, netsukés, specimens of old china, etc., etc. The word is now commonly used on sign-boards exhibited outside the shops of Chinese tradesmen in this particular line who desire to attract foreign customers.

"The vendor of small and second-hand curios, exposes "upon some door-steps his brass trinkets, his vases, his

"little snuff bottles, and a multitude of trifling articles
"difficult to guard from thieves, with no other protection
"than eternal vigilance." *Bits of Chinese Travel.*

CURRY. A corrupted form of the Hindi word *kārhi*, a
stew. Usually written *cari* or *karick* by the French.

CUSPIDOR. From the Portuguese *cuspir* to spit. The
ornamental Chinese vases used as spittoons are usually
so called.

CUSTARD APPLE: 番荔枝—the foreign *lichee*. The
fruit of the *anona squamosa*. Is a native, according to
Dr. H. F. Hance, of the West Indies and of Brazil; but
was introduced into Asia more than a hundred years
ago. So called because the pulp has a white, custard-like
appearance.

CUSTOMS, IMPERIAL MARITIME. See *I. G.*

CUTCH: 兒茶. An extract obtained by boiling the brown
heartwood of the *Acacia catechu*. So called from the
Runn of Cutch, near which the tree grows. Used by the
Chinese as a dye and medicine, and otherwise known as
Terra Japonica, from the old belief that it was an earth.

CUTCHA. The opposite to *pakka (q.v.).*

CYCLE, CHINESE. Consists of 60 years, designated by
the combination of a set of ten and a set of twelve
characters, taken two together in order. Said to have
been invented B.C. 2637, though it is difficult to trace
it back farther than the Historical Records by Ssŭ-ma
Ch'ien, 1st cent. B.C.

DÁBÁN. A Mongol word signifying *mountain pass*; e.g.,
Yanghi Dábán.

DAGOBA *or* DHAGOBA. From *dhâtu garbha* "relic
preserver." See *Stûpa.*

DAI-BUTSU *or* DAIBOOTS: 大佛—great Buddha. A

5

term applied by the Japanese to images of Buddha, and especially to the three principal ones at Nara, Kamakura, and Hiogo. That at Nara, which was the capital of Japan in the 8th cent. A.D., is of bronze, washed with gold, and represents Amida Buddha in a sitting position. It is formed of large plates of bronze, soldered together, is 53 ft. 6 in. in height, and dates from 747. The image at Kamakura is 49 ft. 7 in. in height, and dates from 1251. Its eyes are pure gold, and the boss on the forehead is of silver and weighs over 30 lbs. The length of one of the eyes is 3 ft. 11 in., and the circumference of one of the thumbs is 3 ft. The image at Hiogo is 48 ft. in height and 85 ft. round the waist. It is not gilt, and dates only from 1891. See *Lama Temple*.

DAIDJI: 台 吉. Japanese hereditary nobles who claim descent from the founder of the Mongol empire, or from the Khans or titular princes and dukes of the various Mongol tribes. May be compared with the Chinese "Yellow Girdles."

DAI IN KUN: 大 院 君. The late father of the King of Korea. Some years ago he became involved in political intrigues, and was carried off to China, but was subsequently permitted to return to Korea.

DAIMIO: 大 名—great name. A Japanese feudal chief or prince. Now called *kwazoku* 華 族, the other two classes of Japanese society being the *shizoku* 士 族 or vassals, formerly known as *samurai*, and the *hei-min* 平 民 or people, including manufacturers, agriculturalists, artisans, and citizens generally.

DAISAKAN: 大 屬. The old term for Japanese Government clerks of the 1st grade; now changed to *Ittozoku* (一 等 屬).

DALADA. The left canine tooth of Buddha, now preserved at Kandy, where it was exhibited to the Prince of Wales.

DALAI LAMA: 達賴喇麻. One of the two popes of the yellow or reformed church of the Lamas. Resides at Lhassa, the capital of Tibet. The other is the Lama Panchhan Rinbochhi of Tashilunpo. Also called Teshulama or Panshen Erdeni. *Dalai* is a Mongol word signifying the "Ocean."

DALNY. A corruption of 大利俺灣 Ta-li-an-wan (or Ta-lien-wan), part of Russia's newly-acquired territory at the entrance of the Gulf of Peichili. The town of Dalny is connected with Port Arthur by telephone and by telegraph. The bay affords a good anchorage, although it is rather shallow near the shore.

DAMAR *or* DAMMAR: 吧嗎油. Is a kind of resin dug out of the forests by the Malays, and apparently the fossilised juices of former growths of the jungle, probably of palms. It is used by the Malays for torches, and by the Chinese for caulking boats. D. is the Malayan term for resin generally.

DANCING. Was not unknown to the ancient Chinese, though of a character allied rather to the minuet than to the valse and performed by bands of male dancers only, chiefly as a State ceremonial. May still be seen upon the Chinese stage. For dancing in Japan, see *Fan Dance* and *Jon-nuké*.

DANDY. A name applied to the two-wheeled vehicles of Province Wellesley in the Malay peninsula. In India, the dandy is a hammock slung on a staff, in which the rider sits sideways or lies on his back. Much used by ladies at hill-stations. From the Hindi *dandi* a staff.

DEATH-BLOW TO CORRUPT DOCTRINES: 辟邪紀實. A scurrilous and disgusting Chinese pamphlet published in 1870, by 唐際盛 T'ang Chi-shêng, Provincial

Treasurer of Hupeh, and directed against the propagation of Christianity in China. Translated into English by Dr. Nevius of Chefoo. With the above was incorporated, under the title of 辟邪論, the famous anti-Christian pamphlet entitled 不得已 "I was obliged to" by 楊光先 Yang Kuang-hsien of the 17th cent., to which Fathers Buglio and de Magalhaens replied in 1662.

DEER'S HORNS: 鹿茸. Imported into China (exported from Newchwang) in large quantities, and used as a stimulant medicine, the only explanation for which seems to be the quantity of ammonia therein contained; though it is quite possible that the sound of the character for deer (identical with that of 祿 emolument, and in some dialects 樂 pleasure, ease) and its emblematic meaning have not been without their influence upon a superstitious people.

DELEGATE BIBLE. A version of the Bible in Chinese, originally intended to be the joint work of Delegates from the various Protestant missionary societies in China. On this plan the New Testament was completed in 1850; but at the 9th ch. of Deuteronomy there was a split in the camp, and Messrs Boone and Bridgman retired, leaving the Old Testament to be completed (in 1855) by Messrs Medhurst, Stronach, and Milne. The style is professedly high-class; but the result is for the most part either unintelligible or obscure.

DENGUE. The Indian name of a kind of fever. Pronounced in various ways, but generally *dengee* with a hard g. Has been derived by some amateur philologue from "Aden ague"—Aden being the place from which it was introduced—by an elision of the two *a*'s.

DEVAS. Divine beings, resident either upon earth or in

one of the six celestial worlds (feminine *devi*). They are of three kinds:—(1) *Kamavachera*, or those still under the dominion of the passions. (2) *Rupavachera*, a higher class, though still trammelled with a form. (3) *Ampavachera*, the highest in degree of purification, devoid of form.

DEVILS: 鬼. Strictly speaking, the disembodied spirits of dead people, but popularly applied to all kinds of ghosts, bogies, the denizens of the Chinese infernal regions, and last, though not least, to foreigners (see *Fanqui*) because of their blue eyes and shrill voices. Devils often mingle with the living in order to work some mischief; but they may always be detected by their want of appetite, their dislike to the smell of sulphur, and the fact· that their bodies throw no shadow. Sometimes they are of a milder disposition, a case being on record in which a devil gained a literary degree for his friend and benefactor. They too suffer death and become 聻.

DHOBY. The Hindi word *(dhobi)* for a washerman. Used in Hongkong, but seldom heard in the north of China.

DHYANA: 禪定. A state of abstract meditation, leading to the entire absence of any desire for existence, cultivated by Buddhist priests. There is a Hall of Meditation in all large Buddhist temples, where priests may be seen sitting with their eyes closed, as though wrapt in contemplation.

DIAGRAMS, THE EIGHT: 八卦. Eight combinations or arrangements of a line and a divided line, either one or other of which is repeated twice, and in two cases three times, in the same combination. Thus there may be three lines, or three divided lines, a divided line above or below two lines, a divided line between two lines, and so on, eight in all. These diagrams are said to have been invented two thousand years and more B.C. by the monarch Fu Hsi who copied them from the back of a tortoise. He subsequently increased the above simple combinations to sixty-four double ones, on the permutations of which are based the philosophical speculations of the Book of Changes *(q.v.)*. Each diagram represents some power in nature, either active or passive, such as fire, water, thunder, earth, etc., etc.

"Whoever the author of the Diagrams may have been, "he seems to have arrived, whether by inspiration or "observation, induction, deduction, or whatever process, "at the simple conclusion that all things visible are but "the phenomena consequent on the action of certain "forces." *Alabaster*. See *Yin and Yang*. The following are specimens of these Diagrams:— ☷, ☳, etc.

DIALECTS: 土話. The chief dialects of China Proper are those spoken at Canton, Amoy, Foochow, Ningpo, Peking, and by the Hakkas *(q.v.)*. Natives of these places are mutually unintelligible, although all the dialects are really offshoots from one parent stem. The written language, however, is practically the same all over the empire.

DIAMOND SÛTRA: 金剛經. A favourite Buddhist sûtra in China, first translated into Chinese by Kumarajiva who died A.D. 417. Its concluding words declare that "all objective existence is like a dream, like a vision, "like a bubble, like shadow, like dew, like lightning, and "should be regarded as such."

DICE: 骰子. Said to have been invented by 陳思王 Ch'ên Ssŭ-wang of the 魏 Wei dynasty, 3rd cent. A.D. Chinese dice are peculiar in that the ace and four are invariably red, while the other points are black. That the ace should be thus marked is easily intelligible, both on account of the Chinese fancy for a dab of the auspicious colour on every available object, and also because the ace is in many cases the highest throw; but it is not generally known why the four should be distinguished in like manner to the exclusion of the rest. One day the Emperor 元宗 Hsüan Tsung of the T'ang dynasty was playing a game with his favourite concubine 楊貴妃 Yang Kuei-fei, and wanted three fours to win. As the dice rolled out, one of them settled down at once shewing the desired number, while the others went on spinning round and round. "Four! four! four!" cried out His Majesty much excited, and the dice immediately settled in obedience to the Imperial call. A eunuch standing by suggested that something should be done to mark this extraordinary event, and orders were consequently issued that in future the four should be coloured red. Mr. Stewart Culin, however, is inclined to connect the characteristics of Chinese dice with astrological science.

A slightly varying account is given in the 情史 under the heading 開元. It is also related in the 說郛 that previous to the T'ang dynasty dice were made of wood, and that then the seeds of the *abrus precatorius* were inserted into small holes, hollowed out for that purpose, to mark the various red points required.

DICTIONARIES: 字典. The Chinese language not admitting of alphabetical arrangement, dictionaries are formed by placing together all characters having the same Radical *(q.v.)* and then further sorting these according to the number of strokes in the remaining portion. Or the characters may be arranged in groups according to their Rhymes, forming what are called Tonic dictionaries, which first came into vogue about A.D. 350. Dictionaries have also been arranged under the Initials *(q.v.)*, and again according to the Phonetics. The first dictionary published in China was the *Shuo Wên (q.v.)*. The last of any importance was that of the Emperor K'ang Hsi *(q.v.)*, which contains about 44,000 different characters. Both are arranged under Radicals.

DISTRICT MAGISTRATE. See *Chih-hsien*.

DITCHERS. (1) Calcutta Englishmen are so called, from a fosse dug round the city in 1742, as a defence against the Mahrattas.

(2) The long narrow steamers built for the China trade subsequent to the opening of the Suez Canal, which is the "ditch."

DIVORCE: 出 妻. A Chinaman may divorce his wife for any one of the following reasons:—

(1) Barrenness; (2) Lasciviousness; (3) Neglect of his parents; (4) Talkativeness; (5) Thieving; (6) Jealous temper; (7) Loathsome disease.

But not under any one of the following extenuating circumstances:—

(1) If the wife has been in mourning *(q.v.)* for her husband's parents; (2) if the husband has grown rich since their marriage; (3) if the wife has no home to which she can go back.

DOCTRINE OF THE CH'I (氣). [Before perusing the following quotation from Sir C. Alabaster's exposition of this difficult subject, the reader is requested to refer to (1) *Diagrams* and (2) *Yin and Yang*.] "To class "phenomena was his next thought, but ere he could "conveniently do so, he needed now a name not only "for his symbol but for its parts; and from the sound "of the wind which had breathed the dead water before

"him into life and motion, he called the Initial Force
" *Ch'i*, adding thereto the word by which they already
"expressed grandeur, T'ai Ch'i, the Great Breath, the
"life, the soul, the spirit of the Living Universe."

DOCTRINE OF THE MEAN: 中 庸—invariable medium.
One of the Four Books, the title of which was translated
as above by Dr. Legge. A philosophical work, ascribed
to K'ung Chi, otherwise known as Tzŭ Ssŭ, the grandson of
Confucius. Traces the ruling motives of human conduct from
their psychological source. The following is a specimen:—

In archery we have something like the way of the
superior man. When the archer misses the bull's-eye, he
turns and seeks for the cause of his failure in himself.

How abundantly do spiritual beings display the powers
that belong to them! We look for them, but do not see
them; we listen for, but do not hear them; yet they
enter into all things and there is nothing without them.

DOGS: 犬 and 狗. Are classed among the six domestic
animals of China and are much valued for their fidelity,
although looked down upon for other reasons so that the
word is regarded as a term of abuse. The flesh of dogs
is very sparingly eaten, and then only when the animal
has been fed for the table. The dog-butchers in Canton
are almost as much a curiosity to Chinese from the
north, where there are none, as to foreigners from the
other side of the world.

DOKMA. The Parsi burying-ground or Tower of Silence
(q.v.).

DOLLAR. From the German *thaler*, which word was taken
from the name of the place "Joachims-thal," where, in
the 15th century, the Counts of Schlick coined the silver
extracted from their mines into one-ounce pieces. The

symbol $ has been supposed to be the monogram of U.S.—United States; but others maintain that it is an imitation of the pillars and scroll on the Spanish Carolus or "pillar" dollar *(q.v.)*. Another suggestion is that it is the old cancelled figure of 8, sometimes written /8/, a distinguishing mark in account-books of Spanish dollars which were worth eight reals and were known as pieces of eight (see *Robinson Crusoe*).

DOLON NOR. (See *Lama Miao*). A famous place in Mongolia, so called from the seven lakes *(nor)* there.

DOMA. Court-yard in a Japanese house.

DOMINOES: 牙牌. A set of dominoes, consisting of 32 tablets with 227 spots in all, was presented to the Emperor in the year A.D. 1120. The spots were explained as referring to various categories such as "the four seasons," "the twenty-four solar terms," etc.

DOTCHIN: 度秤 *tu ch'êng*, to weigh. A steel-yard.

DOUBLE ISLAND. (See *Swatow*). The Chinese name *Mah-soo* is either 孖嶼, *lit.* "double island," or 媽嶼 from the name of a goddess who has a small shrine there. Is called 放雞山 "release-fowl-hill" in the Hist. of Chao-chou Fu.

DRAGON: 龍. The Chinese emblem of Imperial power. A fabulous monster whose habitat is in the clouds, by which it is concealed from view. The Imperial dragon is distinguished by the addition of a fifth claw to the usual four.

DRAGON'S BLOOD: 血竭. A resin yielded by the 渴留 *Dæmonorops draco*, a sort of palm found in Sumatra. Used as an astringent, styptic, tonic, etc.

DRAGON BOATS: 龍船. The long boats used for racing at the Dragon Festival.

DRAGON FESTIVAL: 端陽 or 端午. A river festival, annually celebrated with boat-racing on the 5th of the 5th moon in memory of the poet and patriot Ch'ü P'ing of the 4th cent. B.C., who, degraded by his prince and disgusted with the world, drowned himself in the river 汨羅.

DRAGON THRONE: 龍位. So called because the dragon is the Chinese emblem of Imperial power.

DRAMA. See *Theatre*.

DUBASH. A two-tongued man, *sc.* linguist, or interpreter. From the Hindustani *dobāshī*.

DUCKS. See *Bombay Duck*.

DUIT. At Singapore, equals $\frac{1}{4}$ cent.

DUNGANS. Mahommedan subjects of China who in very early times were colonised, under the name of Gao-tchan, in Kansuh and Shensi, and subsequently spread westward into Chinese Turkestan and Jungaria. Some however maintain that the D. are a distinct race, who in the fifth and sixth centuries occupied the Tian Shan range, with their capital at Karashar. But *Tungani* means in the dialect of Chinese Tartary "converts," *i.e.* to Mahommedanism, to which they were converted in the time of Timour by an Arabian adventurer. Were finally destroyed as a people by the Chinese in 1876.

DURIAN *(Durio Zibethinus)*. A fruit found in the Malay Archipelago, of about the size of a man's head, with a thick rind containing a creamy pulp of a delicious flavour but so horribly offensive in smell that few Europeans can bring themselves to taste it.

DUTCH FOLLY: 海珠石 or Sea-Pearl Rock. A small island in the river near the city of Canton, said to have been originally a pearl dropped into the water by a merchant. Another account says it was so named by the

Chinese as resembling a pearl floating on the water. It appears that the Dutch once built a fort on the island; hence the foreign name. In the war which arose out of the "Arrow" case, the island was used as a coign of vantage from which to bombard the adjacent city.

DUTCH FORTS. These remains of the Dutch occupation of Formosa (see *Koxinga*) are still to be found. The best preserved is at Tamsui, where it now forms part of the British Consulate. It is built of red brick, and the walls are 10 or 12 feet in thickness. See *Zealandia*.

DUTCH WIFE. A light frame, either of rattan or lacquered wood, used in bed as a kind of leg and arm rest, with a view to coolness, by persons who sleep badly in hot weather. Those in use among the Chinese are hollow cylindrical frames of bamboo, and are called, by a curious coincidence, 竹夫人 "bamboo wives." Also mentioned by 陸龜蒙 Lu Kuei-mêng, the celebrated poet of the T'ang dynasty, under the name 竹夾膝 "bamboo leg rests."

Apropos of this entry, we may add that a Chinese bed-warmer is called a 湯夫人 or *hot water wife*, being generally a hollow earthenware figure, filled with hot water and used as a hot bottle with us.

DYAKS: 里猫柔. More correctly *Dayaks*. Used by the Malays as a generic term for all the wild races of Sumatra and Celebes, but now especially of Borneo, where they are most numerous, in which sense it is equivalent to our word "savages."

DYNASTIES, CHINESE.

Legendary Rulers		B.C.	2852—2205
Hsia dynasty	夏	„	2205—1766
Shang „	商	„	1766—1122
Chou „	周	„	1122—255

Ch'in dynasty	秦	B.C.	255—206	
Han „	漢	„	206—A.D.	221
Minor dynasties		A.D.	221— „	618
T'ang dynasty	唐	„	618— „	907
Five dynasties	五代	„	907— „	960
Sung dynasty	宋	„	960— „	1260
Yüan (Mongol) „	元	„	1260— „	1368
Ming „	明	„	1368— „	1644
Ch'ing (Manchu) „	清	„	1644—	

DZASSAK: 扎薩克. The chiefs who rule the Mongolian Banners *(q.v.)* are so called. The office is in some cases hereditary; in others, conferred by Imperial appointment.

EARTH, TEMPLE OF: 地壇—altar of Earth. A large enclosure within the walls of the Chinese or outer portion of the city of Peking, dedicated to the worship of Earth as one of the Three Forces 三才, *i.e.* Heaven, Earth, and Man. It is here that the Emperor, ploughing with his own hand, annually turns the first sod of the year, desiring by his example to glorify agriculture, the mainstay of the Chinese people.

EAST INDIA COMPANY. First established a factory *(q.v.)* at Canton in 1684. Monopoly terminated 1834. The character 公 for 公司 *company*, as prefixed to opium (公烟 company opium) and other goods, is a survival of the old days when the name of the celebrated "Kumpani" was sufficient guarantee for the quality of its goods.

EIGHTEEN PROVINCES, forming China Proper.

1.	Chihli	5.	Kiangsu
2.	Shantung	6.	Anhui
3.	Shansi	7.	Kiangsi
4.	Honan	8.	Chehkiang

9.	Fuhkien	14.	Yünnan
10.	Hupeh	15.	Kueichou
11.	Hunan	16.	Ssŭch'uan
12.	Kuangtung	17.	Shensi
13.	Kuangsi	18.	Kansuh

To these might now be added Shing-King *(q.v.)* which is virtually a nineteenth province, its administration having been changed since 1876 from military to civil.

[For Chinese characters, old names, capital cities etc., see under each heading.]

The thirteen provinces of the Ming dynasty may be obtained from the above table by striking out Nos. 1, 5, 6, and 18, and combining Nos. 10 and 11 into one.

ELEUTH MONGOLS: 厄 (*or* 額) 魯特. Same as the "Kalmucks," which is the western name of this division of the Mongols. "Eleuth" or "Oëlot" is probably from Wara or Oirad 瓦喇, the name of the leading tribe known to the Ming Emperors.

EMPERORS OF THE PRESENT DYNASTY, KNOWN AS THE *TA TSING* (Q.V.) OR "GREAT PURE."

Style of reign.	Accession.	Reigned.	Chinese.
Shun Chih	1644 A.D.	18 years	順治
K'ang Hsi *or* Kang Hi	1662 ″	61 ″	康熙
Yung Chêng	1723 ″	13 ″	雍正
Ch'ien Lung *or* Kien Lung	1736 ″	60 ″	乾隆
Chia Ch'ing *or* Kia King	1796 ″	25 ″	嘉慶
Tao Kuang	1821 ″	30 ″	道光
Hsien Fêng *or* Hien Fung	1851 ″	11 ″	咸豐
T'ung Chih	1862 ″	13 ″	同治
Kuang Hsü	1875 ″		光緒

EMPRESS DOWAGER: 慈禧皇太后. The mother of the last Emperor T'ung Chih *(q.v.)*, said to have been sold as a slave-girl at the age of 14, in consequence of the poverty of her parents. She was actually only a concubine of the Emperor Hsien Fêng, but as mother of the Heir Apparent who subsequently ascended the throne, she ranked with the real Empress 慈安; and for many years, until the death of the latter in 1881, the two ladies ruled China together as Joint Regents. During the short reign of T'ung Chih they nominally retired from the government, but resumed power on his death in 1875, when they placed on the throne a four-year old cousin of the late Emperor, now known as Kuang Hsü. In 1889 the Empress Dowager formally relinquished the administration to him, but once more seized the reins in 1898, after a *coup d'état* by which Kuang Hsü was checked in a career of reform and was practically deposed. Is popularly known as 太后佛爺 Her Imperial Majesty Buddha.

ENAMEL: 發藍 *or* 琺琅. The English name for that kind of Chinese ornamental ware which is produced by fixing colours on a copper basis by the application of heat. French, *cloisonné (q.v.)*. The Chinese term *fa-lang* is unquestionably a corruption of *Frank*, through Feringhi [1] 佛狼機, the name under which the early Portuguese traders were known to the Chinese.

ENCYCLOPAEDIAS: 類書. Have been compiled in China on large scale for many centuries, the subjects being arranged under categories, as Heaven, Earth, Man, Sciences, Philosophy, etc. The most famous is the 圖書

---

[1] Now applied contemptuously to the Portuguese by the natives of Calcutta.

集成, arranged as above and profusely illustrated. It was originated by the Emperor K'ang Hsi and completed under his successor in 1726 in 10,000 books dealing with 6,109 sub-heads. Only 100 copies were printed, from movable copper types, for presentation to deserving officials and others. That the types were movable can be proved from the fact that here and there characters will be found upside down or on their sides, which could not possibly occur in block-printing. The whole has been beautifully reproduced by photo-lithography by Messrs Major Bros., Shanghai, and fills 1628 vols, 8vo, of about 200 pp. each.

EPICURUS (of China, The). A name which has been applied, though without the slightest justification, to Lao Tzŭ *(q.v.)*.

ERDENI. See *Panshen*.

ERH YA. See *Urh Ya*.

ETA. A pariah class under the old régime of Japan, whose disabilities have since been removed. Their business was with hides, dead animals, etc.

ETIQUETTE. (Chinese). Never sit down while your visitor is standing, nor pass before him through a door. Never speak to an equal from a chair or from on horseback, but dismount, nor without first removing your spectacles. Always place a visitor on your left; and in handing anything to him, invariably use *both* hands. When he takes his leave, accompany him to the front door.

Chinese servants should not (strictly speaking) appear before their masters in short clothes, nor without socks, nor with shoes down at heel, nor with the tail tied round the head. They should not loll about, but stand in a respectful attitude with their hands down; and on meeting their employers in the street, they should stand aside and yield the path. They should not wear gaudy clothes, nor blue socks, and should be shaved regularly at short intervals.

Chinese street etiquette is also quite different from our own, a fact usually ignored by blustering foreigners who march through a Chinese town as if the place belonged to them, and not unfrequently complain that coolies and others will not "get out of their way." There is, in fact, a graduated scale of Chinese street rights in this particular respect, to which, as being recognised by the Chinese themselves, it would be advisable for foreigners to pay some attention. In England it has been successfully maintained that the roadway belongs to all equally, foot-passengers, equestrians, and carriage-passengers alike. Each is bound to respect the rights of the other, and is responsible for any accident arising from disregard of this principle. Not so in China; the ordinary foot-passenger is bound to "get out of the way" of the lowest coolie who is carrying a load; that same coolie must make way, even at great inconvenience to himself, for a sedan-chair; an empty chair yields the way to a chair with somebody inside; a chair, inasmuch as being more manageable, gets out of the way of a horse; and horse, chair, coolie, and foot-passenger, all clear the road for a wedding or other procession, or for the retinue of a mandarin. Apropos of the custom of getting out of a chair or getting off a horse on meeting a friend who is walking, we have omitted to state that in such cases it is considered the duty of anyone on foot, observing the approach of an acquaintance in a chair or on horseback, to screen his face with his fan and prevent the other from catching his eye, thus saving him the trouble of dismounting. Thus when two high mandarins of equal rank, such as a Viceroy and Tartar General, find themselves face to face in their chairs, those attendants among their retinues who carry the enormous wooden fans rush forward and insert them between the passing chairs, so that their masters may be presumed not to see each other, and consequently not be obliged to get out. No subordinate can ever meet a higher mandarin in this way; the former must turn down some by-street immediately on hearing the approaching gong of his superior officer. At interviews with their superiors, subordinates should not use fans, even in the hottest weather. See *Presents*, *Visits*.

EUNUCHS: 太監. Are employed in the Imperial palace at Peking, for the service (1) of the Emperor, who should have 3,000 in all; (2) of princes and princesses of the blood, sons, grandsons, great-grandsons, and great-great-grandsons, of Emperors; and (3) of the descendants of the eight Manchu chiefs who assisted in the establishment of the present dynasty. The use of eunuchs in China is said to date back to B.C. 1100. From time to time they have played very prominent parts in the history of China, and have even been allowed to adopt sons to inherit their honours. In A.D. 190, a eunuch named Chang Jang actually kidnapped an Emperor. In the early part of the 15th cent., another eunuch named Chêng Ho commanded several important expeditions, even reaching Ceylon and Hormuz in the Persian Gulf. The fall of the Ming dynasty in 1644 has been traced to the pernicious influence of eunuchs in political matters and the present dynasty has kept a tight hand upon them. In 1869 the favourite eunuch of the present Empress Dowager was summarily beheaded for violent behaviour in the province of Shantung, whither he had proceeded to make purchases for his mistress.

EURASIAN. The offspring of a European father and an Asiatic mother. There is a Eurasian school in Shanghai.

EVER VICTORIOUS ARMY: 長勝軍. The Imperial army which ultimately, under the leadership of Colonel Gordon (otherwise known as "Chinese Gordon"), put an end to the T'ai-p'ing *(q.v.)* rebellion. So named because never defeated.

EXAMINATIONS, COMPETITIVE. Have been carried on in China for many centuries, though the modern system, in regard to its various details, dates only from the Sung dynasty, A.D. 960—1260. Three degrees are granted, each of which confers special privileges. They are those of *hsiu ts'ai*, *chü jen*, and *chin shih*, *(qq.v.)*. The examination for the first degree is held twice in every three years by the Literary Chancellor at the prefectural cities of each province. It occupies only one day. The candidates assemble at the place of examination before dawn, and are provided with seats and paper. They are carefully searched on entering, but often find means to elude the vigilance of their searchers; and instead of having the *Four Books* at their fingers' ends, they have them, in the form of diamond editions, concealed up their flowing sleeves. As soon as it is light enough, two themes for prose essays, and one for a poem, are carried round on long poles and are copied down by all. Then ensues a struggle as to who shall finish first, a certain proportion of marks being allowed for speed in composition; and by degrees all the papers are handed in, and the candidates disperse. Some few days afterwards the list is issued; and it is a joyful moment for those who find themselves in possession of the first literary degree, a degree which launches its owner fairly in a recognised career, entitles him to wear official dress with a gilt button of the lowest grade, and exempts him as a prisoner, or as a witness, from the indignity of the bamboo, at any rate until such time as his case shall have been reported to the higher authorities and his diploma cancelled.

The examination for the second degree is held in the autumn of every third year, by an Imperial Commissioner, usually spoken of as the Grand Examiner, who is specially deputed by the Emperor for that purpose. On his arrival from Peking his residence is formally sealed up, and extraordinary precautions are taken to prevent friends of intending candidates from approaching him in an improper sense. At an early hour on the appointed day the candidates begin to assemble, and by-and-by the great gates of the examination hall are thrown open and heralds shriek out the names of those who are to enter. Each one answers 'Adsum' in turn as his name is called, and forthwith receives from the attendants a roll of paper marked with the number of the open cell he is to occupy in one of the long alleys into which the examination hall is divided. Other writing materials, as well as food, he carries with him in a basket, which is always carefully searched at the door. When all have found their seats, the Grand Examiner burns incense and closes the entrance gates, through which no ingress nor egress will now be permitted on any pretence whatever, until the afternoon of the third day, when the first of three bouts or sittings is at an end. In case of death, which is by no means unusual where a large number of human beings are cooped up day and night in a confined space, the body is always hoisted over the outer wall; and this rule would be carried out even were it the Grand Examiner himself, whose place would then be taken by his chief Assistant-Examiner, a functionary who is also nominated by the Emperor and accompanies the Grand Examiner from Peking. The themes are next exhibited and copied down by the candidates. For this first bout there are three for prose essays, always taken from the *Four Books*, and one subject for a poem. An essay should consist of about 700 to 800 characters in length, and the poem of twelve lines, both to be correctly written and the latter in a stated metre; the paper, moreover, not to be soiled or torn. On the afternoon of the third day the candidates hand in their compositions, and are then released until the next morning, when they reassemble for a second bout of three days, as before, to compose five essays on themes taken from the *Five Classics*. On the afternoon of the third day the results of their labours are again handed in by the candidates, and the gates thrown open, to be closed as before on the following morning for a third and last bout of three days, devoted to answering questions on miscellaneous topics selected by the examiners from any source they may choose.

The examination for the third degree is held in Peking once in every three years, in the spring directly following the examination for the second degree. This examination is conducted upon lines almost identical with those of the provincial competition for the preceding degree. It is similarly divided into three sittings, of three days to each, and the subjects, taken from the same sources, are necessarily of the same character. Some 8,000 to 9,000 candidates compete, and among them about 300 degrees are distributed. The winners of this degree are divided into three classes. Upon the first are bestowed appointments in the National Academy of Literature; upon the second, subordinate posts in government offices at Peking; and upon the third, nominations to the ranks of 'expectant' officials, under the various provincial administrations.

Any Chinaman may present himself for the 1st degree who can show that none of his ancestors for three generations have been either actors, barbers, priests, executioners, official servants, etc. There is no limit of age, an instance being recorded of a man who took his third degree at the age of seventy-two.

EXPRESS, AN. A public notification or advertisement of any kind, generally printed and circulated by one of the printing-offices in Shanghai on behalf of those concerned. In an article on *Old Expresses* once published in the *North-China Daily News*, the writer says, "They com-"memorate occurrences that were important at the time "to somebody, and they contain the names of many "persons who have passed away." See *Bunder*.

EXTRA-TERRITORIALITY. The exemption of foreigners residing in China (formerly in Japan, but abolished 1899) from trial and punishment according to the laws of that country.

"British subjects who may commit any crime in China, "shall be tried and punished by the Consul, or other "public functionary authorized thereto, according to the "laws of Great Britain." *Treaty of Tientsin: Art.* XVI.

"What tome or treatise can explain
Thy individuality?"
"I spring from Treaties," whispered back
Exterritoriality.

This word is often written *ex-territorial*; but from the sense it is clearly a similar compound to *extra-parochial*, *extra-provincial*, and such words, and should be spelt accordingly.

FA HSIEN. A Chinese Buddhist priest, who in the year 399 A.D. travelled from China to India overland. He visited Patna, Benares, Buddha-Gaya, and other famous spots, obtaining copies of some of the sacred books of Buddhism, and returning to China by sea, viâ Ceylon and Sumatra, in the year 417 A.D.

FACTORIES, THE. So called from their being the residence of *factors*, or agents of the East India Company, and not because anything was manufactured there. The former residences of foreigners in the western suburbs of Canton, to which they were strictly confined. "The factories were "a series of 13 *hongs (q.v.)*. They were placed side by "side of each other, forming as it were a row or terrace "fronting the river, but each Hong consisted of a series "of buildings placed one behind the other from the river "backwards, for a depth of from 550 to 600 feet to the first "street running parallel with the river." *S. W. Williams.*

FAI TEE: 快 的 —make haste! [Cantonese.]

FAI-T'ING: 快 艇 —fast boat. A small passenger boat in use at Canton.

FA-KEE *or* FA-KI: 花 旗 —the flowery flag. A common Chinese name for the United States, alluding to the "stars and stripes" of the national standard.

FAN CH'IEH. See *Spelling System.*

FAN DANCE (of Japan). The dancer, a girl of about thirteen, is elaborately dressed as a page. Confined by the closely-folded robe, the feet and legs are not much used, the feet, indeed, never leaving the ground. Time is marked by undulations of the body, waving the arms, and deft manipulation of a fan. One movement succeeds another by transitions singularly graceful, the arms describing innumerable curves, and the fan so skilfully handled as to seem instinct with a life and liberty of its own.

FANG TAN: 方單—square document. Local Shanghai term for a title-deed to land, issued in lieu of original deeds which may have been lost. Properly a 執業田單, and called *fang tan* (1) because the character 田 is square, or (2) because it is sealed with a square seal, or (3) because the document itself is square.

FANQUI *or* FAN KUEI-TZŬ: 番鬼—foreign devils, *i.e.*, foreigners. An absurd attempt was once made to shew that the epithet "devils" was applied to foreigners more as a "term of endearment" than anything else, on the ground that the Chinese have good devils as well as bad in their unseen universe, and that there is no reason to believe they necessarily connect us with the latter. Mr. Wu T'ing-fang, Minister to the United States, formerly known as Mr. Ng Choy, thinks that the term *fan-qui* has now lost much of its insulting significance, and that the common word *fan* (see *Barbarians*) is used by the Chinese without the slightest reference to its original meaning; but although there may be much truth in his latter proposition, it is none the less desirable that both these expressions should disappear. The same gentleman states that the Cantonese slang term for missionaries is *Yeh-soo kwai*, "Jesus devils." Pidgin-English-speaking Chinese have mixed up *fan* with our word *foreign*, in which sense it is often used in conversation.

The following story, bearing out the view that the

Chinese often term us "devils" without reference to the meaning of the word, was vouched for by Mr. Mongan, H. M. Consul at Tientsin. Shortly after the opening of the Tientsin Consulate, a Chinaman presented himself before Mr. Mongan with a present of some kind, which he said he had brought from his home, several hundred *li* distant, in obedience to the command of his dying father who had formerly been cured of ophthalmia by a foreign doctor at Canton, and who had told him, upon his death-bed, "never to forget the English." Yet this present was addressed to 大英國鬼子孟大人—"To "His Excellency the Great English Devil, Mongan." See *Devils*.

FANS: 扇. Were made in early ages from feathers, the symbol for which appears in the lower portion of the written character. The Chinese fan proper is now a light frame of bamboo or ivory, round or otherwise, over which silk has been stretched, since the 4th cent. A.D., for purposes of painting or calligraphy. The 摺扇 folding fan was invented by the Japanese, and was first mentioned in the 11th cent. by Su Tung-p'o as having come to China through Korea. In the early years of the 15th cent. folding fans formed part of the tribute sent from Korea to Peking, and one writer mentions, as a curiosity, four Japanese folding fans which had been given to him by Father Ricci, the eminent Jesuit, whom by the way he calls a 外國道人. Fans are used by the Chinese, men and women alike, from the highest officials down to the lowest coolie, and even by the very soldiers in the ranks. Different kinds are used at different seasons by all who can afford to pay for this form of luxury; and it is considered ridiculous to be seen with a fan either too early or too late in the year. They are made to serve the same purpose as an album among friends of a literary turn, who paint flowers upon them for each other and inscribe verses in what is sometimes called the "fan language." They are also used to circulate the news of any important event among the people at large; e.g., the Tientsin Massacre, the brutalities of which were depicted in glowing colours upon cheap paper fans and sold in large quantities until prohibited by the officials. At Canton, and probably elsewhere, fans may be purchased having on one side a plan of the city with the names of the principal streets, temples, yamêns, etc., printed in small Chinese characters.

Mr. Stent published the Index to his vocabulary on photographed slips pasted on to the frame of a common fan. Others are sold which are fans only in form, being really sheaths for daggers, as carried by street rowdies, etc. A deserted wife is spoken of metaphorically as "an autumn fan," 秋後扇. See *Umbrella*, *Red*, and *Etiquette*.

FAN-T'AI: 藩臺. A high provincial authority in China, known to foreigners as the Commissioner of Finance or Provincial Treasurer. Is charged with the fiscal or financial administration of a province. Controls, as head of the civil service, the nomination to, and distribution of, nearly all the minor appointments therein, subject always to the approval of the *Fu-t'ai* or Governor.

FANTAN: 番攤. The celebrated method of gambling with cash *(q.v.)*, common in China. (*Fan* here means "number of times," and *t'an* "to apportion," in allusion to the payment of stakes so many times the original amount according to circumstances). A pile of the coin is covered with a bowl, and the players stake on what the remainder will be when the heap has been divided by 4—namely 1, 2, 3, nothing. The croupier then counts the whole rapidly out by subtracting 4 cash at each sweep of a small rod used for that purpose. Players who stake *on the winning number*, get 3 times the amount of their original stake, less 7 per cent commission for the good of the house. Thus, a dollar will return $ 2.79 clear profit. Suppose however that the dollar is placed *midway between two numbers*, and one of these turns out to be the winning number, the bank pays once the amount of the stake, less commission=$ 0.93 net profit. Again, supposing the dollar to be placed between numbers 1 and 2, so as to be more on 2 than on 1. If 2 cash are left, the player receives twice his stake, less commission, and if 1 is left, he receives his dollar back.

FAR EAST. *Fr.* L'Extrême-Orient. A term which includes China, Japan, the Philippines, the Malay peninsula, Siam, etc.

FA TI: 花地—flower grounds. The well-known Chinese gardens on the opposite bank of the river to the city of Canton are so called.

FAVOURED-NATION CLAUSE. The article in a Treaty —*e.g.*, the Treaty concluded at Tientsin, 1858, between the British and Chinese Governments—by which it is stipulated that "the British Government and its subjects "will be allowed free and equal participation in all "privileges, immunities, and advantages that may have "been, or may be hereafter, granted by His Majesty the "Emperor of China to the Government or Subjects of "any other nation." *Art.* LIV.

The term originated from the frequent occurrence in such clauses of the actual words "favoured nation."

See Treaty between Russia and China, English version, Art. XII.

FEAST OF LANTERNS: 燈節. Held annually on the 15th of the first Chinese moon, *i.e.*, at the first full moon of the year, when coloured lanterns are hung at every door. Originally a ceremonial worship in the temple of the First Cause, dating from about the time of the Han dynasty. The mid-autumn festival of the 15th of the 8th moon is sometimes so called by foreigners.

No respectable Chinaman is ever seen out after dark without a lantern.

FEET. See *Small Feet*.

FEMALE CHILDREN. See *Infanticide*.

FÊNG-HUANG *or* FUNG-HWANG: 鳳凰. A fabulous bird of good omen. Said to appear in times of national prosperity. Generally translated by *phœnix*.

FÊNG-SHUI *or* FUNG-SHWUY: 風水—wind and water, or that which cannot be seen, and that which cannot be grasped. The great geomantic system of the Chinese, by the *science* of which it is possible to determine the desirability of sites whether of tombs, houses, or cities, from the configuration of such natural objects as rivers, trees, and hills, and to foretell with certainty the fortunes of any family, community, or individual, according to the spot selected; by the *art* of which it is in the power of the geomancer to counteract evil influences by good ones, to transform straight and noxious outlines into undulating and propitious curves, rescue whole districts from the devastations of flood or pestilence, and "scatter plenty o'er a smiling land" which might otherwise have known the blight of poverty and the pangs of want. It is said to have been first applied to graves by 郭璞 Kuo P'o, a learned scholar who died A.D. 324, and to house-building by 王伋 Wang Chi, a scholar of the Sung dynasty.

For many years the Chinese urged that the introduction of railways and telegraph poles would seriously injure the Fêng-shui or prosperity of the districts through which they might be carried; but this view is gradually melting away, even in the eyes of the most bigoted of Chinese statesmen, "into the infinite azure of the past."

As one example among many, we may state that the roofs of adjoining houses are never built on the same level. Hence the *Fêng-shui* of Oxford Street would in this respect be considered good; that of most Parisian thoroughfares, bad. For a grave, a wide river in front, a high cliff behind, with enclosing hills to the right and left, would constitute a first-class geomantic position.

Houses and graves face the south, because the annual animation of the vegetable kingdom with the approach of summer comes from that quarter; the deadly influences of winter from the north.

FERINGHEES. Franks. Epithet first applied by the Chinese to the early Portuguese traders. See *Enamel*.

FESTIVALS, CHINESE. See *Moon*. The more important of these are

(1) New Year's Day, when all business is absolutely suspended.

(2) Feast of Lanterns *(q.v.)*, 15th day of 1st moon.

(3) Festival of Ancestral Worship *(q.v.)*, 19th of 2nd moon.

(4) Festival of Dragon Boats *(q.v.)*, 5th of 5th moon.

(5) Festival of Mid-Autumn, 15th of 8th moon.

(6) Festival of All Souls (in Purgatory), 1st to 9th of 10th moon.

FEUDATORIES, THE THREE: 三蕃王. Three powerful leaders who were appointed by the Emperor K'ang Hsi to rule over large portions of the empire in a semi-independent fashion. They were 尚可喜 Shang K'o-hsi, 耿精忠 Kêng Ching-chung, and 吳三桂 Wu San-kuei.

FIG, CHINA. The persimmon *(q.v.)*, is so called; but the Chinese grow real figs, which they call 無花菓 or the "flowerless fruit."

FI-HI: 快蟹—fast crabs. A class of war-junk is so called.

FILIAL PIETY, THE CLASSIC OF: 孝經. A record of a conversation between Confucius and a disciple, named Tsêng Ts'an, on the subject of filial piety. Its genuineness has been doubted, though it is at least as old as the 1st cent. B.C. Confucius declared in the *Analects* that true filial piety does not consist in toiling for and supporting parents, but rather in guarding them from mental annoyance while alive, and in following out their injunctions when dead. He also insists upon a reverential care of the person, as a sacred trust which may not be regarded lightly.

FILIPINOS. The native inhabitants of the Philippines (see *Luzon*). They are of Malay origin, and number from six to eight millions. They are divided into various tribes, scattered over the numerous islands of the Philippine group. Many of them are civilised, while others live in a savage state. Some are not of full Malay blood, but are half-breed Negritos.

FINALS. See *Spelling System*.

FINGERS: 指頭. The following are common names for the fingers: 大指 or 將指 the big finger or commanding finger (= thumb), 食指 the tasting finger, 中指 the middle finger, 無名指 the nameless finger, 小指 the little finger. For purposes of numeration every finger on the left hand represents nine figures, the little finger the units, the ring finger the tens, the middle finger the hundreds, the forefinger the thousands, the thumb the tens of thousands. The three inner joints represent from 1 to 3, the three outer joints 4 to 6, the right side of each joint 7 to 9. The forefinger on the right hand is employed for pointing to the figure to be called into use; thus, 1,234 would at once be denoted by just touching the inside of the upper joint of the forefinger, representing 1,000; then the inside of the second, or middle joint of the middle finger, representing 200; thirdly, the inside of the lower joint of the ring finger, representing 30, and lastly, the upper joint of the little finger touched on the outside, representing 4.

The figures 1—10 are commonly expressed in conversation by the following signs:

1. Close the fist and hold up the thumb.
2. „ „ „ „ „ „ fore and middle fingers.
3. „ „ „ „ „ „ middle, third, and little fingers.
4. Hold up 4 fingers, knuckles towards spectator, thumb concealed.
5. Hold up open hand, palm to spectator.
6. Close the fist, hold up thumb and little finger.
7. „ „ „ „ „ thumb, fore, and middle finger.
8. „ „ „ „ „ thumb and forefinger.
9. „ „ „ „ „ forefinger like a hook.
10. „ „ „ „ „ fore and middle finger crossed.

FIRE-CRACKERS. Are employed by the Chinese at all kinds of ceremonies, religious and otherwise; the idea being to frighten away devils and malicious spirits.

FIRST EMPEROR: 始皇帝. Reigned over China B.C. 221—209. Attempted to make history begin with himself, and accordingly gave orders for the destruction of all literature. See *Burning of the Books*. Built the Great Wall.

FISHES, TWO. Often seen on Chinese envelopes, from an old story of a letter ·having once been conveyed in a fish's belly. Also, as a fanciful shop-sign to aid customers in finding the house they want, when two tradesmen in the same line and of the same name happen to carry on their business in adjoining houses. Huge gilt cash and other ornamental designs are often suspended outside shop doors with the same object.

FISHING CORMORANT: 鸕鷀 *Phalocrocorax carbo*. Found in many parts of China and taught to catch fish, at first with a ring round the neck to prevent it from swallowing the quarry. Also called 烏鬼 the *black devil*, and 釣魚郎 *catch fish gentleman*, the latter term being a borrowed name of the kingfisher.

FIVE CLASSICS, THE. See *Ching*.

FIVE HUNDRED GENII. The Five Hundred Lohan *(q.v.)* are so called.

FIVE RELATIONSHIPS. See *Sacred Edict*.

FLOWER-BOAT: 花艇. A large ornamental barge, used by the *jeunesse dorée* of China for drinking bouts, picnics, suppers, etc. In some districts these boats are painted blue.

FLOWERY LAND, THE: 華國. A common Chinese name for China, similar to *la belle France*, and not necessarily implying the presence of flowers.

FO *or* FOH: 佛 *or* �. See *Characters*. The first of the Chinese characters employed to represent the sound *Buddha (q.v.)*. Now universally used in China for the whole word.

A resemblance has been pointed out in the composition of 佛 to the monogram of the letters I. H. S., which are vulgarly supposed to stand for *Jesus Hominum Salvator*, whereas they are really nothing more than the three first letters of the Greek name ΙΗΣΟΥΣ—Jesus. This faint similarity is of course beneath notice, and not to be compared with the startling resemblances between the instrumental and other parts of the Buddhist and Roman Catholic religions. Among the most striking points may be cited the use of candles, flowers, vestments, beads, holy water, relics, and masses for the souls in Purgatory; not to mention celibacy, fasting, the shaven heads of the priests, the robe folded over the breast in the form of a *cross*, the immaculate conception of *Màyà* 摩 邪 the mother of Buddha, etc., etc.

FOKIEN *or* FUHKIEN: 福 建—happily established. One of the Eighteen Provinces; capital city Fu-chou Fu 福 州 府 on the Min 閩, which latter character is also the old name of the province.

FOOT-BINDING. See *Small Feet*.

FORBIDDEN CITY, THE: 禁 城 *or* 內 宮. The inner area of the Tartar section of Peking, upon which stands the Imperial palace, is so called by foreigners, being a translation of the first Chinese phrase given above. Also known as 紫 禁 城 the Purple Forbidden City.

FORBIDDEN LAND, THE. A name formerly applied to Korea *(q.v.)*.

FOREIGN DIRT. A name for opium *(q.v.)* borrowed from the Chinese use of the word 土 *earth*.

FOREST OF PENCILS. A name applied by foreigners to the Han-lin College, being a literal rendering of the Chinese characters.

FORMOSA. "Beautiful." The Portuguese name for the island of Taiwan *(q.v.)*. Partly occupied in the seventeenth

century by the Dutch (see *Koxinga*); now, by 生番
savages on the hills in the interior, by Japanese and
Chinese along the western seaboard, and by Pepo-hwans
(q.v.) between the other two.

FOUR BOOKS: 四書.

> 1.—The Great Learning.
> 2.—The Doctrine of the Mean.
> 3.—The Confucian Analects.
> 4.—The Works of Mencius.

} See *s.vv.*

The first portion of the Chinese student's curriculum,
from which are invariably taken the themes set at the
examination for the degree of *hsiu-ts'ai (q.v.)* or bachelor
of arts.

FOUR SEAS, THE: 四海. The seas by which the Chinese
believe that the Middle Kingdom *(q.v.)* is bounded. Now
often used for the whole world; *e.g.*—"all within the
"Four Seas are brothers."

FOUR WONDERFUL WORKS: 四大奇書.

> (1) 三國志演義
> (2) 西廂記
> (3) 金瓶梅
> (4) 水滸傳

Four novels which
are held in high
estimation by the
Chinese.

Another classification includes the works designed by
the Emperor K'ang Hsi, namely:

> 康熙字典 see *Dictionaries.*
> 佩文韻府 see *Concordance.*
> 圖書集成 see *Encyclopaedias.*
> 淵鑑類函 an encyclopaedia in 150 vols.

FOXES. Are regarded as uncanny creatures by the Chinese,
able to assume human shapes and work endless mischief
(chiefly in love affairs) upon those who may be unfortunate

enough to fall under their spell. In some parts of China, it is customary for mandarins to keep their seals of office in what is called a "fox chamber;" but the character for fox is never written, the sight of it being supposed to be very irritating to the live animal. A character 胡, which has the same sound, is substituted; and even that is divided into its component parts 古 and 月, so as to avoid even the slightest risk of offence. This device is often adopted for the inscriptions on shrines erected in honour of the fox.

FREEMASONRY, as we understand the term, is unknown in China. Secret Societies *(q.v.)* abound, and some of them (see *Triad Society*) practise rites of initiation and administer oaths similar in character to those which constitute the ritual of Western masonry.

FRIEND OF CHINA. The bamboo *(q.v.)*. This term has been adopted, with less justice, for their journal, by the Society for the suppression of the opium trade in China.

FU *or* FUH: 福 —happiness. Constantly seen on doorposts, vases, etc. The Chinese have a hundred fanciful ways of writing both this and the character for *Show (q.v.)* old age. Another common character of this kind is 喜 *hsi* joy, which often occurs on tea-pots, cuspidors, etc., in a duplicated form, thus 囍 .

FUKEY *or* FOKEE. Native Chinese as opposed to foreign. From the Cantonese pronunciation of 夥計 *a partner* and even *a friend*. Anglicè, *mate*.

British sentry, during occupation of Canton, to passing Celestial:—

> Q. Who goes there?
> A. Fukey—(a friend).

Chinese dogs are usually called *fukey-dogs*, and foreigners may be not unfrequently heard to designate a Chinaman as a "dirty fukey."

FUN *or* FÊN: 分—a share. The 100th part of a Chinese ounce of silver. A candareen.

FUNERALS. At death, the Chinese close the eyes of the corpse, put a little rice and money or powdered jade in its mouth, cover the face with a napkin, clench the two fists, remove all curtains (as likely to retard the passage of the spirit), and then keep watch round it all night. On the second day the body is washed, and dressed in warm clothes lined with red (see *Colours*), the head and face being entirely concealed. Priests are hired, and they begin their duties by "warming the coffin" with small hand-stoves, after which the body is carefully deposited therein. The family tailor then steps forward, and with a pair of scissors rapidly cuts away an oval of cloth so as to expose the face to view. The family crowd round to take a last look, and the lid is fastened down. A curtain is hung up in front of the coffin, and friends are admitted to *kotow (q.v.)* to the spirit of the dead.

Sometimes the coffin remains for months, and even years, in the house, before a burial-ground can be obtained or an auspicious day arranged for the funeral. Sometimes it is deposited on the premises of the Guild *(q.v.)* to which deceased belonged, or in a neighbouring temple; until, preceded by a tablet carried in a sedan-chair, to represent the spirit of the deceased, and accompanied by a train of mourners in coarse ashen-coloured garments, it is gently carried to its final place of interment.

FUNG SHUEY. See *Fêng Shui*.

U-NING FU: 福 甯 府. A Treaty Port near the Samsah inlet in Fuhkien.

FUSAN *or* PUSAN: 釜山. A port in Korea opened by
the Treaty of 26th November 1883.

FUSANG: 扶桑 *or* 佛桑. A country named after a plant
so called which was seen growing there, and is said, but
without foundation, to be the Mexican aloe. Identified
by Klaproth with Saghalien; by Leland, with part of the
American continent; and by others, with Japan. Visited
by a Chinese Buddhist priest in the 5th century, to whom,
were Leland's view correct, would be due the honour of
the discovery of America.

FUSIYAMA: (1) 弗似山—the incomparable hill; (2) 富
士山—learned scholar's hill. The celebrated mountain
—an extinct volcano—of Japan. Is about 12,600 feet
above the level of the sea, and is composed chiefly of
cinders which swarm with myriads of small insects. Lady
Parkes was the first European lady who ever reached its
summit. Last eruption took place in 1707. The following
is an imitation of a Japanese ode in which the word is
introduced as a pun.

> Now hid from sight are great Mt. Fusi's fires—
> Mt. Fusi, said I? 'Tis myself, I mean!
> For the word *Fusi* signifies, I ween,
> *Few see* the constant flame of my desires.
> > *B. H. Chamberlain.*

FUSUMA. Japanese sliding screen, covered with wall paper.

FUT'AI *or* FOO-YÜEN: 撫台 *or* 撫院—the tranquilliser.
Governor of a province. Ranks with the Governor-General
or Viceroy, and exercises much the same functions in a
slightly inferior degree; but in provinces where there is
no Viceroy, wields the supreme power.

FUTURE STATE. The belief in spirits and in a future
state generally has prevailed in China from the earliest
ages, though not in any way recognised by Confucianism

which preserves an agnostic attitude towards all spiritual questions. A heaven and a hell were introduced by the Buddhists, and borrowed by the Taoists *(q.v.)* as a defensive measure against their more attractive rival. The popular belief now is that there is a world of shades, an exact model of the present life, with penalties and rewards for wicked and deserving persons.

GAGS: 枚. Are used to prevent soldiers from talking during a night attack, in ambuscade, etc. They are first mentioned in B.C. 208, and as late as 1874 when Li Hung-chang made his famous forced march to Peking to the aid of the Empress Dowager.

GALANGAL: 艮薑 — "Liang" ginger, or ginger from 高艮府 Kao-liang Fu, which is the old name of the modern 高州府 Kao-chou Fu in the province of Kuang-tung. The word *Galangal* is probably a corruption of *Kao-liang-kiang* or Kao-liang ginger.

GALAW: 喀咯. A meaningless term peculiar to the Cantonese dialect, employed to finish off a sentence euphoniously, at the same time adding an indefinable something to the force of the words spoken. May be compared, in some respects, with the French *allez; e.g.*, "Je me moque pas mal de lui, allez!" Has been introduced into pidgin-English; *e.g.* "You too muchee saucy, galaw!"

GARDEN OF ASIA. A name given to the vicinity of the three cities of Kashgar, Yangy Hissar, and Yarkand, from the great fertility of that region, which was artificially induced by the admirable irrigation system of the Chinese settlers.

GARDEN OF CHINA. The province of Shansi has been so called. So also the province of Ssŭ-ch'uan; see *Shanghai Mercury*, 14 November 1884.

GÂUTAMA: 喬答摩 or 瞿曇. From *gâu* earth and *tama* most victorious. The sacerdotal name of the Shakya family *(q.v.)*, that family being said to be the most victorious on earth.

GEGEN. A living Buddha or Hutukhtu *(q.v.)*.

GEISHA: 藝者. A Japanese singing or dancing-girl.

GENGHIS KHAN—the "greatest" Khan. Written 成吉思汗 in the 通鑑綱目. Also known as *Temujin* 鐵木眞 or 特穆眞. The great Mongol conqueror of China, A.D. 1162—1227.

GENJI MONOGATARI. The first Japanese novel, by Murasaki no Shikibu, a woman. It is assigned to the close of the 10th cent.

GENSAN *or* WONSAN: 元山. A port in Korea opened to foreign trade by the Treaty of 26th November 1883.

GEOMANCY: 堪輿. See *Fêng Shui*.

GHARRY. A kind of four-wheeled carriage in use at Singapore. From the Hindi *gâri*.

GIALBOS: 贊普. The descendants of the ancient kings of Tibet, who ruled that country before the Lamas *(q.v.)* began to usurp temporal power.

GIBRALTAR OF CHINA. See *Hongkong*.

GINGALL *or* GINJAL. See *Jingal*.

GINSENG: 人參—image of man. A plant *(Panax repens)* found in Manchuria, Korea, America, and elsewhere, the root of which is believed to resemble the human body in shape. It is much valued by the Chinese as a strengthening medicine, and the Emperor, to whom all ginseng found in China belongs of right, occasionally bestows small quantities on deserving officials who may happen to be in failing health.

Popular superstition says that after three centuries the

ginseng plant changes into a man with white blood, which is the veritable elixir of immortality, a few drops being sufficient to raise a dead man to life.

Ginseng is of two distinct kinds, viz., that which is found wild and commands fancy prices, and that which is cultivated for the wholesale trade and is of incomparably less value. The latter fetches from two to twelve taels a catty, while the former is sometimes worth as much as one thousand taels a catty. The older the plant, the more it is valued; and the age of the wild root may be ascertained by marks upon the stem and other peculiarities of structure.

Ordinary ginseng is prepared by simply drying the root in the sun, or over a charcoal fire. To prepare the red or clarified ginseng, the root is placed in wicker baskets which are put in a large earthen vessel with a close-fitting cover and pierced at the bottom with holes. This is set over boiling water, and the roots are steamed according to their age, about four hours being an average time.

GIORO *or* GHIORO: 覺羅. The Manchu surname of the present Imperial family of China. The legendary progenitor of the Manchu chieftains who subsequently reached the throne bore the surname of *Aisin Gioro* 愛新覺羅 or "Golden Race," and the Manchu nation was known to the Chinese at the time of the Sungs *(q.v.)* as the 金朝 or "Golden Dynasty." All Red Girdles *(q.v.)* are called *Gioros*, as opposed to Yellow Girdles who are 宗室—"of the Imperial family." As to pronunciation, this word would be more accurately written *giolo*, the *g* being soft. Is often seen on visiting cards, as a title, preceding the name.

GIRAFFE: 惡那西約. This animal is figured and

described in the *T'u shu* (see *Encyclopaedias*) as a native of Libya. It is there said to turn round and show off its beauty to spectators, as though quite enjoying being looked at. See *Kilin*.

GIRDLE, RED: 紅帶子. A distinctive badge worn by members of the collateral branches of the present Imperial family of China in the male line for ever, dating from the Manchu chieftain now known as 天命 "By Heaven's command," A.D. 1616. Those entitled to wear the red girdle are also called Gioros *(q.v.)*.

GIRDLE, YELLOW: 黃帶子. Is worn by the direct issue of the Emperors of the present dynasty and their descendants in the male line for ever, dating from the Manchu chieftain 天命, A.D. 1616. See *Gioro*. "Each "generation becomes a degree lower in rank, until they "are mere members of the family with no rank whatever, "though they still wear the girdle and receive a trifling "allowance from the Government. Beggars and even "thieves are occasionally seen with this badge of relationship "to the Throne."—*G. C. Stent*.

"The imperial family wear a golden yellow sash, and "the gioro a red one; when degraded, the former take "a red sash, and the latter a carnation one."—*Chinese Chrestomathy*.

GLASS: 玻璃 *po-li*. First manufactured in China, A.D. 424. The term *po-li*, which occurs as early as A.D. 643, and which is evidently of foreign origin, has been the subject of much discussion, and has been identified with the Turkish *billur*, with *polish*, with *vidro*(!) and recently by Dr. Hirth with "*belor* or *bolor*, meaning glass or crystal "in several Central Asiatic languages." See *Mirrors*.

GO-BANG. The now celebrated Japanese game recently

introduced into England. Called by the Japanese *gomo-ku narabé* 五 目 並, *i.e.*, five eyes in a row, the book name being 畫 五 "draw five."

Go-bang is simply 碁 盤 or checker-board. The object of the game is to get five checkers or counters in a row.

GO ON : 吳 音. The pronunciation of Chinese as first learnt by the Japanese at the end of the 3rd and beginning of the 4th centuries, A.D., representing the dialect of modern Nanking and Soochow. See *Kan On* and *To On*.

GOD. See *Heaven* and *Term Question*.

GODOWN : 土 庫 *or* 棧 房. (1) Originally a cellar or place to which it was necessary to *go down*. Now, a warehouse. (2) From the Malay *gĕdong*, a warehouse.

GOL. A Mongol word signifying *river; e.g.*, the Erguo gol.

GOLD, SWALLOWING : 吞 金. Euphemistically used among the Chinese for suicide by poison, chiefly in the case of high officials who have received intimation from Peking that their lives are no longer wanted: Absurdly supposed by some foreigners and many ignorant natives to signify death from swallowing lumps of gold, or inhaling, or suffocating oneself with, gold-leaf. This mistake has been made by most writers on Chinese subjects, such as Doolittle, Williams (*Middle Kingdom*, II. 543) and others; and a qualified European practitioner wrote as follows in the Customs' Gazette, No. XXXIII, January—March, 1877 :—

"Gold-leaf poisoning appears to be seldom practised "here (Kiukiang) as a method of committing suicide, "as I have heard of only one case during my three years' "residence . . . . Gold-leaf, where it does not suffocate, "must act simply as an irritant, and therefore I should "consider that the rational treatment would be the

"continuous exhibition of alkalies, with demulcent drinks
"and emetics."

But it might just as well be argued that 賜 帛 "to
present silk" must necessarily mean an Imperial gift of a
few bales to a deserving mandarin, instead of, as it
actually does, a peremptory command to strangle himself
forthwith.

The *Hsi-yüan-lu*, or Instructions to Coroners, uses the
term in the sense of lump gold or silver, and gives
directions for *softening* the swallowed metal so as to
make it pass easily through the intestines. And a case
is quoted of a Brigadier-General who swallowed three
finger-rings and died after severe vomiting.

GOLD FISH: 金 魚 or *Cyprinus auratus*. First mentioned
by Su Tung-p'o, A.D. 1036—1101, as follows:

> Upon the bridge, the live-long day,
> I stand and watch the gold fish play.

GOLDEN FOOT, THE. Generally and wrongly used for
the King of Burmah. Mgr. Pallegoix, in his *Description
du Royaume Thai ou Siam*, p. 260, speaking of the King
of Siam says, "Il n'est pas permis de le nommer par son
"propre nom; il faut le désigner par les titres rapportés
"ci-dessus," and then he gives a list of ten titles, the first
of which is *phra-bat* or the "divine feet." Now Rees'
Encyclopædia, under the word *Prabat*, after explaining
that *pra* means anything worthy of veneration and that
bat means "foot," refers the term to one of the famous
footprints of Buddha to which the king renders homage
once a year when he visits it with great pomp and parade,
and which has been covered with a plate of gold. Thus
it is this footprint which is the "Golden Foot," the proper
title of the King of Siam being "Divine Feet;" but both

are in Siamese called *Phra-bat*; hence the confusion. Again, Rees says (see *Birman*) the queen and princes have the title of "*Praw*," and it is probably from the similarity of this word to *Phra* that a further confusion arose between the title of the King of Siam and that of the queen and princes of Burmah. Of the Siamese, Captain James Low writes, "everything holy or magnificent is "with them, as with the Burmese, *golden*."

GOLDEN LILIES: 金蓮. A poetical name for the cramped feet of Chinese women. From an expression used by the monarch Tung Hun Hou 東昏侯, A.D. 498—502, in admiration of his concubine P'an 潘妃 as she danced upon a stage ornamented with lilies:—"Every footstep "makes a lily grow."

GOLDEN ORCHID SOCIETY: 金蘭會. A secret association of unmarried girls who bind themselves not to cohabit with their husbands after matrimony (which they are unable to avoid), but to leave them and return to their old homes or go elsewhere. Strictly prohibited by the officials in China.

GOLDEN SAND, RIVER OF: 金沙江. The name of the Yang-tsze *(q.v.)* above Hsü-chou Fu in Ssǔ-ch'uan. Thence to the borders of Kokonor, the name is further changed to 布叠楚河. In Kokonor it is known as 木魯烏蘇 and 穆魯伊烏蘇, *i.e.* Murus-usu; and near its source as 客齊烏蘭 Kachi-uran.

GOLDEN TARTARS: 金人. A tribe of Tartars, also known as 女眞 Nü-chên, who under the leadership of a chieftain named 阿骨打 Akuta, threw off allegiance to the Kitans and established an independent empire, A.D. 1114. In 1122 Peking was captured, and the Kitan power came to an end.

GOLDEN YOUTH, THE. A name applied to Hung Wu, the founder of the Ming dynasty, A.D. 1368, in reference to the good luck which attended him. See *Beggar King*.

GONGEN. General designation of native Shintô *(q.v.)* gods in Japan.

GONGS: 鑼. Are beaten at intervals before the cavalcade of a Mandarin to warn the people to stand aside. For the Viceroy and officials of equal rank 13 consecutive blows are given; for the Fan-t'ai, Tao-t'ai, etc., 11; for the Prefect 9. Officials below this rank are only entitled to use gongs beyond the limits of the capital of a province, e.g., in District cities, where 7 blows would signal the coming of the magistrate. Gongs are much used in religious ceremonies, and as salutes by passing junks belonging to the same fleet. Hence the proverb 不 搥 鑼 *not to beat gongs*, i.e., *not to salute* said of persons no longer on speaking terms. As to etymology, Webster gives "Malayan (Java) *gong*;" but the Chinese word 更 *kêng* (the *ê* pronounced like the *u* in *sung*) the night-watch, may possibly be the true source of the term, and the origin of the Malay word. Substituted by foreigners in China for

> "...that all-softening, overpowering knell,
> "The tocsin of the soul—the dinner bell."

At wrecks of junks the Chinese are very careful to save the gongs, and will not ever part with them under any consideration. To do so would entail "bad joss" on further enterprises.

GONSAI. (Jap.) A concubine, as opposed to the *honsai* or real wife.

GON-TENJI: 權 天 女. The Imperial concubines of Japan.

Gon is an honorary prefix, almost equivalent to Her Highness.

GOOSEBERRY, THE CANTON. See *Carambola*.

GOSSAMER. Is supposed by the Chinese to be the remains of birds which have flown too high and become dissipated in mid air. Compare the German belief that it is the winding-sheet of the Virgin Mary, which fell off when she was taken up to heaven.

GOVERNMENT OF CHINA. Is nominally an autocracy, but really a democracy. The Emperor is supposed to be the Vicegerent of Heaven, with the lives and properties of the Chinese people at his absolute disposal. He reigns however rather than rules, leaving the administration in the hands of the Six Boards *(q.v.)*. The provinces are under the charge of Viceroys and Governors, responsible only to the Throne (see *Tartar General*). Below them come the Treasurer, Judge, and Salt Commissioner. Then come the Tao-t'ais, Prefects, District Magistrates, *(qq.v.)*, and a host of subordinate officials, each of whom is responsible to his immediate superior for the proper administration of his department and the peaceful behaviour of the people with whom he is brought in contact. Anything in the way of oppression or injustice is met by a popular rising, and the career of the official in question is generally at an end. Taxes are rarely imposed or increased without a previous consultation with the local merchants or elders concerned, or they would be resisted to the death. In other words, the people tax themselves (see *Likin*).

GOVERNOR. See *Fut'ai*.

GOVERNOR-GENERAL. See *Tsung-tuh*.

GRAMMAR. Every word in Chinese being a monosyllable, incapable of inflexion, agglutination, or change of any kind, there cannot possibly be such a thing as grammar in our sense of the term. The Chinese have no grammar of their own language, nor any equivalent by which the idea could be expressed.

"Jetez vos grammaires au feu." *Prof. Schlegel.*

"We should like to see all so-called Chinese grammars in the flames: they are quite as dangerous as they can be advantageous." *E. H. Parker.*

GRAND CANAL: 運河 —transport river *or* 閘河 river of locks. Extends from Tientsin to Hang-chou Fu, the capital of Chehkiang, a distance of about 650 miles, and completes an almost unbroken water communication between Peking and Canton. Designed and executed by the first Mongol Emperor of China, Kublai Khan *(q.v.)*, who was materially assisted in his project by the canals dug during the reign of Yang Ti in the early part of the seventh century, to connect the Yellow River with the Yangtsze.

GRAND EXAMINERS: 主考. Officers imperially commissioned to hold examinations at the various provincial capitals for the purpose of conferring the *chü jen* or master's degree. These examinations take place once in every three years.

GRAND SECRETARIES: 大學士. The four principal members of the Chinese Cabinet Council. Two are Manchus and two Chinese. There are also two Assistant G. Secretaries, one Manchu and one Chinese. The term was first used under the T'ang dynasty.

GRAPE, THE: 葡萄 or *Vitis vinifera*, L. Said to have been introduced from Central Asia into China about B.C. 126, subsequent to which date bunches of grapes appeared for a time in ornamental designs, *e.g.* on the backs of mirrors *(q.v.)* as first pointed out by Dr. Hirth. Grape-wine was also made, and it is frequently mentioned as in use under the T'ang dynasty. The Chinese term *p'u-t'ao*, which is evidently of foreign origin, has been identified with the Greek βότρυς a cluster of grapes.

GRASS CHARACTER: 草 字—plant character. The Chinese running hand. So called because of its irregular plant-like appearance. Chiefly used in business; never in official documents. Dates from the Han dynasty, previous to which there was a kind of writing known as 藁 書·

GRASS-CLOTH: 夏 布—summer cloth. A kind of linen made from the fibre of a hemp-producing plant called China Grass *(q.v.)*.

GREAT DEVELOPMENT: 大 乘—Mahayana. Also called *vehicle* and *conveyance*. The system developed by the northern Buddhists of India about the time of the Christian era, and propagated in China, Japan, Mongolia, Tibet, and Nepaul. Its chief features were the addition of a number of new Buddhas and Bodhisatvas, new worlds for them to live in, and a general extension of the mythological element. The *Lesser Development* 小 乘 or Hinayana, is based upon the original books of Buddhism, and is the system of the Cingalese, Siamese, and Burmese.

GREAT LEARNING: 大 學. One of the Four Books *(q.v.)*. "What the Great Learning teaches is—to illustrate "illustrious virtue; to renovate the people; and to rest "in the highest excellence."—*Legge's Translation*.

Its author is unknown. Chu Hsi attributes a part to Confucius himself, regarding the rest as commentary; but Dr. Legge thinks it was more probably the work of K'ung Chi 孔 伋, grandson of Confucius and author of the *Doctrine of the Mean*. The following is a specimen:—

"There is no evil which a mean man will not perpetrate "when he is alone. But when he sees a superior man, he "instantly tries to dissimulate, concealing what is evil and "displaying what is good. The other, however, sees into "his very soul; so that dissimulation avails him naught. "So true is the saying that that which is really within "will be manifested without. Therefore the superior man "must be watchful over himself when he is alone."

The term Great Learning, adopted by Dr. Legge, rather obscures the meaning of the Chinese, the latter being in reality 大人之學 Learning for Adults. See *The Little Learning*.

GREAT WALL, THE: 萬里長城—the ten thousand mile rampart. Designed and for the most part built by the first universal monarch of China, Shih Huang-ti 始皇帝, who came to the throne B.C. 221, as a means of defence against the Mongolian hordes, and named by him the "Red Fort" 紫塞, as being an addition to the nine old frontier forts which guarded the Empire of China. Is about 1400 miles (English) in length, twenty-two feet in height, and twenty feet in thickness. Passes over hilly districts, sometimes to an elevation of 5,000 ft. At intervals of 100 yards or so are towers, some forty feet high; the whole being built of brick, except towards its western extremity, where it is barely more than a huge mud bank. Is the most noticeable work of man on the globe.

GREEN HEADS, THE: 綠頭. A *sobriquet* given to the Anglo-Chinese contingent at Ningpo, long and ably commanded by Colonel Cooke, formerly of the "Ever Victorious Army" *(q.v.)*.

GREEN TEA. Generally believed to be prepared from the leaves of a different species of plant from that which furnishes black tea, whereas the distinction between the two lies only in the mode of preparation.

> "... for I grow pathetic,
> Moved by the Chinese nymph of tears, green tea."
> *Byron.*

GRIFFIN. A new arrival in the East; equivalent to a "freshman" at Oxford. See title-page.

    Also, a racing pony that runs for the first time.

GROSVENOR MISSION. A mission consisting of the Hon. T. G. Grosvenor, A. Davenport, and E. C. Baber, sent to Yünnan to enquire into the circumstances of the murder of Mr. Margary. See *Yünnan Outrage.*

"GUESS FINGERS." See *Chai Mui.*

GUILDS: 會館—meeting houses. The trades'-unions of China, except that there is here no combination of Labour against Capital as with us, but merely a union of merchants or traders in any particular branch of commerce, with a view to facilitate and render more successful the business operations of each individual member. The buildings in which these associations meet are often very handsomely decorated, and are always provided with a stage for theatrical performances.

GUNONG. A Javanese word meaning hill or mountain, commonly occurring in names of places.

GUNPOWDER. Under the name of *huo-yao* 火藥, first occurs early in the seventh century, when it was used for fireworks. Guns, said to be of western origin, were first used by Genghis Khan and Kublai Khan; but were first systematically employed in warfare during the reign of Yung Lo of the Ming dynasty (15th century).

GUP. The Hindustani for gossip or scandal.. A few years ago some letters were addressed to one of the Shanghai papers under this *nom de plume*, and Florence Marryat has published a novel with this title.

GUTZLAFF : 馬蹟—horse footstep. An island off the mouth of the Yangtsze, so called after a well-known missionary of that name.

HADAKA-ODORI. A dance *in puris naturalibus*, performed by Japanese courtesans. See *Yoshiwara.*

HADJI. A Mahommedan who undertakes the pilgrimage to Mecca, the name being kept for the remainder of the pilgrim's life. Is a common term of respect in the Malay peninsula.

HAIFANG: 海防. A Sub-prefect in charge of a maritime Sub-prefecture, or *t'ing*. Literally: Coast-defence.

HAIKAI. A Japanese triplet of 5, 7, and 5 syllables only. It was introduced about the close of the 15th cent. A.D., chiefly by a Buddhist priest named Yamazaki Sō-kan.

HAIKWAN, THE : 海關. Superintendent of Chinese Maritime Customs. Always a Chinese official, as distinguished from his European colleague, the Commissioner of Customs 稅務司. This title is curiously applied by the people of Swatow and Amoy to the British Consul, in preference to the official 領事官, which is actually not understood.

HAINAN, ISLAND OF : 海南—south of the sea. Commonly known to the Chinese as K'iung-chou 瓊州, being a prefecture of the Kuang-tung province.

HAIPHONG: 海防. A port in Tongking, the trade of which is chiefly confined to rice, with a small quantity of silk, gambier, tin, varnish, and lacquer oil; all of which come from the interior.

HAIR, FALSE. Is occasionally worn by Chinamen who for some reason or other have not presentable cues *(q.v.).*

Thieves invariably wear false cues which come off in the hand when seized. The famous Empress Wu, who ruled China from A.D. 684 to 705, used to wear a false beard when presiding at State Councils.

HAKKAS: 客家—strangers. A race said to have migrated from the north of China (Kiangsu or Shantung) to the Kuang-tung province at the time of the Yüan dynasty, A.D. 1206—1368. For an elaborate account of this people, see an article in *Notes & Queries on China and Japan*, Vol. 1, No. 5, by Dr. Eitel.

HAKODATE: 箱館. A port in the northern island of Japan.

HAMPALANG: 喊嘭唅. A common expression in the Canton and Swatow dialects meaning "all." Like much of the *patois* of China, it cannot, properly speaking, be written; the three characters above giving only the sound without conveying any meaning. Said by Mr. G. Minchin to be a corruption of the Cantonese 咸埋包來 "wrap up all and come," as used by the bum-boat men at Whampoa when directing their assistants to take away whatever old clothes, etc., the sailors on the foreign ships might have given them in payment for their eatables. Being subsequently imitated by the Jacks themselves, their corruption "hampalang" passed into the Cantonese dialect as a convenient expression for "all."

HAN, SON OF: 漢子. That is, a man who lived under the Han dynasty, B.C. 206—A.D. 221, the epoch of the *Renaissance* of Chinese literature, often spoken of as the brightest page of Chinese history. The name of the dynasty came to be used as a synonym for China, in which sense it is still employed.

HANG-CHOW: 杭州. The capital of Chehkiang, remarkable

for the beauty of its surroundings. Divides with Soochow
the honour of being a terrestrial paradise.

上 有 天 堂 下 有 蘇 杭

Above, there is the Hall of God; below, there is
Soochow and Hangchow.

HANKOW: 漢口—mouth of the Han (river), which here
joins its waters with those of the Yang-tsze. A port on
the Yang-tsze, opened by the Treaty of Tientsin in 1858,
though not occupied until 1861. Is 582 geographical
miles from Shanghai; one of the five commercial centres
of China, and once the starting-post for the great annual
Ocean Race *(q.v.)*.

HAN-LIN: 翰林—forest of pencils. A College in Peking,
the members of which are charged with the compilation
of dynastic history, Imperial decrees, and literary matters
in general. They draw up prayers and sacrificial addresses,
honorary titles for Dowager Empresses, patents of dignity
for the chief concubines of a deceased Emperor, make
offerings at the tomb of Confucius, etc., etc., while a
number of them are required to be in attendance on the
Emperor as readers, instructors, advisers, and so forth.
Admission to this body is the highest literary honour
obtainable by a Chinese scholar. Established early in
the 8th century by the emperor Hsüan Tsung of the
T'ang dynasty.

Seniority in the Han-lin College being determined by
date of entry, it often happens that an older man in
years has to address his younger but senior colleague in
a form which in every other Chinese walk of life would
be due from the younger to the older.

HANOI: 河內. The capital of Tongking.

HAPPY VALLEY, THE: 黃泥涌—yellow mud creek.

A valley in the island of Hongkong, covering about thirty acres of ground, and used as a race-course. At one side of it lies the beautiful cemetery where foreigners are buried. The term *Happy Valley* belongs originally to Dr. Johnson's *Rasselas*, the history of a prince of Abyssinia who travelled far and wide in search of true happiness.

HARA KIRI: 腹 切—belly cutting. Disembowelment; the form of suicide formerly in vogue among the Japanese. Familiarly known to Europeans as the "happy despatch."

HARE, THE: 兔 or *Lepus sinensis*. Much legend and superstition has gathered around this animal, which has been for many centuries associated with the moon, the first mention being in the poems of Ch'ü P'ing, 4th cent. B.C. In later times the hare in the moon was believed to be occupied in pounding drugs for the elixir of life. The Chinese do not seem to make any distinction between hares and rabbits.

HATOBA: 埠 頭. A pier, or landing-place. [Japanese.] Used much as *matow (q.v.)* in China.

HATS, CHINESE OFFICIAL. Are of two kinds, for winter and for summer; called "warm hats" 煖帽 and "cool hats" 凉帽, respectively. The latter are made of a yellow grass: the former of black cloth, velvet, and satin. Both have red tassels. The days for changing from one to the other in spring and autumn vary in various parts of the empire, as fixed by the provincial officials in each case; but they are always (1) very shortly before or after the "Beginning of Summer" at the end of the 3rd or in the early part of the 4th moon, and (2) some time between the mid-autumn festival on the 15th of the 8th moon and the 9th of the 9th moon.

HEATHEN CHINEE, THE. The title of Bret Harte's celebrated satire on the outcry against the employment of Chinese labour in the Western States of America.

WHICH I wish to remark—
   And my language is plain—
That for ways that are dark
   And for tricks that are vain,
The heathen Chinee is peculiar,
   Which the same I would rise to explain.

Ah Sin was his name;
   And I shall not deny
In regard to the same
   What that name might imply,
But his smile it was pensive and childlike,
   As I frequent remarked to Bill Nye.

It was August the third;
   And quite soft was the skies;
Which it might be inferred
   That Ah Sin was likewise;
Yet he played it that day upon William
   And me in a way I despise.

Which we had a small game,
   And Ah Sin took a hand:
It was Euchre. The same
   He did not understand;
But he smiled as he sat by the table,
   With the smile that was childlike and bland.

Yet the cards they were stocked
   In a way that I grieve,
And my feelings were shocked
   At the state of Nye's sleeve,
Which was stuffed full of aces and bowers,
   And the same with intent to deceive.

But the hands that were played
   By that heathen Chinee,
And the points that he made,
   Were quite frightful to see—
Till at last he put down a right bower,
   Which the same Nye had dealt unto me.

Then I looked up at Nye,
   And he gazed upon me;
And he rose with a sigh,
   And he said, "Can this be?
We are ruined by Chinese cheap labour,"
   And he went for that heathen Chinee.

In the scene that ensued
   I did not take a hand,
But the floor it was strewed,
   Like the leaves on the strand,
With the cards that Ah Sin had been hiding,
   In the game "he did not understand."

In his sleeves, which were long,
   He had twenty-four Jacks—
Which was coming it strong,
   Yet I state but the facts:
And we found on his nails, which were taper,
   What is frequent in tapers—that's wax.

Which is why I remark,
   And my language is plain,
That for ways that are dark,
   And for tricks that are vain,
The heathen Chinee is peculiar,
   Which the same I am free to maintain.

HEAVEN: 天. This term as used by the Chinese may mean either (1) the sky as seen overhead which is personified into the Deity, "old Bluecoat" 穿藍衣裳, or the "old gentleman of the sky" 老天爺, 天公, 上天 etc., and in large number of cases can only be rendered intelligibly by "God." (2) Abstract right 理. When Confucius said, "He who offends against Heaven has none to whom "he can pray," the learned commentator Choo He *(q.v.)* added 天即埋也 "by Heaven is meant abstract right." (3) Fate, Kismet; e.g., the phrase used in deeds of sale of girls: "If she should die, both parties agree to accept "such event as the will of Heaven."

In illustration of No. 1, the character 天 is often drawn with men and women leaning against it eating from the usual rice bowl, the whole forming a picture conundrum and explained by 靠天喫飯 "they rely on Heaven for "their daily food."

HEAVEN, TEMPLE OF: 天壇—altar of Heaven. A large enclosure within the Chinese or outer portion of the city of Peking where the Emperor sacrifices and performs various religious ceremonies in honour of Heaven, the great unseen Power which directs the affairs of men, from which the Emperor himself holds his commission to rule over the whole world (天下), and to which he is personally responsible for the well-being of his people.

A list of all those executed during the year and of their crimes, is burned by the Emperor on the *Altar of Heaven* at the winter solstice; he is thus supposed to inform heaven of the manner in which he has used its delegated authority.

HEAVEN-SENT BARRIER. A name applied by the Chinese to the Wu-sung *(q.v.)* Bar, as protecting Shanghai from the promiscuous ingress of large ships of war. Compare—"Many of us have thought that our sea-wall is a "specially divine arrangement to make and keep us a nation "of sea-kings after the manner of our forefathers, secure "against invasion and able to invade other lands when we "need them." *Impressions of Theophrastus Such.*

HEEN *or* HIEN. See *Hsien.*

HEH-LUNG-KIANG : 黑 龍 江—black dragon river. One of the Manchurian provinces, and a favourite destination for banished Chinese officials.

HEIMIN : 平 民. The so-called "common people" or working classes of Japan.

"The shizoku *(q.v.)* have ceased to carry swords, but "they retain power over the *heimin*, as they did in former "times."—*Hiogo News*.

HELL. See *Chamber of Horrors*.

HERBAL, THE CHINESE. See *Pun-ts'ao*.

HERMIT LAND, THE. A name formerly applied to Korea *(q.v.)*.

HIBATSHI : 火 鉢—fire bowl. A portable stove used in Japan for warming rooms, etc.

HIEN FUNG *or* HSIEN FÊNG : 咸 豐—general abundance. The style of reign adopted by the Emperor who ruled China from 1851—1862. Fled from Peking on its capture by the allied forces, and died at Jehol *(q.v.)*.

HININ : 非 人 — "Not humans." A class of Japanese paupers, formerly allowed to squat on waste lands.

HIOGO : 兵 庫. A port in Japan. Same as Kobé 神 戶.

HIOUEN THSANG. French orthography of Hsüan Tsang *(q.v.)*.

HIRAGANA *or* HIRAKANA : 平 假 字. The Japanese running hand or simplified form of the Kana *(q.v.)*. The common symbols used in writing the native language, resembling the Chinese "grass" character. Said to have been introduced into Japan by Kobodaishi who died A.D. 835.

The Hiragana consists of 48 primary characters, but numbers nearly 150, if varieties of form be included With the addition of some 500 cursive characters, it forms the syllabary employed by women, and in novels and all publications for the illiterate. Chinese characters are added where necessary to prevent confusion.

HISTORY, BOOK OF. See *Shoo King*.

HISTORY, FATHER OF. A name given to 司馬遷 Ssŭ-ma Ch'ien, who flourished B.C. 145—87 and produced the first systematic history of China, known as the 史記 Historical Record, covering a period from the earliest ages down to his own day. It contains 526,500 words. Since then, histories of the various dynasties, twenty-four in all, have been regularly published after the close of each dynasty, and fill, in the uniform edition of 1747, no less than 216 large volumes.

HIUNG-NU: 匈奴. See *Hsiung-nu*.

HIYAKSHO: 百姓. The Japanese "farmer" class.

HOANG-HO: 黃河—yellow river. So called from the yellowness of its water, caused by the vast quantity of mud which is swept down by its rapid current to the sea. Pronounced *Hwong haw* in the Mandarin dialect. Known to the Mongols as Kara mouran or the Black River.

It is now nearly fifty years since the Yellow River deserted the channel through which it formerly found its way across Kiangsu into the Yellow Sea; and, turning northward at a point near Lan-yi, in the north-east of Honan, found for itself a new outlet into the Gulf of Peichili. Several times before the river has deviated in a similar way, always with disastrous results. Its present channel is so narrow that, even at normal height, the water is level with either bank; but when it rises with the slightest increase in volume, it spreads out like a sea over some thirty miles of ground. See *China's Sorrow*.

HOEY: 會. A commercial Guild. A secret society.

HOIHOW: 海口—sea port. The port of Kiung-chou Fu *(q.v.)* in Hainan.

HOKLOS: 福老—the old ones of Fu, i.e. Fuhkien. A tribe said to have come originally from that province. Now found chiefly in the Prefecture of Hui-chou 惠州. Williams writes 學老; but the last character should be 佬, which is a Cantonese colloquial word meaning *man*. 學 is the attempt of the Cantonese to write the Fuhkienese sound of the character 福.

HOKUSAI. A.D. 1760—1850. The famous Japanese artist, known by many fancy names. He was the son of a mirror-maker, and excelled in painting trees, flowers, fruit, birds, beasts, fishes, and men and women. On his tomb are the words *Gwaikio Rojin Manji*, the Old Man mad on Painting. At the back is written, "My soul turned "will o' the wisp can come and go at ease over the "summer fields."

HOLY CITY, THE. A title bestowed in 1585 upon the city of Macao by the Portuguese settlers residing there. Above the entrance to the Senate House may still be seen—"*Cidade do Nome de Deos—não ha outra mais leal*," i.e., "City of the Name of God—there is not another more loyal."

HONAM. Name of an island close to Canton opposite to which formerly stood the celebrated foreign "factories" *(q.v.)*.

HONAN: 河南—south of the (Yellow) river. One of the Eighteen Provinces, capital city K'ai-fêng Fu 開封府. Old name 豫.

HONG: 行—a row, or series. Chinese warehouses were so called because consisting of a succession of rooms, and the old "factories" *(q.v.)* being similarly built, the Chinese called each block a *hong*. Now used of all kinds of mercantile houses.

HONG-BOAT: 三机—three oars. A Chinese sampan with a small wooden house in the middle, capable of holding about eight persons. Said to have been rowed originally by only *three* men sitting in the bow, with a fourth sculling at the stern—whence the Chinese name; but now the number varies according to the fancy of the owner. Used by foreigners residing at Canton. Same as *Matrimonial*.

HONGKEW *or* HONGQUE: 虹口. The site of the American Settlement at Shanghai. From the local pronunciation of the above two characters, literally, *rainbow mouth* or *port*, the Chinese name of the place.

HONGKONG: 香港—fragant lagoon. There has been much controversy as to the correct interpretation of the above two characters. "Fragrant Streams" and "Incense Harbour" are among those given. The use of the term "lagoon" is based upon the fact that the inlet of water which forms the harbour of Takow, Formosa, and is unquestionably a lagoon, is written down in Chinese maps of the place as a 港. Our word *Hongkong* is a corruption of the local pronunciation of the Chinese name. See *Petticoat String*.

Hongkong was ceded to the English in 1841 and by Treaty of Nanking in 1842, but is still frequently spoken of by the inaccurate as being in "China," and sometimes even as a Treaty Port. Was formally erected into a British Colony 5th April 1843. Is 26 miles in circumference, and nine in length by eight in breadth. The "Peak," upon which stands the signal staff, is 1825 feet high. There is now a funicular railway to the summit. Just as

Gibraltar dominates the entrance to the Mediterranean Sea, so does Hongkong dominate commercially the entrance to the China Seas. Like Gibraltar it is close to the mainland of an alien power, and has similar physical aspects—a rocky height rising abruptly from the sea, with the town at the foot of its slopes. Like Gibraltar too it is almost entirely unproductive.

HONG MERCHANTS. The security merchants of former days, who, for the privilege of trading with foreigners coming to Canton, became security to the mandarins for their payment of duties and their good behaviour while on shore. Monopoly broken up by Treaty of Nanking 1842.

HONSAI. See *Gonsai*.

HOO-SZE: 湖師. Abbreviation for 湖絲師 "silk expert' or "silk toucher." Compare *chaa-sze*. Known in Canton as 絲師 *or* 湖絲客, 湖絲 standing for raw silk from Hu-chou Fu in Chehkiang.

HOPPO, THE. The Haikwan *(q.v.)* or Superintendent of Customs at Canton, has been so called for many years. The term is said (1) to be a corruption of *Hoo poo* 戶部 —the Board of Revenue, with which office the Hoppo, as collector of duties, is in direct communication; (2) to be from *Ho poh* 河泊 originally "god of the rivers" but subsequently applied to the Canton river-police magistrate. A well-known native work, however, states that 關部 the Superintendent of Customs is called in English 合煲 *Hoppo*.

HOTOW: 河頭—head of the river. Name of a large kind of boat used by foreigners at Canton for going up country, picnics, etc. So called from the name of the place at which they are built. Are usually distinguished by three or four red doors, called 馬門, on each side.

HOUSE-BOAT. The common name among foreigners in China for small sailing boats housed over and fitted up with sleeping bunks, cook's galley, and other European appliances. Are much used on the river Yang-tsze by the "shootists" of Shanghai, Chinkiang, etc.

HOWQUA: 伍官. The popular designation of the famous co-hong merchant, named 伍怡和 Ng E-wo (in Pekingese Wu I-ho), who was one of the intermediaries, under the old system, between the Chinese officials and foreigners at Canton, and whose house there is still one of the show sights. He died in 1843. Howqua was an Amoy man, and the word seems to be an attempt at representing the Amoy sounds of the above two characters. Mr. Parker writes in the *China Review*, XVII, p. 53, "Is evidently the word 家 *ka* as written by the Portuguese." The Portuguese, however, sound *qua* not as *ka* but as *kwah*; *e.g.* quadrado.

HSIEN: 縣. A district under the immediate control of a magistrate called a *chih-hsien (q.v.)*, or simply a *Hsien*.

HSIEN PI: 鮮卑. A tribe which originally occupied the mountains and glens of south-east Mongolia, and gave great trouble to the Chinese for some centuries after the Christian era. They were the progenitors of the Kitans *(q.v.)*.

HSIN CHING LU: 尋津錄. The *Book of Experiments*, or first handbook of the Court Dialect published by Sir T. Wade. Was wittily travestied into 新京路 "the new road to Peking," the sounds of the two sets of characters being sufficiently near, for a foreign ear, to admit of such a pun.

HSIU-TS'AI: 秀才—cultivated talents. A graduate of the lowest rank. Generally translated *bachelor of arts*.

This was the general term for scholar or man of letters

until the time of the Emperor Kuang Wu (A.D. 25—58), when it was changed to *mao-ts'ai* 茂才, on account of the character 秀 forming part of the Emperor's name. The old name was restored some two centuries later.

HSIUNG-NU: 匈奴. A Tartar tribe from Eastern Mongolia, probably the Scythians of Herodotus, known in early ages as 山戎 or 熏粥, under the Hsia dynasty as 淳維, under the Yin dynasty as 鬼方, under the Chou dynasty as 獫狁, and under the Han dynasty as 匈如. They first began to give trouble in the 3rd cent. B.C., disappearing from history in the 5th cent. A.D. See *Ouigours*.

HSÜAN CHUANG *or* YÜAN TSANG: 玄奘 *or* 元奘. The famous Buddhist priest who left China for India in A.D. 629, returning after an absence of seventeen years and bringing with him 657 volumes of the Buddhist scriptures.

HU-KUANG: 湖廣. The old name of a province now divided into Hu-pei and Hu-nan *(q.v.)*, but still used collectively of the two. Also called the Two Hu, 兩湖.

HUÉ: 交州府. The capital of Annam. Locally known as 許愛, whence the name Hué.

HUNAN: 湖南—south of the (Tung-t'ing 洞庭) lake. One of the Eighteen Provinces. Capital city Ch'ang-sha Fu 長沙府. Old name 楚. See *Chou Han*.

HUNDRED FAMILY NAMES: 百家姓. Correctly speaking, "the family names" of China, hundred being merely a round number used to express "all." The title of a small work several centuries old which contains 408 ordinary Chinese surnames, and 30 double names or such as we should unite in English by a hyphen. In K'ang Hsi's lexicon, however, we find no less than 1,678 characters mentioned as surnames, besides 168 double and 8 triple names; while in the biographical section of the *T'u shu* (see *Encyclopaedias*) there are 3,038 single names and 1,619 double, triple, and quadruple names, making a grand total of 4,657 in all. Chinese of the same surname (with some few exceptions) may not intermarry. The four common names—our Brown, Jones, and Robinson—are Chang 張, Wang 王, Li 李, and Chao 趙. These names are in many cases translatable, and yield such meanings as *Field*, *Fox*, *Crab*, *Spring*, *Home*, *Bellyful*, *Farmer*, *White*, *Gold*, *Joy*, *Ball*, etc. Tradition says that there were originally only eight clan-names, all of which are written with the Radical *(q.v.)* woman; and this, taken in connection with the fact that the Chinese word for "surname" contains the same Radical, seems to show that in early times the family line was traced through the mother. It is also noticeable that in the majority of cases surnames were derived from places, and not place-names from persons as with us.

HUNG-LOU-MÊNG: 紅樓夢. A famous Chinese novel in the Peking dialect, popularly known as the Dream of the Red Chamber, dealing chiefly with events of domestic life which are very graphically described, and attributed to Ts'ao Hsüeh-ch'in of the 17th cent. Many Chinese are said to have died for love of the heroine, Miss Lin, so exquisitely has that young lady been portrayed by the author; but the book being considered a dangerous one to fall into the hands of youth was accordingly placed in the *Index Expurgatorius* of China, though at present its sale is carried on much the same as that of any other work. It is generally issued in 24 vols, 8vo, containing about 4,000 pages, and the number of personages introduced to the reader runs to over 400. There is something distinctive in the delineation of each of these; in view however of the confusion likely to arise from such a bewildering maze of names, a small dictionary has been published in which each individual is more or less described. The title should properly be "The "Dream of the Red-storeyed Mansion," the allusion being to the wealthy establishment at which the scene of the story is laid, and to the pomp and power of its inmates, destined by the inevitable turn of Fortune's wheel to lapse into poverty and decay.

HUNG-MÓ *or* HUNG-MAO: 紅毛—the red-haired. A term first applied by the Chinese to the Dutch, in the 17th century, and now to all white foreigners. Is slyly used to a great extent, as also *fan* 番 barbarian, among the Chinese of Hongkong. The writer has even received a letter from his washerman addressed 紅毛二江臣 *The red-haired Vice Consul*, though even this will hardly bear comparison with a title he once obtained in Swatow, where it is commonly used, namely 耶穌官 *The Jesus Mandarin*—an appellation which tells its own tale. In Amoy and Swatow, the term "red-haired" is now reserved for the English.

HUNS, THE. See *Hsiung-nu.*

HUPAO, THE: 滬報—Shanghai News. Name of a Chinese newspaper issued from the *Daily News* office. First appeared 18th May, 1882.

HUPEH *or* HU-PEI: 湖北—north of the (Tung-t'ing 洞庭) lake. One of the Eighteen Provinces. Capital city Wu-ch'ang Fu 武昌府. Old name 鄂 ngO.

HUTUKHTU: 呼圖克圖. The cardinals, or second order in the hierarchy of Lamaism *(q.v.).* The three chief

9

Hutukhtus reside at Urga, Kuku Khoto, and Peking; the latter representing Lamaism at the Court. In Tibet they wield temporal as well as spiritual power, the administration being entirely in their hands. Popularly known as "Living Buddhas." The term H. is derived from a Mongolian word which is interpreted in Chinese as signifying *tsai lai jên* 再來人—*i.e.* one who returns again, an Avatar.

HWANG-POO *or* WANG-PU: 黃埔—Yellow Reach. The river whereon, at a distance of about 12 miles from the Yang-tsze into which it flows, stand the town and foreign settlements of Shanghai.

HWANG-TI: (*a*) 黃帝—the Yellow Emperor. A legendary ruler, who is said to have flourished nearly 3,000 years before Christ and to have been the pioneer of the early civilisation of mankind by the invention of wheeled carriages, a medium of exchange, music, astronomical instruments, etc., etc. Was called "yellow" because he reigned under the influence of *earth* (whatever that may mean), and yellow is the colour of earth. Must not be confounded with the next.

HWANG-TI: (*b*) 皇帝—Supreme ruler. The title of every Emperor of China since the days of the First Emperor (*q.v.*), before which time the title 王 *wang* "prince" was employed. When the Mongols conquered China in the early years of the 13th century, and adopted the title Hwang Ti, they analysed the character 皇 into its component parts 白 *white* and 王 *prince*, and translated them literally into Mongolian as Tchagan Khagan or "White Khan." This was subsequently adopted by the Russians for Asiatic use in the various forms of Ak-khan, Ak-Padshah, and Biely Tsar or "White Czar."

HWEI-HWEI *or* HUI-HUI: 囘 囘. Generally used of all classes of *Mahommedans* found in China. The character 囘 is sometimes written with *dog* by the side 狟.

HYPNOTISM. See *Mesmerism.*

HYSON: 熙 春—flourishing spring. A kind of tea.

HYSON, YOUNG: 雨 前—before the rains. A kind of tea so called because it was picked early. Formerly called by foreigners *uchain.*

IBN BATUTA. An Arabian traveller who visited China in the fourteenth century, and whose narrative corroborates several of the statements of Marco Polo.

ICHANG: 宜 昌. A port in the province of Hupeh on the upper Yang-tsze, opened to trade by the Chefoo Convention of 1876.

ICHIBU: 一 分—one *bu (q.v.).*

ICHI-ROKU: 一 六—one six. All days of the month which contain one or other or both of these numbers; *e.g.*, the 1st, 6th, 11th, 16th, etc. These days were adopted as official holidays on the establishment of the present Government in Japan, but recently Sundays have been substituted.

"Our readers have doubtless been unaware that their "Majesties the Emperor and Empress, desirous of instructing "themselves in European science, were accustomed to take "lessons regularly every day, excepting those of *ichiroku.*" —*Echo du Japon.*

The Japanese also use the expressions *ni-hitchi* 二 七 2nd and 7th, *sam patchi* 三 八 3rd and 8th, *shi-ku* 四 九 4th and 9th, and *go-juh* 五 十 5th and 10th in the same manner. The same kind of phraseology is also common in China.

I. G., THE. Abbreviation for *Inspector General* of the

foreign department of the Chinese Customs. During the occupation of the native city of Shanghai by the T'ai-p'ing rebels 1853—55, the collection of the Customs' revenue was temporarily placed in the hands of three foreign officials deputed by the British, French, and American Consuls; and this system was found to answer so well that it was continued, even after the evacuation, under the guidance of Mr Horatio Nelson Lay at the head of a small staff of European assistants. The arrangement was finally extended to all the Treaty Ports, and has developed into what is now known as the Chinese Customs' Service —hitherto one of the most ably conducted organisations in the world.

IKKU. A well-known Japanese poet and humorist. Died 1831.

IMMORTALS, THE: 仙人. A term which is somewhat loosely applied to the *richi* of Buddhism and to the saints of Taoism *(q.v.)*.

INCHHON. Same as *Jenchuan (q.v.)*.

INDIAN INK. A misnomer for the slabs of *Chinese* ink used all over the empire since the third century of our era; though, according to one native authority, it was manufactured as early as B.C. 140. It is prepared chiefly in Anhui, from a lampblack produced by burning either sesamum oil or the oil of the seeds of *sterculia platanifolia*, Linn. f., with varnish and pork-fat. A paste is made from this lampblack and some glue is added, also musk or Baroos camphor to scent it, and some gold-leaf to give it a metallic lustre. The paste is beaten on wooden anvils with steel hammers, and then placed in wooden moulds and ornamented with gold or coloured characters etc. From their habit of putting the writing brush or pencil into the mouth in order to give a fine point, the

Chinese have come to employ the phrase "eating ink" as a metaphorical equivalent for study.

INFANTICIDE. The prevalence of this crime in China has been greatly exaggerated, while the harrowing stories connected with Baby Towers *(q.v.)* have been shown to be ridiculously untrue. It is now quite an open question whether infanticide is more practised in China than in Europe and elsewhere. Foreigners often fail to understand how it is that, if infanticide does not exist, stone tablets engraved with warnings against this crime can still be set up near ponds, and endless pamphlets be produced illustrating the crime and the dire effects upon those who perpetrate it. The explanation however is simple. Any Chinaman who makes money is compelled by public opinion to do something in the philanthropic line. He may build a needed bridge, or mend a road, or publish a pamphlet setting forth the terrors of Purgatory (see *Leprosy*). Infanticide (girls only), which of course does occur, as in every other country, is one convenient outlet for such philanthropy. Happily for the honour of the Chinese people, who are very fond of children, it is possible actually to prove a negative, and show that extensive infanticide cannot be practised in China, as follows. Every Chinaman throughout the empire, with the very rarest exceptions, marries young. If his wife dies, he marries again; it is not thought proper for widows to remarry, though some do so. Many well-to-do Chinamen take a concubine; some two, three, and even four. Therefore, unless there is an enormous disparity in the numbers of boys and girls born, infanticide must be reduced to very narrow limits. Yet, as late as May 1897, Mrs Isabella Bishop said at a meeting of the Zenana Missionary

Society that "of eleven Bible women whom she had seen "at a meeting in China, there was not one that had not "put an end to at least five girl babies." It is a work of supererogation to add that few Chinawomen bear five children.

INITIALS. See *Spelling System*.

INLAND SEA, THE. The sea which is almost surrounded by the three southernmost islands—Nipon, Sikok, and Kiusiu—of the Japanese empire. It is about 250 miles in length, and contains some fine pieces of scenery.

INNER LAND, THE. See *Nui ti*.

INQUESTS. Are held in China upon the bodies of all who die by violence or are found dead under suspicious circumstances. Also, in cases of grievous bodily injury, when a limit is fixed within which the accused is responsible, and during which the injured man is handed over to his charge. The inquest is held by the District Magistrate or his Deputy, without a jury, within view of the body, on the very spot where found or struck down.

INTERCALARY MONTH: 閏月. (Accented on the second syllable). A thirteenth month inserted seven times in nineteen years, or about once in every third year, in order to make up the annual deficiency of the lunar year of twelve months as compared with the solar year. The four following methods, the last of which is still in use, have been adopted at various times for determining the incidence of this month.

(1)—The reduplication of every 33rd month. Thus in the 3rd year there would be an intercalary 9th month, in the 6th year an int. 6th, in the 9th an int. 3rd, in the 11th an int. 11th, in the 14th an int. 8th, in the 17th an int. 4th, and in the 19th an int. 12th.

(2)—Addition of a month at the end of the proper year.

(3)—Reduplication of the month, the numerical order of which was the same as the number of days from the winter solstice to the end of the current month, no matter whether a month of 29 or of 30 days, and no notice being taken of any remainder exceeding 12. Thus if the winter solstice fell on the 24th of the 11th month of 30 days, the following 6th month would be reduplicated.

(4)—Selection of a month under which the following conditions would be fulfilled:—That the winter solstice shall always fall in the 11th month, the summer solstice in the 5th month, the vernal equinox in the 2nd month, and the autumnal equinox in the 8th month. Also, that the month intercalated shall be one during which the sun does not pass from one sign of the zodiac to another; and provided always that the 1st, 11th, and 12th moons be never reduplicated. [By a mistake the intercalary month for the year 1813 was calculated for the 8th moon, but as this brought the winter solstice into the 10th month, the Emperor cancelled the calculation and made the 2nd moon of the following year the intercalary month instead, which fulfilled all the conditions required.]

INVITATIONS (CHINESE). If declined, should be sent back in the original envelope, with an ordinary visiting card bearing the two characters 辭 謝 *tz'ŭ hsieh*, "declined with thanks." If accepted, should be kept and taken with the guest for presentation to the host. In neither case is any formal answer expected.

IQUON: 夷 官. A name under which Chêng Chih-lung, the father of Koxinga, was known to the Portuguese.

I-RO-HA KANA. A form of Japanese writing said to have been invented by Kūkai, a Buddhist priest who died

A.D. 835. It was an attempt to assimilate the letters as much as possible to the Bonji (*i.e.* Pali) used in the sacred books of the Buddhists.

ISHI-DŌRŌ: 石燈籠. A stone lamp. [Japanese].

JADE: 玉 *Yü* (said to mean *the* gem *par excellence*). A species of nephrite, the green and white kind of which (翡翠 *fei ts'ui*, kingfisher plumes) is highly valued by the Chinese. Rings, bracelets, vases, and various other ornaments are made of this stone, which is also largely imitated. The Chinese word is extensively employed in ceremonious language; *e.g.*, 玉體 "jade (*i.e.* honourable) person" and 勿吝玉趾 "do not spare your jade footsteps," *i.e.* "come and see me," etc., etc., jade being considered as emblematical of most of the virtues, and as a product of Heaven and Earth. Whole ship-loads of it have been brought as ballast from other countries to China, but have found no market, the Chinese declaring that it was not the same article as their own, which comes from the mountain-ranges of Tibet.

JAMBARREE. A festive party, involving much noise. [Slang.] Analysed by a wag at Swatow:—

Alcohol	75 parts.
Vox humana	24 „
Water	1 „

JAPAN: 日本—Sun Root. Hence it is called "Land of the Rising Sun," the extreme Orient. Our word is from *Jeh-pun*, the Dutch orthography of the Japanese *Ni-pon*, as represented by the above two Chinese characters.

Formerly known to the Chinese as 倭 *Wo*, the Country of Dwarfs, which character was altered by the Japanese to 和. Also called 神國 the nation of gods, and 皇國 the Imperial nation. [See *Nipon* and *Yamato*.]

The Chinese written language and Confucian books were introduced into Japan in A.D. 286, on the advice of Atogi, son of the King of Korea, who visited that country. Until they became acquainted with Chinese, the Japanese had no written character. When the Japanese began to write their own language phonetically, they used Chinese characters (see *Kana*). Later on they limited the number of characters for use as phonetic signs, and then wrote these in an abbreviated form (see *Katakana*) or in a cursive form (see *Hiragana*). The Japanese alphabet, consisting of 47 syllable-letters, was invented by Kudu-no-Madu, A.D. 693—755; and the first Japanese written book dates from 712 (see *Kojiki*). The Japanese, like the Chinese, write from right to left in vertical columns. Diplomatic relations between China and Japan began about the end of the 6th century, and continued for some time under the T'ang dynasty, during which period Japanese students were sent to China to study the Chinese language and literature. Kublai Khan sent an armada against Japan in A.D. 1281. It was destroyed in a storm, aided by the attacks of the Japanese, and only 3 men out of 100,000 are said to have escaped.

JEHOL: 熱 河—hot river. A summer residence of the Emperors of China, lying about 100 miles north of Peking, beyond the Great Wall, and built in 1780 on the model of the residence of the Panshen Erdeni *(q.v.)* at Tashilumbo in Tibet, when that functionary proceeded to Peking to be present on the seventieth anniversary of the Emperor Ch'ien Lung's birthday. It was here that the Emperor Hsien Fêng died in 1861, subsequent to the capture of Peking by the British and French forces. Our name is an imitation of the Chinese sounds, through the

French, the final being due to the French transliteration of the Peking 兒 *eul*, which is usually added in the north to the two characters given above.

JENCHUAN: 仁川. A Prefecture in Korea, in which is situated the port of Chemulpo *(q.v.)*.

JESUITS, THE. This term, as used in China, refers to the highly-educated Romish missionaries of that particular society, who resided at Peking during the seventeenth and part of the eighteenth centuries, and employed themselves chiefly in the translation of scientific works, in teaching astronomy, etc., etc. Matteo Ricci and Adam Schaal are among the most famous. They have found not unworthy successors in the Jesuits of today, among whom may be mentioned PP. Zottoli, Couvreur, Havret, and others. See *Sicawei*.

JEWS: 挑筋教 *T'iao-chin-chiao*—sect of those who take out the sinew. Are said to have carried the Pentateuch to China shortly after the Babylonish captivity. They founded a colony in Honan in A.D. 72, and erected a synagogue at K'ai-fêng Fu in A.D. 1164. Were discovered by Ricci (see *Jesuits*) in the 17th century. Hebrew rolls of parts of the Pentateuch in the square character, with vowel points, were obtained in 1850. The Jews are mentioned in the *Hist. of the Yüan (Mongol) Dynasty*, 1329 and 1354 A.D., as 朮忽, the equivalent of the Chaldæan *Jĕhud*.

JIGGY JIGGY *or* JIKI JIKI: 直直 Japanese equivalent for "make haste!"

JIMMU TENNO. The first Mikado of Japan, B.C. 660, with whose reign the historical period begins.

JINGAL. The Chinese blunderbuss. From the Hindustani *jangâl*, a swivel, a large musket. Generally fired in China from a swivel fixed on a wall or in a wooden post, but sometimes with the barrel resting on a second man's shoulder, in which case it is called a 抬鎗 *t'ai ch'iang*.

"There is very little recoil with these weapons, as "they weigh about twenty pounds, and the charge is not "rammed home, but just dropped down the muzzle."— *Shanghai Courier*.

JINRICKSHA *or* JINRIKISHA: 人力車—the man's strength cart. A small gig, invented about 1872 and constructed to carry one or more persons, drawn by a coolie in shafts and sometimes pushed by another from behind. From the Japanese pronunciation of the above three characters. Now largely used in Shanghai, Hongkong, Amoy, and some Indian hill stations. The Japanese name is *Kuruma* "a vehicle," and the coolie is called *Kurumaya*.

JOHN TUCK. A slang name for the Viceroy at Canton, being the corruption of *Tsung-tuk* 總督, Governor General, as pronounced by the sailors of H. B. M.'s fleet during the occupation of Canton.

JON-NUKÉ. The famous, but immodest, "forfeit dance," performed by Japanese courtesans, who pay forfeit for any failure to imitate each other's gestures when challenged by a loud "Hoi!" by throwing off one article of clothing each time, until nothing remains, when they disappear behind a curtain at the back. Part of the performance consists of singing a song, beginning with the words "Jon-kino, jon-kino." See *Yoshiwara*.

JOO-EE *or* JU-I: 如意—as you desire. A kind of sceptre often given as a present among the Chinese, and signifying that the recipient will attain his wishes. To be seen in the hands of idols at Chinese temples. The term is sometimes used by Chinese shop-keepers as a shop-sign; *e.g.* 如意襪 "as you wish stockings (sold here)."

The Buddhist Mani 摩尼, a gem which was said to remain always brilliant, was called the Ju-i Pearl. It is enumerated as one of the Seven Precious Things.

JO-RO: 女郎. A prostitute [Japanese]. So *Joroya* a house of ill fame.

JOSS. A Chinese idol; also applied to the Christian God. The word is a corruption of the Portuguese *Deos*, God, and has come to be used in pidgin-English in the sense of luck, as good joss or bad joss, according to circumstances.

JOSS-HOUSE. A Chinese temple; *e.g.*, the "Treaty Joss-house" where the Treaty of Tientsin was signed. Also used by the natives to designate all foreign churches and chapels.

JOSS-HOUSE MEN. Missionaries are so called by pidgin-English speaking Chinese.

JOSS-PAPER. Pieces of gold and silver paper worked into the form of shoes of sycee *(q.v.)* and burnt by the Chinese at masses for the dead, before the shrine of the God of Wealth (財神), etc., etc.

JOSS-PIDGIN. Any form of religious ceremony, foreign or native, including cracker-firing, processions, etc., etc.

JOSS-STICK. A stick of incense made from the dust of various scented woods mixed with a little clay, and used in temples for worship, in houses for lighting pipes, etc. Some for the latter purpose are prepared so as to hang over a wire frame in a spiral form; and being lighted at the bottom, burn slowly upwards and last for many hours. Carefully regulated joss-sticks for marking the time are sold at the famous "Water Clock" in the city of Canton.

JUDGE, PROVINCIAL:按 察 使 *or* 臬 司. A high official, ranking with the Treasurer or Fan-t'ai *(q.v.)*, who is responsible for the due administration of justice in the province to which he has been appointed.

JUDICIAL PROCEDURE. In the case, for instance, of a murder, a preliminary investigation is held before the District Magistrate, and if there is sufficient evidence against the accused, he is committed for trial before the Prefect. If the Prefect confirms the view of the Magistrate, the case is sent on to the Provincial Judge; and, similarly, by him to the Fu-t'ai or Governor. The Governor then holds a trial and reports to the Board of Punishments in Peking, and the Board lays the case before the Emperor. The Emperor commands the Board to examine and report; and if the Governor's view is confirmed, the latter receives instructions to that effect. Otherwise, the case is referred back for reconsideration, the Governor usually getting a strong hint as to the direction his reconsideration is expected to take. He himself refers back to his subordinates, and so on.

JUDY. Slang term for a Chinese courtesan. See *Punch and Judy*.

JULAI. See *Tathâgata*.

JUNK. According to Ibn Batuta, only the larger kind of Chinese sailing-vessels should be so called; but the term is now used of all sea-going boats and of the more bulky of the river craft. It is a notable fact that single junks are rarely seen at sea; they generally sail in pairs, even down to the small fishing-junks which ply their trade along the coast, the object being no doubt that of mutually rendering assistance. Probably from the Malay *ajong* or *jong*, which means a large boat, corrupted by the Portuguese into *junco*.

KABAYA. The long upper dress worn by Malay women and largely adopted as a déshabillé by the Dutch ladies in Java.

KAGO: 駕籠—riding basket. A bamboo palanquin formerly used in Japan, but now superseded by the *jinrikisha (q.v.).*

KAKEMONO. A Japanese hanging picture.

KAKI. The Japanese name for *persimmon (q.v.).*

KAKKE: 脚氣—foot humour. The Japanese name for *Beriberi* (said to be a Cingalese word meaning "weakness"). A locally endemic contagious disease, probably of a malarial character, showing itself in two forms, the dropsical, and the atrophic (the so-called wet and dry forms). It is now believed to consist essentially in a multiple degenerative inflammation of the nerves.

KALMUCK TARTARS. See *Tartars* and *Eleuth Mongols.*

KALPA: 却波. [Sanskrit]. An immense period of time. A "great" Kalpa = 1,344,000,000 years, or 80 small kalpas.

KAMAKURA. Residence of the Shoguns *(q.v.)* of Japan from the close of the 12th cent. A.D. to 1867.

KAMI: 神. A god or spirit of the ancient religion *(Shinto)* of Japan.

KAMPONG. See *Campong.*

KAN ON: 漢音. A pronunciation of Chinese according to the dialect of Singan Fu, capital of Shensi, introduced into Japan through Korea about A.D. 600, and especially used by Confucianists. See *Go on.*

KANA: 假字—borrowed words. Contraction for *Karina.* Chinese characters used phonetically to represent Japanese sounds. These are of two kinds; *Katakana* and *Hiragana (q.v.).*

KANG *or* K'ANG: 炕. A brick bed, with a fire underneath it. Used all over the more northern parts of China.

KANG HI *or* K'ANG HSI: 康 熙—lasting and prosperous. The style of reign adopted by the second monarch of the present dynasty, A.D. 1662—1723. It was under the auspices of this Emperor that the great Chinese lexicon was compiled which is known as the *K'ang Hsi Tzŭ Tien* (see *Dictionaries*). Twenty specimens of the cash *(q.v.)* cast by this Emperor have each a different character on the reverse, which, read in the proper order, form a poetical quatrain. Complete sets of these are now rather rare. See *Lohan.*

KANGAKUSHA. A term applied to the Japanese scholars of the 18th century, who were crazy on Chinese literature and Chinese ideals generally. See *Wagakusha.*

KANGURA FUYE. The Japanese flute. *Koma fuyé* is the Korean flute.

KANSUH: 甘 肅—voluntary reverence. One of the Eighteen Provinces. Capital city Lan-chou Fu 蘭 州 府. Old name 隴 *Lung.*

KAO-LIANG: 高 粱—tall millet. The *Sorghum vulgare* or Barbados millet.

KAOLIN: 高 嶺. The Chinese name for what is known to foreigners as China Clay *(q.v.)*. So called from the name of a ridge of hills near a great porcelain factory in Kiangsi.

KAPAN: 夾 板. Chinese name for a European sailing-vessel, taken from the old-fashioned clinker or ribbed build as distinguished from the build of junks.

KAPPORÉ. A Japanese dance performed by geisha.

KATAKANA: 片 假 字—side-borrowed words. (See *Kana*). A form of Japanese writing derived from the Chinese, only a part of each character being taken. It consists of 48 symbols, and is seen only in conjunction with Chinese characters (*kaisho*). Invented by Kibidaishi, who died A.D.

776. Little used except in dictionaries for explanatory purposes, to express grammatical terminations, and to spell foreign names.

KAUTCHEWS. The people from 高州 *Kau-tchew* (in mandarin *Kao-chou*) to the south-west of the Kuang-tung province. They emigrate in large numbers to the Straits' Settlements.

KAY-TOW: 客頭—head of the strangers. An employer of Chinese labour in the Straits.

KEIBU: 警部. A Japanese sergeant of police.

KELUNG: 岐籠 *or* 基隆 *or* 雞籠. Subsidiary port to Tamsui at the north end of Formosa, opened to trade by the Treaty of Tientsin, 1858. Was once a Spanish and subsequently a Dutch settlement. Coal is found in the neighbourhood. The name *Kelung* was once applied to the whole island of Formosa.

KEN: 間. Japanese term for a "district." Equivalent to the Chinese *hsien (q.v.)*.

KEN: 間. A measure of six Japanese feet ($= 71^1/_2$ inches).

KENCHO: 縣廳. A Japanese magistrate's office.

KENREI: 縣令. A Japanese District Magistrate.

KHALKAS, THE: 喀爾喀. The Khalka nation comprises those tribes of Mongols which, owing probably to their remoteness, maintained to a late date their independence of the Manchu sovereignty.

KHAMBALU. From *Khampalik* or *Khan baligh*, the city of the Khan. The Mongol name for what is now the Tartar portion of the city of Peking. Mentioned by Marco Polo as *Cambaluc*.

KHAN: 可汗 or more often 罕 and 汗. A Mongolian term for "prince." The Pathan Mahommedans in India are called "Khan."

KHATA *or* KHADAK. Ceremonial scarves interchanged between a Mongol host and guest.

KHATEEB. The Mussulman preacher in a Malay village. See *Billal.*

KHUTUKHTU. See *Hutukhtu.*

KIANGNAN. The old name of Anhui and Kiangsu See *Two Kiang.*

KIANGSI: 江 西 —west of the river. One of the Eighteen Provinces. Capital city Nan-ch'ang Fu 南 昌 府. Old name 豫 章 *Yü-chang.*

KIANGSU : 江 蘇. One of the Eighteen Provinces. From the first syllables of Kiang-ning Fu 江 寧 府, the capital, and Su-chou Fu 蘇 州 府, the celebrated city of beautiful women. Old name 吳 *Wu.*

KIAO-CHOU:膠 州. A port on the southern shore of the Shantung Promontory, ceded to Germany in 1898. It was reached by traders from the Erythraean Sea, B.C. 680—642; and the Buddhist monk Fa Hsien landed there at the end of his voyage from Ceylon in A.D. 414.

KIAO-TCHI *or* GIAO-TCHI : 交 趾. A name formerly believed to have been given by the Chinese to the inhabitants of Cochin-China *(q.v.)* because in that country the sexes bathed together. Now ascertained to be a native name for the aborigines of Annam, derived from the separation of their big toes from the rest of the foot, like thumbs.

KIEN LUNG. See *Ch'ien Lung.*

KI-LI-SSŪ-TANG : 基 利 斯 當. The Roman Catholic pass-word among converts in China, being an imitation of the Latin *Christianus.* Thus, "Lao-tang" (the last syllable with "old" prefixed) is used as a form of address among native converts, as opposed to "Lao Pai" or "Old

Gentile," the *Pai* representing the first syllable of Pontius Pilate's name.

KILIN *or* CH'I-LIN (in Japanese *Kirin*): 麒麟. One of the four fabulous creatures of China, generally translated "unicorn." It is mentioned in the Odes, and is also said to have appeared just previous to the death of Confucius. The Spring and Autumn Annals *(q.v.)* end with the record of this fact. An attempt has been made by some foreign scholars to identify the Kilin with the giraffe.

KIMONO. A long robe with sleeves, open in front and folding, worn by Japanese of both sexes, with a girdle.

KIN: 斤. A catty *(q.v.)*.

KING, THE. See *Ching*.

KINGHITAO. See *Seoul*.

KINSATSZ: 金札. Japanese bank-notes first issued in 1868, when the Daimios who overthrew the Tycoon found it necessary to raise a loan.

KINSAY *or* QUINSAY: 京師 —capital. The modern city of Hang-chou Fu, the capital of the empire at the time of the Sung dynasty. *Kinsay* is a corruption of the sounds of the above two characters.

KIŌJEN. A Japanese farce, in colloquial.

KIOKA. A comic variety of the Japanese Tanka *(q.v.)*.

KIOTO *or* KIYOTO: 京都. The capital of the Mikados of Japan from A.D. 794 to 1868. Also known as Heian-jo or the City of Peace. See *Kamakura*.

KIRGHIS *or* KASAKS. Nomads who inhabit the great desert lying between Siberia, China, Turkestan, and the Caspian Sea. *Kir* means field, and *gis* or *gez* is the root of the word *gizmelt* to wander. Hence, *Kirghis* is a man that wanders over fields: a nomad.

KIRIN: 吉林 —joyful forest. One of the Manchurian provinces.

KITAN TARTARS: 契 丹. A tribe of Tartars who, under the leadership of a chieftain named 阿保機 Apaoki, united with themselves the Golden Tartars *(q.v.)* and then threw off their allegiance to the House of Liang, founding in A.D. 907 what is known as the 遼 Liao dynasty.

KITES, PAPER: 紙鳶 or 風箏. Are said to have been known as early as the 2nd cent. B.C., and to have been often used for political or military signalling. Kite-flying is thought to be good for boys, as it makes them throw their heads back and open their mouths, thus getting rid of internal heat. The Chinese are very expert at it, and make kites to resemble the kite, as expressed by the first term above, and also in all manner of quaint shapes. To some kites a kind of Æolian harp is attached; hence the second term above. Messengers, consisting of bamboo frames with fire-crackers attached, are sent up the string, the crackers being timed to explode on reaching the top.

KITTYSOL. The Chinese bamboo-made umbrella is so called. From the Spanish or Portuguese *quitasol*. "Eran seis, y venian con sus quitasoles." *Don Quixote*, ch. IV.

KIUKIANG: 九江—(1) nine rivers; (2) crooked river, from the shape of the character 九. One of the ports on the Yang-tsze, opened to trade by the Treaty of Tientsin, 1858, though not occupied until 1861. It lies near the outlet of the Poyang 鄱陽 lake, with which certain Chinese commentators have wrongly identified the "nine rivers" mentioned in the Book of History (禹貢—Tribute of Yü). These were believed by the scholars of the Sung dynasty to refer to the Tung-t'ing lake, a view fully confirmed by Baron von Richthofen in his recent work on China. Etymology No. 2 is of course absurd.

K'IUNG-CHOW: 瓊州—red marble region. A port in the I. of Hainan, opened to trade by the Treaty of Tientsin, 1858, but not formally occupied until 1876. It was proposed in Sir R. Alcock's unratified Convention of 1869 to substitute Wênchow *(q.v.)* as more likely to be a profitable centre of trade.

KLINGS, THE. The common term in the Straits' Settlements for all Indians. (See *Chetties*). The German traveller, Jagar, suggested Telinga, a part of the Coromandel coast, as the original word of which *Kling* may be a corruption.

KNIFE MONEY: 刀錢. Some of the earliest Chinese coins, dating as far back as 2,000 and more years before Christ, were cast in the shape of a razor blade; hence the name. Genuine specimens of "knife money" are exceedingly rare and much prized by Chinese numismatists; but the market is flooded with spurious imitations of all kinds.

KNOTTED CORDS: 結繩. Said to have been used by primitive man in China before the invention of writing; but how or to what extent, there is no record to show.

KOBANG: 小判—small division. A Japanese gold coin equal to 4 *bus (q.v.)*.

KOCHO: 戶長. The superintendent of a street or block in a Japanese town. Cf. Chinese *ti-pao*.

KODSKI: 小使. A servant. [Japanese.]

KOIAN. See *Coyan*.

KOJIKI: 古事記 *or* Records of Ancient Matters. The earliest surviving book written in Japanese, containing the first traditions of the Japanese race, from the myths which form the basis of the Shinto religion down to A.D. 628. Completed in 712, by Yasumaro who declared that he took it down from the words of one Hiyeda no Are.

KOKINSHIU: 古今集. A famous Japanese anthology, issued in the 10th cent. A.D. and covering the previous 150 years. Arranged under categories.

KOKUSHI: 國司. The title of the eighteen principal *Daimios (q.v.)* of Japan.

KO-LAO SOCIETY: 哥老會—elder brother society. One of the numerous secret fraternities of China, membership of which is strictly forbidden by the Government, and is punished on discovery by death. *Penal Code*, Bk. II., Sect. 162.

"The arrest and execution of an individual found guilty "of connection with the secret Brotherhood known as the "*Ko Lao Hwei.*"—*Peking Gazette*, 8 Sept. 1877.

KONG: 缸. A large glazed earthen jar for holding water.

KONGSI *or* KONGSEE: 公司—company or guild. An association of Chinese formed for purposes of mutual protection, etc.

KOOSBEGE: "lord of the family." A title bestowed in 1847 upon Yakoob Beg, and equivalent to "Vizier."

KOREA. An imitation of the sounds *Kao li* 高麗, the common Chinese name for this country, pronounced *Kori* by the Koreans. [高 was formerly written 槀 *a quiver*]. It is incorrect to speak of *the* Korea, which is merely a word-for-word rendering of the French *La Korée*, just in the same way as it is strictly speaking wrong to say *the* Tyrol.

Otherwise known as 朝鮮 Chaosien, a name adopted in A.D. 1392, from the name of a district in the north-west of the peninsula, signifying the country nearest to the rising sun. The Koreans themselves employ both names, the official designation being Chaosien. The Japanese pronunciation of this name is Chosen.

The kingdom of Korea, for many centuries a vassalage of the Chinese empire, is said (but without foundation) to have been established about 1100 B.C. It is known in the historical annals as 韓 *Han*, the name of the Three States which formerly divided the Korean peninsula, until one of them, Ko-rye, absorbed the other two, about the close of the 11th cent. A.D. Hence the name Korea. In A.D. 1392, the capital was fixed at 諱 陽 Han-yang or Seoul *(q.v.)*, and the country was divided into 8 provinces, 80 districts, and 360 cities. Korea was conquered by the Chinese under the T'ang dynasty, and remained more or less in subjection until quite recently, when its autonomy was restored. The population is estimated at 7 to 8 millions; including islands, 15 millions.

Korea was visited by Henrik Hamel, a Dutchman, in 1653, and since then by voyagers of various nationalities. In 1866, a French expedition to avenge the murder of some priests was repulsed. In 1868, an American expedition, said to be of a filibustering character in connection with treasure hidden in some mausoleum, returned without having accomplished anything. In 1835, two Catholic missionaries entered the country, and many afterwards maintained an incognito there by the adoption of mourning, which completely covers the face, and in the case of a noble, exempts the mourner from all stoppages and questionings at Customs' barriers, etc.

Chinese is the official language of Korea, but proclamations appear in Chinese and Korean, side by side. The native language is alphabetic, having 11 vowels and 14 consonants, and is thought to have been based on the Sanskrit. It is written vertically, from left to right, and is said to have been invented about the 8th or 9th century of our era by a learned Buddhist priest named 薛綜 Hsieh Tsung.

KOREYA. The cry of a Japanese policeman = Move on!

KORU: 斛 *or* 石. A Japanese grain measure = 5.13 bushels.

K'OT'OU *or* KOW-TOW *or* KOTOO: 磕頭 and 叩頭—knock the head. The ceremony of prostration common in China. Chiefly performed (1) before the Emperor (three kneelings, nine knockings 三跪九叩), (2) before any mandarin as H. I. M.'s representative, (3) in religious ceremonies, (4) to friends and relatives seen for the first time after the death of one's father or mother, (5) by inferiors to superiors as a humble apology, and in some other cases. The term is also conventionally used in a ceremonious sense = thank you. Our word is an imitation of the Chinese sounds.

KOU-LAN HU-T'UNG: 勾欄衚衕—enclosure street, *or* houses-of-ill-fame street. The name of a street in Peking, part of which was formerly occupied by the Inspector-General of Maritime Customs and his staff. For the meaning of this term, as commonly understood by all educated Chinese, see the 南宋市肆.

"The correct form is 勾闌, and I think there can be "little if any doubt that the name is a vestige of the "Yoshiwara *(q.v.)* of the Mongol period." *Mayers.*

With this term may be compared the signification of Shameen *(q.v.)*, it being worthy of note that both localities have been set apart for the use of foreigners.

KOUMISS: 馬乳酒 *or* 酥酪. An ardent spirit distilled

chiefly from mare's milk, and largely consumed by the Mongols. Said to be beneficial in some forms of phthisis.

KOWLOON: 九龍. A peninsula on the mainland of China, opposite to the island of Hongkong. A portion of it was leased to England in 1860, and a further slice was added in 1899.

KOXINGA *or* KOSHINGA: 國姓爺—lord of the country's families. The celebrated chieftain 鄭成功, who expelled the Dutch from Formosa in 1662. *Koxinga* is derived from the Portuguese method of writing the first three characters given, a title by which this leader was commonly known. Known to the Japanese as Kokusenya. His battles formed the subject of a play published in 1715 by the famous Japanese playwright Chikamatsu *(q.v.)*.

KRIS *or* KÂRIS. Pronounced *krees* or *creese*. A dagger of irregular shape, worn by the Malays in a sheath at the girdle. That a mere scratch may be effective, it is occasionally kept poisoned; and streaks of blood upon it are carefully preserved as honourable marks. Its blade is wavy or flame-shaped, from 1 to $1\frac{1}{2}$ inches wide and from 14 to 18 inches in length, capable of inflicting a dreadful wound. The finer specimens are often beautifully damascened. Etiquette demands that during a friendly interview the kris should be concealed and the handle turned with the point close to the body; otherwise it is exposed, with the handle turned the reverse way. The *Kris panjang* and the *Kris pandak* are the long and short kinds, respectively.

KU-LANG SU: 鼓浪嶼—drum-wave island. A small island to the west of the harbour of Amoy, nearly 3 miles in circumference, and about 1 mile in length by $\frac{3}{4}$ mile in breadth, upon which stand the Consulates and private residences of merchants and others connected with the trade of the port. The name "drum-wave" has been given to this island from a certain drum-like noise made by the plashing of the waves at a particular point upon its western shore. Upon a rock near the German Consulate, the following legend is carved in large characters:—

Ku-lang-su is a Paradise upon earth;

The Egret River is second to none.

Chinese population, about 3,000.

KUANG HSÜ *or* KWANG SÜ: 光緒—brilliant succession. The style of reign adopted by the present Emperor of China, who came to the throne in 1875, aged four. His name is *Tsai T'ien* 載湉, and he is the son of the late Prince 醇 Ch'un, familiarly known as the "seventh Prince," seventh son of the Emperor Tao Kuang. The style Kuang Hsü is from a sentence in a State paper of the Sung dynasty: 光丕復緒 "brilliantly renew the dynastic succession."

KUANGSI: 廣西. The western division of the ancient 廣州. One of the Eighteen Provinces. Capital city Kuei-lin Fu 桂林府, or Cassia-forest; so called from the cassia which grows in the neighbourhood. Old name 粵西 *Yüeh-hsi.*

KUANG-TUNG: 廣東. The eastern division of the ancient 廣州. One of the Eighteen Provinces. Capital city Kuang-chou Fu 廣州府 (Canton). Old name 粵東 *Yüeh-tung.*

KUBLAI KHAN: 忽必烈汗. The founder of the Mongol dynasty in China, A.D. 1280. Grandson of Genghis Khan.

KU-CHŌ: 區長. The superintendent of one of the "quarters" or parishes (區) into which all Japanese towns and cities are divided.

KUGE: 公家—noble family. The name of the ancient nobility of Japan, residing at Kiyoto and attached to the Court of the Mikado, as opposed to the territorial nobles or Daimios *(q.v.)*. The Kuge are hereditarily noble, by virtue of their blood-relationship (however distant) to the Mikado.

KÜ JEN. See *Chü-jên*.

KUMPANI. See *East India Company*.

KUMQUOT. See *Cumquat*.

KUNG: 貢. Tribute.

KUNSAN. A port on the left bank of the Changpo river in Korea, about 10 hours by steamer south of Chemulpo.

KUO TZŬ CHIEN: 國子監. The Imperial Academy of Learning. "Rather an assemblage of titled literary dignitaries "than a body of officials with active functions." *Mayers*.

KURA. A Japanese "godown" *(q.v.)*.

KURUMA. See *Jinricksha*.

KUWAZOKU: 華族—noble class. The modern name of the Daimios *(q.v.)*.

KWAN TI: 關帝. The Chinese Mars or God of War. A celebrated warrior, named Kuan Yü 關羽, who lived at the close of the second and beginning of the third century of our era. Originally a hawker of bean-curd, he was one of the three heroes who entered into a confederacy to support the Han dynasty against the rebellious Yellow Turbans. He played a leading part in the wars of the Three Kingdoms (see *San-kuo-chih*) until he was finally taken prisoner and beheaded, after which he was canonised, and subsequently (A.D. 1594) raised to the rank of a God. A particular cash, struck during the reign of the Emperor Ch'ien Lung, is called "Kwan Ti's knife" from its supposed resemblance to that weapon.

KWAN-YIN: 觀音—she who observes or pays attention to sounds; *i.e.,* she who hears prayers. The Chinese Goddess of Mercy. Sometimes represented in white clothes with a child in her arms, and worshipped by those who desire offspring. Corresponds to the *Avalôkitês 'vara* of Buddhism, and in some respects to the *Lucina* of the Romans. Also known as 大悽大悲 "great mercy, great pity;" 救苦救難 "salvation from misery, salvation from woe;" 自在 "self-existent;" 千手千眼 "thousand arms and thousand eyes," etc. But down to the early part of the 12th century Kwan-yin was represented as a man.

KWANG-CHOU-WAN. A bay on the Lien-chou peninsula, ceded by China to France as a naval station.

KWASHA or QUASSA. A power of Attorney. The term is much used by Straits'-born or other Chinese who have mixed with Malays, from whose language it is derived.

KWEI-CHOW *or* KUEI-CHOU: 貴州—noble region. One of the Eighteen Provinces. Capital city Kuei-yang Fu 貴陽府. Old name 黔.

KWEI-TSZE *or* KUEI-TZŬ: 鬼子—devils. A Chinese term for foreigners. Sometimes used in ignorance, and for want of a better expression; but usually, as an insult. Sir C. Alabaster reported that once when travelling in the interior he was politely saluted as 鬼子大人—His Excellency the Devil. See *Devils* and *Barbarians*.

K'WI-K'WI *or* K'UAI-K'UAI: 快快 — make haste! [Mandarin.]

KYFONG: 街方—neighbourhood. Any portion of a Chinese town, even the whole of it, as in Hongkong, may be called a *Kyfong*.

"A Kyfong meeting took place to-day."—*China Mail*, 16 Jan. 1878.

LAC *or* LAKH. A Hindi word, meaning 100,000. Correctly written *lakh*. The Malay *laksa* = 10,000.

LACQUER: 漆. From the Arabic *lak*. A lustrous, highly-polished kind of wood-ware, peculiar to China and Japan. This lustre is due to the use of the sap of a varnish-tree *(Rhus vernicifera)*, which is dissolved in spring-water and mixed with oil and other ingredients, and then laid on to the article in question with as many as ten or fifteen applications for the best specimens. The lacquer made in Foochow is the only kind which can compete with the Japanese; and this is said to be itself of Japanese origin.

LADRONES, THE; *i.e.* "The Pirates." The group of islands which includes Hongkong has been so called, in imitation of the more celebrated group discovered by the Portugese-Spanish voyager Magalhaens in 1521, and for precisely the same reason—the piratical disposition of their inhabitants.

LAI-OK: 黎岳. A fast-sailing, heavily-armed boat, built, expressly for smuggling purposes, at Lai-ok near Canton; whence the name. The smugglers were protected by shields, from behind which they could work their guns; and this made them very difficult of capture. Their boats have now disappeared, their very existence being prohibited by the authorities.

LALLY-LUNG *or* LA-LI-LOONG: 剌戾龍. Pidgin term for a thief. Said to be a corruption of the Portuguese *Ladrão*. See *Ladrones*.

LAMA: 喇嘛. A priest of the Tibetan form of Buddhism. This word, "according to the Chinese, has the meaning "of *wu shang* 無上, *i.e.* 'unsurpassed' or 'without a "superior.'"—*Mayers*. Colonel Yule, on the other hand, says it means "spiritual teacher."

LAMA MIAO: 喇嘛廟. (See *Dolon Nor*). A famous mart upon the plains of Mongolia, so called because of the two temples *(miao)* there.

LAMA TEMPLE: 永和宮. A monastery at Peking in which about 1500 Mongol and Tibetan priests study the Law of Buddha and other subjects. It is remarkable for a colossal figure of Mâitrêya Buddha, 70 ft. in height. See *Daibutsu*.

LAMAISM. The form of Buddhism prevailing in Mongolia and Tibet. "Is the Romanism of the Buddhist church."— *Koeppen*.

LANGSON 諒山 AFFAIR, THE, which resulted in hostilities between France and China, occurred on the 23rd June, 1884, and arose out of an alleged breach of the Li-Fournier Convention *(q.v.)*. Colonel Dugenne, commanding a small French force, was marching to occupy Langson, a town near the borders of Tongking, which it was known was garrisoned by Chinese regular troops. According to the official report, the French column was fired upon a day or two before it reached the defile where the Chinese opposed the advance in force, but it was subsequently contended by the Chinese that this firing was by banditti not under the control of the mandarins. When Colonel Dugenne found his advance opposed by a large Chinese force some parleying took place. The French themselves admit that the Chinese asked for a delay of two or three days in which to obtain instructions and to evacuate their position. Colonel Dugenne sent an ultimatum later on in the day stating he would continue his march forward in an hour. He did advance at the end of that period, the result being that his column was received with a heavy fire, and had to beat a hasty retreat.

LAO TZŬ: 老子—the old philosopher. The founder of Taoism, and reputed author of the *Tao Tê Ching (q.v.)*. He was the old philosopher of China *par excellence*, and fragments of his wisdom have been preserved in the works of Chuang Tzŭ as well as in the treatise mentioned above. His birth has been fixed at B.C. 604. Said to have had an interview with Confucius, who remarked afterwards that he could understand the flight of birds and the movement of fishes, but could not comprehend Lao Tzŭ; concluding by saying that he could only compare him with the dragon. The story of this interview however has now been recognised to belong to the category of pious frauds. He is said to have foreseen the fall of the Chou dynasty, and to have finally taken his departure on a journey to the west, after which he was never seen again. As a mythological being, he is known as the Old Boy, because born with white hair and eyebrows. This event took place at the village of Oppressed-Virtue, in the parish of Cruelty, in the district of Bitterness, which was in the state of Suffering. His mother conceived him in consequence of the emotion she felt at the sight of a falling star, and she is said by some to have been a virgin (或云其母無夫. See art. in 太平廣記). He was carried in the womb for 81 years, and had large ears with three orifices, jagged teeth, a square mouth, and ten fingers on each hand.

LAO-YEH:老爺—old father. Equivalent to "His Honour." The title of Chinese officials below the grade of Subprefect. Assistant Subprefects, Department and District Magistrates are, however, accorded by courtesy the higher title of *Ta-lao-yeh*.

LARN-PIDGIN, A. An apprentice "boy," who attaches

himself to a household with a view of *learning* the *pidgin (q.v.)* required of a servant by foreign masters, receiving little or no wages for the services he is able to render.

LASCAR. A general denomination for Indian sailors. Used among the Malays in the sense of servant or slave, contemptuously spoken. Said to be derived originally from a Persian word meaning *army*, and correctly written *Lashkar*. But the *Pioneer* of 11th December 1877 says this term "is probably slang for Anglo-Indians."

LATAH. A form of nervous paroxysm, common among the natives of the Malay peninsula, under which the victim will commit all kinds of absurdities and even crimes.

LEKIN. · See *Likin.*

LÉLANG *or* LELONG. Used in the Straits for an auction. See *Yé-lang.*

LEPROSY: 麻瘋. Has been known for many centuries in China. Lepers are so far as possible isolated though allowed to intermarry, and the Asylum for these sufferers at Canton dates from A.D. 1380. The disease has received scant attention at the hands of Chinese physicians; however a few years ago a thousand copies of an illustrated pamphlet dealing with the subject were distributed by a wealthy man at Amoy. The treatment consisted in rubbing the hands or feet on bamboo rollers to keep off numbness, and in taking doses of a decoction made from a variety of herbs.

LESSER DEVELOPMENT. See *Greater Development.*

LI: 里. About one third of a mile English. $27^4/_5$ *li* = 10 miles. This word occurs in (Count) Palikao, which is *Pa-li-ch‘iao* 八里橋 "eight *li* bridge," the name of a village near which that general gained a victory over the Chinese in the campaign of 1860.

LI: 理. Abstract right. The phrase "I don't see the *li*, *i.e.* the force, of doing so and so" is not unfrequently heard among foreigners in China.

LI: 禮. Etiquette; politeness.

LI KI. See *Rites, Book of*.

LI'S LAMBS. A satirical term formerly applied by foreigners to the soldiers under the command of Li Hung-chang, late Viceroy of Chihli, and expressive of their ferocity towards innocent tradesmen rather than of any signal prowess on the battlefield.

LI SHU. See *Seal Character*.

LI T'AI-PO: 李太白. A celebrated poet, the Anacreon of China, who flourished A.D. 669—762. He was admitted to a close intimacy with the reigning Emperor, but ultimately lost favour and ended his days in obscurity.

LIANG *or* LEANG: 兩. A Chinese ounce. A tael.

LICHEE *or* LYCHEE: 荔枝. A fruit found in the south of China, and eaten both in its fresh and dried forms. The "foreign lichee" 番荔枝 is the custard-apple.

LIE TEA. A mixture of willow and other spurious leaf with genuine tea leaf, to be fraudulently sold as tea. The spurious leaf is fired and carefully manipulated in the same way as the genuine leaf, but its true character is easily detected by a tea-taster.

LI-FAN YÜAN: 理藩院—the manage-feudatory-(states) office. The Chinese "Colonial Office," now replaced, as far as western nations are concerned, by the Tsung-li Yamên *(q.v.)*. Has general supervision over the nomad tribes of Mongolia and other dependencies of the Chinese Empire.

The Russian Treaty, signed at Tientsin in 1858, contains (Art. II.) the following words:—"Dorénavant

"les communications entre le Gouvernement suprême de
"Russie, et le Gouvernement suprême de Chine, ne se
"feront plus comme cela était jusqu'à présent par le
"Sénat d'une part et le Tribunal *Li-fan-yuan* de l'autre
"mais. . . . ."

LI-FOURNIER CONVENTION, was a settlement of the
Franco-Chinese difficulty in Tongking, drawn up and signed
at Tientsin, 11th May 1884, by H. E. Li Hung-chang,
Viceroy of Chihli and Captain Fournier of the *Volta*.
The Convention provided for the immediate withdrawal
of the Chinese forces from Tongking; respect for French
treaties with Annam past and future; a treaty of commerce
opening for free trading in merchandise, with guarantees,
the frontiers common to Tongking and China throughout
their length; and the waiving of the indemnity claimed
by France. One of the most extraordinary diplomatic
incidents on record occurred in connection with this
Convention. Captain Fournier drew up a memorandum,
when the Convention was signed, fixing a date for the
evacuation of Tongking by the Chinese troops. After the
Langson affair had occurred Li Hung-chang officially
declared that Captain Fournier had erased the important
clause relating to the evacuation in this memorandum
and had attached his initials to the erasures. A facsimile
of the memorandum with the erasures was published.
On the other hand, Captain Fournier declared on his
honour that he made no such erasures, and he has fought
a duel with a Parisian journalist who commented on his
declaration. There was no European present but Captain
Fournier when the erasures are alleged to have been
made, but two Chinese officials who were with Li Hung-
chang at the time have placed on public record their

corroboration of Li Hung-chang's declaration. Either Li Hung-chang or Captain Fournier must have been guilty of the gravest falsehood.

LIKIN *or* LEKIN: 釐金—thousandth *or* cash money; from *li* the thousandth part of a tael *(q.v.)* which is nominally one *cash (q.v.)*, and *kin* metal, here used for money. [Also written 釐捐—cash contribution.] A tax, originally of one cash per tael on all sales, voluntarily imposed upon themselves by the people, among whom it was at first very popular, with a view of making up the deficiency in the land-tax of China caused by the T'aip'ing and Nienfei troubles. It was to be set apart for military purposes only—hence its common name "war-tax;" and was said by the Tsung-li Yamên to be adopted merely as a temporary measure. Is now collected at rates differing in different provinces and at different times. The Chefoo Agreement *(q.v.)* makes the area of the Foreign Concessions at the various Treaty ports exempt from the levy of *likin.*

"Instead of abolishing the tax, the Chinese, through "the kind offices of Sir Thomas Wade, are endeavouring "to legalize it."—*Shanghai Courier.*

LIN, COMMISSIONER: 林則徐. The special Commissioner sent by the Emperor to Canton in 1839 to put an end to the opium trade. These orders he attempted to carry out by seizing and destroying some 20,000 chests of the drug, owned by foreigners, an act which led to the so-called "Opium War" of 1841—42. While in office he dispatched a long letter to Queen Victoria, calling upon her to prohibit the export of opium from her dominions to China.

LING CHE *or* LING CH'IH: 凌遲. The "ignominious

slashing" or so-called "lingering death," which should, strictly speaking, consist in a fearful mutilation of the limbs before giving the *coup de grâce*, but which is now generally modified into a few cuts on the body just before decapitation. Is the punishment for parricide and similar heinous crimes. Possibly the victims are drugged previous to the operation. At any rate, in the only authentic account we have from a foreign eye-witness (T. T. Meadows), it is expressly stated that the man who was thus sliced to death was not heard to utter even a groan.

LING-TOW: 寵頭—dragon's head. The chief landing-place upon the I. of Kulangsu *(q.v.)* is so called, being the head of the dragon to which the whole island is said to bear some resemblance.

LINGA: 龍牙—dragon's tooth. A stone column, the symbol of Siva, worshipped by the Hindus and found also in western China.

LINGUISTS: 通事. English-speaking Chinese, of more or less capabilities, employed as interpreters for the local dialects. The intermediaries of trade between foreigners and Chinese in the old days were so called.

LITERARY CHANCELLOR: 學臺. A high provincial official, specially appointed by the Emperor to superintend the advancement of learning in his particular province. Holds annual examinations at each of the chief towns therein for the purpose of bestowing the degree of *Hsiu-ts'ai* or B.A.

LITERARY EXPOSITOR. See *Urh Ya.*

LITERATI, THE. This term, while really including all literary men of no matter what rank or standing, is more usually confined to that large section of unemployed scholarship made up of (1) those who are waiting to get started in an official career, (2) those who have taken one or more degrees and are preparing for the next, (3) those who have failed to distinguish themselves at the public examinations and prefer to eke out a small patrimony by taking pupils rather than engage in the pettifoggings of trade, and (4) those who, though possessed of sufficiently high qualifications, have no taste for official life, and are in a position to pass their time in the enviable seclusion of "retired scholars" 隱士.

LITTLE LEARNING: 小學 *or* Learning for Children (see *Great Learning*). An elementary treatise, prepared by Chu Hsi as a first reader for boys and a stepping-stone to the Four Books, but superseded some five to six centuries ago by the Trimetrical Classic *(q.v.)*. It is written in a difficult style, quite out of keeping with the subject matter. The following is a specimen:—

"Do not snatch your food, or eat or drink to excess.
"Do not make a noise when eating, or gnaw bones, or
"take food out of your mouth, or throw bones to dogs, etc."

LIVING BUDDHA: 活佛. A popular name for the Hutukhtu *(q.v.)*.

LOCKS, THE RIVER OF: 閘河. A translation of a Chinese name for the Grand Canal *(q.v.)* upon which there are a considerable number of large *locks*, each being under the control of an official appointed for that purpose.

LOHAN: 羅漢. Same as *Arhan*. "Lohan cash" were cast in the reign of the Emperor K'ang Hsi, and were thus honourably named because believed to contain gold. The character for Hsi appears upon them in its proper form 熙 and not 凞 as it was subsequently written. The change is said to have been made in order to mark the reign of this truly great Emperor.

LOKSOY: 綠水—green water. A green dye. From the Cantonese pronunciation of the two Chinese characters.

LOLOS: 猓猓 *or* 猓猓 *or* 玀玀. Wild hill-tribes of Ssŭch'uan and Yünnan. Sub-divided into White and Black Lolos, the latter being so called from the independence of their character and the efforts which they have made so far to avoid intermarriage with the Chinese. The word "Lolo" is a term of reproach, said to be a reduplicate of the native word *Na*. Hence *Laos*.

LONG ELIZAS. The trade term for certain blue and white vases ornamented with figures of tall, thin Chinawomen, is a name derived undoubtedly from the German or Dutch. German sailors and traders called certain Chinese vases, from the female figures which distinguished them, 'lange Lischen'—Dutch, 'lange lijzen',—*tall Lizzies*, and the English sailors and traders promptly translated this into 'long Elizas.'

LONIN. See *Rōnin*.

LOO-CHOO *or* LEW-CHEW: 琉球. A group of islands, sovereignty over which was in recent years claimed by China against Japan, and at one time nearly brought the two countries into hostile collision. It is clear, however, even from Chinese historical sources, that the dress, manners and customs, language, and currency of Loo-choo are of Japanese origin; and by a treaty made in 1874, subsequent to the dispute above-mentioned, China formally acknowledges the Loochooans to be subjects of Japan.

LOQUAT: 盧橘—rush orange. A fruit found in the south of China. Our word is the Cantonese pronunciation of the above two characters. The story of the supposed resemblance of the loquat leaves to a donkey's ear is apocryphal.

LORCHA: 划艇. A vessel of about 100 tons burthen,

having a hull of European build, and originally commanded by a European captain; but rigged with Chinese masts and sails, and manned by Chinese sailors. The word *lorcha* is usually believed to have been introduced from South America by the Portuguese; but Mr. Justin McCarthy says it is taken from the Portuguese settlement at the mouth of the Canton river.

LO-TI SHUI: 落地稅 —arrive at destination duty. A duty originally levied by Chinese officials on foreign-owned goods sent into the interior under Transit Pass, *after the said goods had passed into native hands* at their place of destination. Now irregularly levied at some ports on goods brought from the interior by natives for sale to foreign merchants. The term 坐賈 has been substituted in certain parts of Kuangsi, with a view to shew that the tax is incident upon the resident merchant and not upon the foreign importer.

LOUVRE *or* LOUVER. The half-doors, common in the East, which prevent people from seeing into bedrooms as they pass by, while at the same time admitting the necessary current of air. Used chiefly in the south of China. From the French *l'ouvert*, from *ouvrir* to open.

LOWDAH: 老大 —the old great one. Captain of a junk. Foreigners call their head boatmen *lowdahs*, chiefly in Shanghai and at the Yangtsze ports; *tai-kong (q.v.)* being heard more frequently in the south.

LUCRABAN SEEDS: 大楓子. Brought from Siam, and used as a medicine by the Chinese.

LUKONG *or* LOKONG: 老更 —old watchman. The Hongkong native constables are so called. Satirically spoken of as "look-ons," from absence of energy in the discharge of their duties.

LÜ LI: 律例. The Penal Code of China.

LUNGAN *or* LUNG-NGAN: 龍眼—dragon's eyes. A fruit found in southern China, and sometimes called the wild lichee.

LUNGCHOW: 龍州. A Treaty Port in Kuangsi.

LU-PAN: 魯班. The Archimedes of China.

"Wonderful stories are related of his ingenuity; among "others it is said that his father having been put to death "by the men of Wu 吳, he carved an effigy in wood of "a genie whose hand pointed in the direction of Wu, "where, in consequence, a drought prevailed for the "space of three years."—*Mayers.*

He is now regarded as the patron saint of carpenters; and the expression 魯班門前弄斧子 "to brandish "a hatchet at Lu-pan's door" is the exact equivalent of "teach your grandmother to suck eggs."

LUZON *or* LUÇON: 呂宋. The native name for the Philippine Islands, discovered by Magalhaens in 1521, annexed by the Spanish in 1569, and ceded to the United States in 1899. From the fact of these islands being in the possession of the Spanish, the Chinese came to apply this name to Spain itself, prefixing the word 大 great. Luzon appears to have been originally peopled by Negritos, who were ultimately subdued by invading Malays. See *Filipinos.*

MA: 碼. Used in Canton in the sense of a "yard" English.

MACAO: 澳門. A small peninsula to the extreme south-west of the Kuang-tung province, first occupied by the Portuguese trading with China in 1557. It appears that Macao was actually ceded to the Portuguese in 1566, on condition of payment of an annual tribute to the Chinese Government, which was to be represented in Macao by a resident mandarin. The said payment ceased in 1849, after the war between Portugal and China, and the barbarous assassination by the Chinese of Ferreira de Amaral, Governor of Macao. Meanwhile, the colony was (until 1844) under the jurisdiction of Goa, and was in every way the property of Portugal. Of late years China has endeavoured to resume her lost suzerainty, and the inability of Portugal to negotiate a Treaty with China is due solely to the fact that the former refuses to surrender Macao. The Portuguese name is said to be derived from *A-ma-ngao* 亞媽澳—the port of the goddess A-ma. Is sometimes called the Holy City (*q.v.*).

The term *ma-ku* as applied to tobacco (孖姑烟) and seen in Canton at shops and stalls where cigarettes are sold, is probably a reproduction of the European word Macao, especially as cigarettes are so commonly smoked by the Portuguese.

"The birthday of the King of Portugal was celebrated "yesterday in the usual way, a goodly number of Chinese "merchants assembling to make the customary *kotau* "(see *kotow*) to the effigy of the King."—*China Mail* 1st Nov. 1877.

MACARTNEY'S EMBASSY, LORD. A mission dispatched from England to China in 1792, at the close of the glorious reign of the Emperor Ch'ien Lung, for the purpose of placing mercantile relations between the two countries on a better footing. Sir C. Staunton, who had picked up a knowledge of Chinese in Italy, was a page in Lord Macartney's suite and was specially noticed by His Imperial Majesty who patted him on the head and gave him an ornamental purse from his own person.

MACE: 錢 *Ch'ien*. The tenth part of a Chinese tael or

ounce. From the Sanskrit *māsha* a bean; hence a weight of gold or silver.

MADAT *(Malay)*. An inferior preparation of opium, made from the covering which encloses the drug.

MAFOO: 馬 夫 —horse-man. The Chinese groom or "horse-boy."

MAGISTRATE, DISTRICT. See *Chih-hsien.*

MAGO. Japanese term for a pack-horse leader.

MAHARAJA. A Sanskrit compound, meaning Great King. Maharani=Great Queen.

MAHOMMEDANS: 囘 囘 . First settled in China in the Year of the Mission, A.D. 628, under Wahb-Abi-Kabcha, a maternal uncle of Mahomet, who was sent with presents to the Emperor. Wahb-Abi-Kabcha travelled by sea to Canton, and thence overland to Si-ngan Fu, the capital, where he was well received. The first mosque was built at Canton, where, after several restorations, it still exists. Another mosque was erected in 742, but many of these M. came to China simply as traders, and by and by went back to their own country. The true stock of the present Chinese Mahommedans was a small army of 4,000 Arabian soldiers sent by the Khaleef Abu Giafar in 755 to aid in putting down a rebellion. These soldiers had permission to settle in China, where they married native wives; and three centuries later, with the conquests of Genghis Khan, large numbers of Arabs penetrated into the Empire and swelled the Mahommedan community.

MAI-PAN. See *Compradore.*

MA-KWA *or* MAGWA: 馬 褂 —horse jacket. The short outer jacket, chiefly worn by the northern Chinese. A yellow *ma-kwa* is a distinction conferred by the Emperor on high officials; sometimes called the *Yellow Riding*

Jacket, and said to have been first bestowed on the famous Viceroy Tsêng Kuo-fan in 1855 by the Emperor Hsien Fêng, who drew off the jacket he was wearing at the time and placed it on the shoulders of his great Minister and General. It is supposed to bring the wearer into close proximity with the Emperor and Imperial interests. Hence, in Cantonese slang, a Yellow Jacket is a person chosen from among the near relatives of a merchant or shop-keeper to exercise certain responsible functions connected with the business that could hardly be delegated to a stranger.

MAITRÊYA BUDDHA: 彌勒佛—the Merciful One. The coming Buddha, expected to appear and open a new era about 3,000 years hence. Is often depicted as a laughing god in Chinese temples.

MAKURA-KOTOBA. See *Pillow-Words*.

MAKURA ZŌSHI *or* Pillow Sketches. A collection of miscellaneous jottings by Sei Shōnagon, a Japanese lady of high rank who lived in the 9th and 10th cent. A.D.

MALAY: 無來由. From the native word *Malâiu*.

MALOO, THE: 馬路—horse road. Name of a street running east and west through the middle of the British Settlement at Shanghai. From the Mandarin pronunciation of the above two characters, which were used for "high road" as early as the 6th century B.C.

Hence the term 土庄茶 Maloo Mixture or 還魂茶 Resurrection Tea, a medley of used tea-leaves, the leaves of various other plants, and rubbish of all kinds, manufactured in Shanghai and shipped to England as tea.

MAMEY: 妹妹—little sister. A common Chinese term, learnt by European children in the north of China from native nurses, and applied to their younger sister.

MANCHU: 滿 洲. A native of Manchuria, whence came the conquerors of China and the founders (1644) of the present dynasty. Manchu garrisons are stationed at the most important points in the Empire, such as Canton, Foochow, etc. (see *Tartar General*). In 1599 Nurhachu, the famous chieftain who really founded the Manchu power, gave orders to the Erdeni 巴 克 什 Pakosh and another scholar to provide the increasing Manchu nation with a written language. This they did by basing the new script upon Mongol, which was based upon Ouigour, which in turn had been based upon Syriac. Manchu is written in vertical columns like Chinese but reads from left to right.

MANDARIN. Any Chinese official, civil or military, who wears a button *(q.v.)* may be so called. From the Portuguese *mandar* to command. A comparison has also been suggested with the Sanskrit *mandtrim*.

" 'I am an old friend of the family: his son is now a " 'major.' The little boy did not know what was meant " by a *major*, so the trader told him it was the title of " a Chinese mandarin (官). 'And what is a *mandarin?'* "asked the boy. 'A mandarin,' replied the trader, 'is " 'one who rides out in a sedan-chair or on a horse; who " 'when at home sits in a lofty hall; whose summons is " 'answered by a hundred voices; who is looked at only " 'with sidelong eyes, and in whose presence all people " 'stand aslant:—this is to be a mandarin.' " *Strange Stories from a Chinese Studio*, Vol. I, p. 403.

MANDARIN DIALECT: 官 話. The common language spoken by educated persons all over the Chinese Empire, as opposed to the various local dialects. Pekingese, shorn of its *patois*, may now be considered as the standard "Mandarin" which it is most desirable for foreigners to acquire. Southern Mandarin is based upon the Nankingese pronunciation; and differs from the northern dialect in the substitution of *k* and *ts* for *ch*, *e.g.*, *kin* for *chin* "gold," *ts'ien* for *ch'ien* "a thousand," and other similar letter-changes. Strictly speaking, "Mandarin" is a mistranslation of 官, which is here equivalent to 公 "public" or "common to all"—the vulgar tongue, the use of which dates from the 13th cent. A.D.

MANDARIN DUCK: 鴛鴦. A beautiful species of duck *(anas galericulata)*, so called because of its superiority over other kinds of ducks, and not because it is set apart for mandarins. Emblem of conjugal fidelity. Hence, a kind of sword, with two blades in one sheath, is known to the Chinese as 鴛鴦劍 "mandarin duck sword."

MANDARIN ORANGE: (1) 柑 (2) 硃砂橘. The loose-skinned orange of China. The first kind is sometimes called the "coolie-mandarin," because resembling the coolie orange *(q.v.)* in colour and having a rather tighter skin than the latter which is also of a much deeper hue. The slang phraseology of Europeans at Canton divides the two species into "tight" and "loose" mandarins.

MANDOLIN. The Chinese guitar is sometimes so called. From the Italian *mandolino*.

MANDOR. A Malay corruption of the Portuguese *mandador*. A superintendent; an inspector of workmen; a headman or "boss," etc., etc. "Yesterday afternoon, the Mandor, "who is a Hadji *(q.v.)*, applied for his own and the "other coolies' wages......"—*Hongkong Daily Press* of 22 Sep. 1877 (from the *Straits' Times*).

MANGO: 芒菓 *or* 檬菓. The fruit of the *Mangifera indica*. From the Malay *mangga*, of which the Chinese characters imitate the sound.

MANGOSTEEN. The fruit of the *Garcinia mangostana*. From the Malay *manggistan*.

MANICHAEANS: 摩尼 *or* 末尼. These worshippers of the Chaldaean Mani or Manès, who died about A.D. 274, appear to have found their way to China in the 6th cent., a Manichaean temple at Si-ngan Fu, the capital of Shensi, being mentioned as early as 621. In 807 they made formal application to be allowed to have recognised places of meeting.

MANILA LOTTERY. A lottery formerly held once every month at Manila under the sole management and proprietorship of the Hispaño-Philippine Administration. The number of tickets (which were at $ 5.00 each, but subdivisible into ten parts at $0.50 apiece) was 12,000 monthly. The highest prize for ten months of the year was $ 16,000; the total amount of the monthly prizes being $ 45,000, divided between 487 tickets, the rest being blanks. But in June and December the price of a ticket was $ 20, and $ 180,000 was divided between 453 winning tickets, the highest being $ 60,000, the next $ 25,000, the five next $ 5,000 each, etc., etc. The profits of the Government were 4 per cent. Some said the drawings were fairly conducted; others maintained a contrary opinion. The tickets and coupons, the sale of which was illegal in China, were at first numbered in the ordinary way, but an attempt at forgery by the addition of a figure compelled the management to adopt the system of having all marked with *the same number of places*; hence 123 was written 00123, etc., etc. Moreover, the line where the ticket was separated from the foil was wavy, not straight; holders had therefore to be careful not to attempt to improve the edges of their paper.

MANJI *or* MANZI. Old name for that part of China south of the Hoang-ho. From 蠻子 *man tzŭ*, the savages of the south.

MANJUSRI. See *Wên Shu*.

MAN-MAN: 慢慢—go slowly. A common phrase in use all over China. To go slowly; to wait—*e.g.*, tell my chair-coolies to *man-man*, *i.e.*, to wait for me.

MANTRA. The name of a charm practised by the Hindus, in which sense it is found in Buddhistic writings.

MANTUY *or* MANTOO. A corruption heard in Central Asia of the Chinese *man-t'ou* 饅頭 steamed flour dumplings.

MĀNYOSHIU. A collection of Japanese poetry of the 7th and 8th cent. A.D. The modern official edition runs to 122 vols, containing 4000 pieces in all, mostly Tanka.

MAO-TZŬ: 毛子—hairy ones. A common term for foreigners among the Chinese at Tientsin. Mr. Swinhoe is said to have translated this expression by "hats" (帽子), from the identity in sound, but not in tone *(q.v.)*, of the two characters 毛 and 帽.

MAQUI *or* MA-K'UAI: 馬快—swift as a horse. A kind of detective policeman employed at all Magistrates' Yamêns in China. Sometimes used for the constable of a foreign Consulate, in which sense 巡捕 would be a more appropriate term.

MARCO POLO: 博羅. The celebrated Venetian traveller who visited China in 1274, bearing letters from Pope Gregory X to Kublai Khan *(q.v.)*, and who spent 24 years in the East. During three years of this time he held high civil office, and was also sent on a mission to the king of Annam under the title of 樞密副使博羅 Privy Councillor, Assistant Envoy, Polo. Was afterwards known to his countrymen as Messer Marco *Millione* from his frequent use of the word million as applied to the wealth of China and the Great Khan.

MARRIAGES in China are arranged by go-betweens who are legally responsible for their share in the transaction. One important preliminary consists in comparing the year, month, day, and hour, at which the two parties were born, to ascertain that they are in astrological harmony.

If these negotiations are followed up by acceptance, on the part of the bride's family, of marriage-presents, and if no misrepresentation of facts can be proved by either side against the other, the marriage-contract is held to be complete, and neither party is allowed to draw back. A day is fixed, and the bridegoom fetches the bride in a gaudy red sedan-chair from her home to his own, where they worship together in the ancestral hall, and rise up man and wife.

The re-marriage of widows is not prohibited, but strongly discountenanced by public opinion. Marriage may not be celebrated during the period of mourning for a parent and certain other near relations; nor (with notable exceptions) between people bearing the same surname; nor between first cousins either on the father's or the mother's side. Custom, however, interprets this last clause as applicable only to first cousins of the same surname. No *legal* objection was raised to the suggested marriage of the hero and heroine of the *Hung-lou-mêng (q.v.)* nor to the hero's actual marriage with Pao-ch'ai. See *Polygamy* and *Divorce*.

MARU: 丸—revolving, referring to the paddle-wheels or screw. Japanese suffix to the names of steamers; *e.g.* Genka-maru.

MASAMUNÉ. A famous Japanese swordsmith, A.D. 1264—1343.

MASKEE. Pidgin term for "never mind," "no matter," etc. Possibly from the Portuguese disjunctive *mas*.

MASSANPO. A port on the south-west coast of Korea, possessing one of the finest harbours in the Far East.

MASTER OF HEAVEN. An inaccurate rendering of the term 天師 or Divine Teacher, found in the works of Chuang Tzǔ (ch. 徐無鬼). It has long been applied to the Taoist pope, in whose body is supposed to reside the soul of a celebrated Taoist, 張道陵 Chang Tao-ling, who discovered the elixir of life and became forthwith an immortal, some eighteen hundred years ago. The people believe him competent to effect marvellous cures and work other miracles; and from the proceeds of an extensive business in charms etc., he manages to derive a not inconsiderable income. At his death, the precious soul above mentioned will take up its abode in the body of some youthful member of the family whose name will be hereafter revealed.

MATA-MATA. *Lit.* "all eyes." A policeman. From the Malayan *mata* an "eye."

"In any case I can allege from personal knowledge "that bribery is an every-day matter in Singapore from "the lowest *mata-mata* to the highest—(better not say "what, perhaps)."—*China Mail* (copied from *Straits' Times*).

MATE-MATE. Japanese for "wait a little;" equivalent to the Chinese *man-man*.

MATOW: 馬頭—horse's head. The Chinese for jetty or pier, in common use among foreigners. No satisfactory explanation of this term has been found hitherto. The execution ground at Canton is called 天字馬頭, probably from the name of a jetty or landing place at no great distance. 天字 here means *chief*, this being the point at which all high officials land, and near which their boats may be seen anchored in large numbers.

MATRIMONIAL. Another name for the hong-boat *(q.v.)* in use at Canton. So called because well adapted for ladies.

MAUM CHOW. See *Chowfah*.

MÂYÂ: 摩耶. The immaculate mother of Shâkyamuni Buddha, whose name is strikingly similar to that of Mary the mother of Jesus. Among other similarities existing between the Roman Catholic and Buddhist churches may be mentioned celibacy, fasting, use of candles and flowers on the altar, incense, holy water, and ceremonials generally. See *Fo*.

MENCIUS: 孟子—the philosopher Mêng, often spoken of as 亞聖 the Second Sage, Confucius being the first. The Chinese sounds *mêng-tzŭ* were latinised by the Jesuit missionaries into their present form. Flourished B.C. 372—289. His works form one of the Four Books *(q.v.)*, and the following are specimens:—

"Mencius said, I like fish and I also like bear's paws. "If I cannot have both, I will forego the fish and take "the bear's paws. Similarly, I like living and I like doing "my duty to my neighbour; but if I cannot do both, "I will forego life in preference to foregoing my duty.

"Mencius said, Take a man whose third finger is bent "and cannot be stretched out straight. It is not painful, "neither does it interfere with his work; yet if there were "any one who could make it straight, he would think "nothing of journeying such a distance as from Ch'in to

"Ch'u, simply because his finger is not as good as
"those of other people. But to be grieved because one's
"finger is not as good as other people's, and not to be
"grieved because one's heart is not as good as other
"people's—this is called ignorance of the relative importance
"of categories."

MÊNG-TZŬ: 蒙自. A Treaty Port in the province of
Yünnan.

MERMAN or MERMAID. The Chinese have for many
centuries believed in the existence of creatures half human
half fish. A nation of such beings is described and figured
in the 異域圖 of the 14th cent., under the name of
氏人國.

MESMERISM: 罡符. Was once widely known in China
as a cure for various diseases, but is now prohibited and
only practised in secret. The *modus operandi* is as follows.
A Taoist priest, known for his skill in the art, is requested
to attend at the house of a sick person for the purpose
of administering *kang-fu*; and accordingly, after arranging
what is to be paid for his services and securing part of
the sum in advance, he proceeds to fit up within the
patient's room an altar for burning incense and joss-paper
and for worship generally. Muttered incantations follow,
as the priest walks slowly and with prescribed steps round
and round the room. By-and-by, he approaches the sick
man and partly raises him, or turns him on his back or
side, or lifts up a leg or an arm, or gently shampoos
him, the object being all the time to bring the sick
man's mind into *rapport* with his own. When the priest
thinks he has accomplished this, he commands the patient
to perspire or to become cool, or gives instructions for
the regulation of pulse and heart, in each case according

to what he conceives to be the exigencies of the disease. The whole scene is rendered as impressive as possible by silence, and by darkening the room, with the exception of one oil-lamp by the light of which is dimly visible the silhouette of the robed priest waving his large sleeves in the air. The imaginative faculty of the sick man is thus excited.

MEXICANS. Abbreviation for Mexican dollars.

MIAO-TZŪ: 苗子—shoots *or* sons of the soil. The aboriginal tribes of certain mountainous districts in the south and south-west provinces of China.

MIDDLE KINGDOM, THE: 中國. A translation of the common Chinese name for China; it being generally believed that China is situated at the centre of the earth, surrounded by the Four Seas, beyond which lie a number of small islands inhabited by the red-haired barbarians who come to the Middle Kingdom to trade. The term is of great antiquity, but at one time seems to have been confined to Honan. It was also applied by early Buddhist writers to Central India.

MIH-HO-LOONG: 減火龍—extinguish-fire-dragon. The celebrated European volunteer fire brigade of Shanghai. [A Chinese fire-engine is called a "water dragon."]

MIKADO: (1) 御門 Imperial gate. The ruler who, as spiritual Emperor, formerly shared the sovereignty of Japan with the Shōgun *(q.v.)* or temporal Emperor; and who at death became a *kami* 神 or god. Known to the Chinese as the 文王 Civil Sovereign. Since 1867, when the Shōgun submitted and retired into private life, the Mikado has been sole Emperor of Japan. The first Mikado is said to have sprung from the sun. (2) Also derived from *mika* great, and *to* (*do* in composition) a place.

MIKOTO: 尊. An honorific epithet of a *kami (q.v.)*. Has been wrongly believed to be a title of the Mikado.

MING DYNASTY *or* THE MINGS: 明 *ming*, bright. A dynasty which ruled China from 1368 to 1628 and was noted for the severity of its laws. A piece of pottery or a curio of that date is often spoken of as "a Ming;" at the same time, not one-tenth of the china stamped with the 大 明 *great Ming* brand really belongs to that epoch; in fact, it is roundly asserted that the presence of the stamp is now conclusive evidence of a spurious imitation. See *Blue*.

MING TOMBS: 明 陵. The tombs of the Emperors of the Ming dynasty. Some of these are near Nanking; the rest, and by far the finest, about one day's journey from Peking, whither the Emperor Yung Lo transferred his court in 1411. The chief objects of interest at these tombs are the avenues of enormous animals and human figures carved in stone. See *Stone Figures*.

MIRROR OF HISTORY: 通 鑑. Name of a famous history of China from the 4th cent. B.C. to the 10th cent. A.D., completed by 司 馬 光 Ssŭ-ma Kuang in 1084. It was subsequently revised by Chu Hsi, which work is known as the 通 鑑 綱 目.

MIRRORS: 鏡 or 鑑. Circular mirrors of polished metal, often beautifully chased at the back, have been known to the Chinese from the earliest ages, though now superseded by glass.

Confucius said, "As you look into a bright mirror to "see your face, so you must look back into the past to "know the present."

Chuang Tzŭ, 3rd and 4th cent. B.C., wrote, "The "perfect man employs his mind as a mirror. It grasps

"nothing; it refuses nothing. It receives, but does not
"keep."

"To a beauty, mankind is the mirror in which she
"sees herself. If no one tells her that she is beautiful, she
"does not know that she is so."

MISSIONARIES. See *Protestant* and *Roman Catholic*.

MIXED COURT, THE: 會番公堂. A tribunal, instituted
at Shanghai in 1869, for the hearing (1) of all cases between
Chinese resident within the settlements, (2) of all civil and
criminal cases (except murder and certain serious charges
between Chinese and foreign residents), in which Chinese
are defendants, and (3) of cases in which foreigners are the
defendants, provided always they are unrepresented by a
Consul on the spot. The Court consists of a Chinese official
having the rank of sub-Prefect and a foreign Assessor, the
latter being always, in civil suits, a representative of the
nationality involved. Otherwise, a British Assessor sits
three times, an American twice and a German once,
a week. The Court was formerly held at the British
Consulate, but has since been transferred to a building
in the Maloo *(q.v.)*, at the entrance to which may usually
be seen a number of convicted prisoners wearing the
cangue *(q.v.)*. The punishments inflicted range from 20
blows with the bamboo to three or four years' penal
servitude. Over the outer gates may be seen the following
legend: 遠來近悅, 物阜民康, "men flock from afar
"while those who are near rejoice. Business brisk and the
"people prosperous."

MODEL SETTLEMENT, THE. A local name for Shanghai,
once characterised by the Duke of Somerset in Parliament
as a "sink of iniquity," this generous estimate having
been based, as the Duke himself explained, upon the

reports of *naval officers and others who had visited the place.*

"I am not burning to return to the *Model Sink.*—" Letter from E. C. Baber in the *North-China Herald.*

MOGUL, THE GREAT. The Persian corruption of Mongol *(q.v.).* The title of the Emperors who, after the conquest of Hindustan, ruled at Delhi from A.D. 1526 to 1803. The first occupant of the Imperial Throne was Baber, and among his most illustrious successors may be mentioned Akbar and Aurungzeb.

MO-LI-HWA *or* MOLY: 茉莉花. The jasmine. Name of a celebrated Chinese tune. Compare *Odyssey,* X, 305,

μῶλυ δέ μιν καλέουσι Θεοί

identified with the mandrake. See Pliny, *Nat. Hist.,* XXV, 4.

MOMEIN. The Burmese name for 騰越 T'êng-yüeh in the province of Yünnan.

MONGOL: 蒙古. Said to be an imitation of *moengel* celestial, or as some writers say, "brave." The great Turanian stock, whence have come, at different epochs of the world's history, the Scythians, the Huns, the conquerors of China (see *Genghis Khan*), and of India (see *Mogul*).

"Baschpa" Mongol is the name of a form of writing, invented A.D. 1269 by 巴思巴 Baschpa or 'Phagspa, a Tibetan lama, under the direction of Kublai Khan. It was based upon Ouigour which had been based upon Syriac (see *Manchu*), and is written in vertical lines and connected by ligatures.

MONSOON. From the Arabic *mausim* "season;" the season winds.

Monsoons are shifting trade winds in the East Indian ocean, which blow periodically, some for half a year one way, others but for three months, and then shift and blow for six or three months directly contrary. These winds are constant and periodical, as far as the thirtieth degree of latitude, all round the globe.

MONTO. A Buddhist sect, founded in Japan in A.D. 1262 by a man named Shinran. Celibacy, fasting, monastic life, and the sacred books in Sanskrit, are the chief features of ordinary Buddhism against which the Monto sect protests.

MOON: 月. Symbol of the Female or Negative Principle in nature. Is popularly thought to be inhabited. Used in the sense of month, the Chinese being a *lunar* year of 12 months, with an intercalary month *(q.v.)* in every third year to rectify the calendar. Chinese servants struggled at first against the payment of their wages according to the European year as they thus lost a month (*i.e.* the intercalary) once in every three years. The first, fifth, and ninth moons are considered specially unlucky. In these months Chinamen will not marry, nor change houses, neither will Mandarins take over their seals of office. The first moon of the year was known as 正 *chêng*[4] until the First Emperor *(q.v.)* altered the sound to *chêng*[1], because part of his own name was sounded *chêng*[4], though differently written. There seems to be a tradition that the ancient Chinese year consisted of ten months only. Many fanciful names are applied to the months, often associated with flowers and fruits.

The 1ST MOON is called 正月, 端月, 泰月*, 元月, 正陽月, 三陽月, 春王.

The 1st day of the 1st is called 元旦, 端日.

„ 7th „ „ „ 人日, 靈辰.

„ 15th „ „ „ 上元, 元宵.

The 2ND MOON is called 花月, 大壯月*, 仲陽月,
杏月 or *Apricot month.*

„ 1st day of the 2nd   „   中和.

The 2nd day of 2nd is called 踏青, 桃荣.

„ 12th   „   „   花朝, 眞元.

„ 3RD MOON   „   桐月, 夬月*, 蠶月, 桃月
or *Peach month.*

„ 3rd day of the 3rd „   上巳.

„ 4TH MOON   „   乾月*, 麥秋, 清和, 槐月
or *Sophora month.*

„ 8th day of the 4th „   浴佛.

„ 5TH MOON   „   蒲月, 垢月*, 鬱燕, 滿月,
榴月, or *Pomegranate
month.*

„ 5th day of the 5th „   端午, 天中.
„ 13th   „   „   竹醉.

„ 6TH MOON   „   暑月, 遯月*, 荷月 or
Lotus month.

„ 6th day of the 6th „   天貺.
„ 24th   „   „   觀蓮.

„ 7TH MOON   „   否月*, 蘭秋, 桐月, 巧月,
瓜月 or *Melon month.*

„ 7th day of the 7th „   巧日, 七夕.
„ 15th   „   „   中元, 大慶.

„ 8TH MOON   „   觀月*, 仲商月 桂月 or
Cassia month.

„ 5th day of the 8th „   千秋.
„ 15th   „   „   中秋, 月夕.

The 9TH MOON is called 剥月*, 季商月, 菊秋, 菊月 or *Chrysanthemum month.*

„ 9th day of the 9th „ 重陽,重九.

„ 10TH MOON „ 間月,坤月*,正陰,陽春, 小陽月,梅月 or *Plum month.*

„ 15th day of the 10th „ 下元.

„ 11TH MOON „ 復月*, 仲冬月, 葭月 or *Hibiscus month.*

„ 12TH MOON „ 臨月*,椒月,嘉平月,臘 月 or the *Sacrificial month.*

„ 8th day of the 12th „ 臘日.

„ 30th „ „ 除日,除夕.

N.B.—Those names marked with an asterisk are taken from the 易經 or Book of Changes *(q.v.).*

MOORMEN (corrupted to Morramen): 白頭人—white head men. A common term in Canton for the miscellaneous natives of India who go there to trade. The Chinese name is taken from the turban worn by Mahommedans and others; while our word has been fancifully derived from 貌陋 *mao lou* men, or "ugly face" people. The Parsees, formerly called 波斯, a name now used for Persia, are included in this category.

MORTGAGES of land or tenements in China should, according to the Penal Code, be duly registered at the office of the local magistrate. Second mortgages are illegal. If the mortgagor, at the end of the period specified in the deed, is unable to discharge the mortgage, he may either retain his right to recover the land at any future period, in which case the mortgagee may re-mortgage to another party; or he may surrender the land absolutely, in consideration of a further sum to be agreed upon between himself and the mortgagee.

MOSQUITO. From the Latin *musca* a fly, through the Italian, Spanish, or Portuguese, *mosca*. The English orthography should therefore be *muskito*. Tincture of *Pyrethrum roseum* applied to the skin is recommended as an excellent protection against mosquito bites. The best local sedative of the irritation caused by bites is liquid ammonia, but any strong spirit is also effectual.

For a valuable discovery, by Dr. P. Manson formerly of Amoy, that a certain species of mosquito is the intermediate host of the *filaria sanguinis hominis*, and probably the carrier of infection in elephantoid diseases, see the Chinese Customs' *Medical Reports*, No. 14, page 10.

MOTH EYEBROWS: 蛾 眉. Eyebrows which resemble the markings over the eyes of the silkworm moth, considered a great beauty by the Chinese. This similitude is a favourite with poets:—

> And as the strains steal o'er me
> Her moth-eyebrows rise before me.

The term has been wrongly referred to the antennae of the same insect.

MOTOŌRI. 1730—1801. A voluminous Japanese writer. His chief work was the Kojiki-den, a commentary on the Kojiki *(q.v.)*.

MOUKDEN. The Manchu name of Fêng-t'ien Fu 奉 天 府, the capital of Manchuria.

MOURNING. On the death of a parent the Chinese son refrains from shaving either head or beard for one hundred days, and dresses in complete white, even down to the silk with which he finishes off his queue. It is only the white hat and white shoes, however, which infallibly betoken mourning, white jackets being commonly worn by the people. The duration of this period is from a nominal three years (actually, 27 months) for a father or mother, down to three months for more distant relatives. A child mourns three years for its parents in memory of the three years of infancy when it was wholly dependent upon their aid. See *Cards.*

MOW *or* MOU: 畝. The Chinese acre. About $\frac{1}{6}$ of an English acre; but varies in different places. In Shanghai the official mow is held to contain 7,260 sq. ft. English, and is subdivided into *fun, haou, le, sze,* and *hoo.* The Municipal mow is taken at 6,600 sq. ft. See *Weights and Measures.*

The subjoined Notification published in 1861, by H.M. Consul, defines the area of a Shanghai *mow* :—

"The following definitions of the contents of a Shanghai "*mow,* obtained from the official land measurer of the "district, and checked by careful examination of his "measuring instruments, is published for general information.

"Each *mow* is 240 *poo* long by 1 *poo* broad, and "contains therefore 240 square *poo.*

"The *poo* measures 5 feet Chinese Government rule (官 尺), equal to 66 inches English. A square *poo* therefore contains 30.25 square feet English, and a square *mow* 7,260 square feet English. It follows that a square piece of ground measuring 85.20569 feet, or $85\frac{1}{5}$ feet every way, contains exactly one Shanghai *mow.*"

MOXA 艾, BURNING THE. A form of actual cautery used by the Chinese and Japanese. From the dried and beaten leaves of *Artemisia Moxa* are prepared pastilles, which being applied to the skin and set on fire (properly, with the aid of a burning-glass), burn slowly down and leave eschars. At one time Moxa acquired a considerable reputation amongst French physicians; but both that and acupuncture—equal favourites with Far-Eastern practitioners—are too heroic remedies to find favour with Europeans. Is employed chiefly for neuralgia, sciatica, and such complaints; and also among Buddhist priests, for branding the heads of novices when taking the usual vows on entry into a religious life. Corruption of the Japanese *Mookasa.*

"Moxa, præstantissima cauteriorum materia, Sinensibus "Japonibusque multum usitata."—Kaempfer's *Amœnitates Exoticæ*, fasc. iii, obs. 12.

MUCK-AND-TRUCK. A department of trade in the Far East, which deals with hides, bristles, bones, etc., and is much looked down upon by the ordinary British merchant.

MULLS. Madras Englishmen are so called because of their good mulligatawny.

MUNDOO *or* MENDU. A Mongolian form of salutation= How d'ye do?

MUNSHANG: 門上. The door-keeper of a yamên *(q.v.)* or any large establishment. This functionary receives no pay, but takes squeezes from suitors, commission from tradesmen on sales, etc. etc.

MUSIC: 樂. (1) *Ancient.* Said to have been invented by Hwang Ti[a] *(q.v.)*, but few traces of it survived the Burning of the Books *(q.v.)*. We know that it was reckoned very powerful as an agent of good government, and was part of the ordinary curriculum of an educated man in early ages. As to quality, Confucius himself was so impressed by the execution of a piece composed by the Emperor Shun, sixteen centuries previously, that "for "three months he could not tell one kind of meat from "another." This too when there were only 5 notes.

(2) *Modern*. Sub-divided into ritual music, which is generally of a minor character, and popular or theatrical music. The notation is cumbrous. A note indicates simply a certain sound at a certain height, but there is no indication of its value. Thus, it is quite impossible to learn a tune from the written notes. The characters 合四乙上尺工凡六五 correspond to our five lines and four spaces. Rests are marked, but their duration is a matter of taste. The only recognised measure is in four time; others are however admitted, especially that in three time. There are no sharps, flats, or naturals. The scale is neither major nor minor but participates in the two. It is not tempered. There is nothing like *harmony*; the only association of different and simultaneous sounds being that produced by two strings at a distance of a fourth, a fifth, or an octave.

MUSICAL INSTRUMENTS. According to the Chinese these are of eight kinds, being made either from the gourd, earthenware, leather, wood, stone, metal, silk, or bamboo, and comprise such varieties as the reed-organ, the ocarina, the drum, castanets, the musical stone or stone-chime, cymbals, the guitar, and the flute.

MUSK: 麝香. A favourite perfume with the Chinese, obtained from the civet *(Viverra zibetta)*, which animal, when pursued by hunters, is fictitiously said to tear out its scent-gland with its claws and so escape death.

MÛSMEE: 孃. A waitress at a Japanese tea-house. Literally: a girl.

NACODAH. Correctly *nakhoda*: a Persian word meaning the captain of a boat.

NAGAS. The "dragon race." A tribe of the Tibeto-Burman family, now occupying the eastern boundary of Bengal, said to be a remnant of the powerful people who inhabited the Gangetic valley before the Aryan invasion of India.

NAGASAKI: 長崎. A port in Japan.

NAGA-UTA. The "long" poetry of the Japanese. In point of metre it is the same as the Tanka *(q.v.)*, with an additional phrase of 7 syllables, making 38 syllables to each stanza, but without any limit to the length of the poem.

NAGOYA. That quarter of the *yashiki* or feudal mansion of a *daimio (q.v.)* occupied by his two-sworded retainers.

NAKÔDO. Matrimonial go-betweens employed by the Japanese.

NAILS. Many educated and wealthy Chinese allow one or more of their finger-nails to grow long, as a sign that the owner does not earn his living by manual labour. These nails are occasionally from $1\frac{1}{2}$ to 2 inches in length, and are guarded by elegant silver sheaths.

> Est-ce par l'ongle long qu'il porte au petit doigt
> Qu'il s'est acquis chez vous l'estime où l'on le voit?
> Molière, *Le Misanthrope*, Acte ii. Sc. 1.

NAI-MAH: 奶媽. A wet-nurse.

NAMAH (in Pali "namo") AMITABBHA: 南阿無彌陀佛 "Hear us, O Amida Buddha!" A formula of adoration used by Chinese Buddhists in their liturgies, at the invocation of the Trinity, etc.; also frequently seen written on walls, or cut on stone tablets both in town and country. (See *O-me-to fu*).

NAN-NING FU: 南寧府. A new Treaty Port in the province of Kuangsi.

NANKEEN. Cloth made at Nanking from unbleached cotton.

NANKING: 南京—southern capital. Now known as Kiang-ning Fu, the capital city of Kiangsu. Until 1411 the residence of the Court; hence the name. In 212 A.D., Sun Ch'üan, the first Emperor of the 吳 Wu dynasty, established his capital at Nanking, which he founded under the name of 建業. Variously known as 白門, 白下, 秣陵, 金陵, 應天府, etc. See *Porcelain Tower*.

NATS: 仙. The spirits of nature as worshipped by the Burmans. These are not in any way connected with Buddhism, but are relics of their old Turanian nature-worship. They are believed to injure people unless propitiated.

NAVY, THE CHINESE. Apart from the few men-of-war of modern type now possessed by the Chinese, there should be some 2,000 vessels of various kinds constituting the navy proper. These include junks armed with nets for catching the enemy's ships, etc. etc.

NESTORIAN CHRISTIANS. The church which first introduced Christianity into China, A.D. 631, under the title of 景教 "luminous teaching." The "Nestorian Tablet," with a bilingual inscription in Chinese and Syriac, put up A.D. 781 and discovered at Si-ngan Fu in the province of Shensi, A.D. 1625, gives a general idea of the object and scope of the Christian religion. The genuineness of this tablet was for many years in dispute, Voltaire, Renan, and others of lesser fame, regarding it as a pious fraud. The last hopes of its opponents have now been dispelled by the exhaustive monograph of Père Havret, S. J., entitled *La stèle de Singan.*

NETSUKÉ *or* NETSZKE: 根 附 . Small Japanese carved figures, of wood or ivory, used as buttons for suspending to the *obi* or belt the tobacco pouch, pipe, snuff or water bottle, medicine or seal or brush case, etc. Their use is said to date from about the middle of the 17th cent., when tobacco was first introduced into Japan. Known colloquially as 小 止 .

NEWCHWANG *or* NIUCHUANG: 牛 莊—cow town. The inland town in the extreme N. E. of China, opened by the Tientsin Treaty of 1858; but which, from the silting up of the river, was unfit for trade, and was exchanged for Ying-tzŭ 營 子 five miles from the mouth of the river. The present port, however, is still called *New-chwang* by foreigners.

NEW YEAR, CHINA. Begins on the first day of the lunation in which the sun enters Pisces, which may be any date between 22 January and 20 February, inclusive. This is the season chosen for the great annual holiday of the Chinese. For a month no official documents are stamped, and to obviate inconvenience blank forms are previously prepared; but it is obvious that such a rule could not be strictly adhered to. All accounts have to be settled up by New Year's Eve, on which night no Chinaman goes to bed. On New Year's Day, absolutely no work is done from one end of the empire to the other. Fire-crackers, feasting, and congratulatory visits are substituted for the ordinary routine of life. See *Moon.*

NGO-ERH-CH‘IN: 額 爾 沁 . The name given to the Tibetan envoy to China.

NIEH T‘AI. See *Judge, Provincial.*

NIEN-FEI: 捻匪. Mounted banditti who for several years committed much havoc in the northern provinces of China. In 1868 they approached within a few miles of Tientsin; and Mr. Burlingame, then proceeding with his family as Chinese Ambassador to foreign nations, had a narrow escape from falling into their hands. Said to have been so called because they wore twisted greased turbans: 幅布以油捻爲記. A history of the suppression of this rebellion has been published in Peking entitled 勦平粤匪方畧.

NIGORI: 濁 = thickening. A term used by the Japanese to denote the transformation of a surd (*e.g.* thi) into a sonant (*e.g.* dhi).

NIHONGI. A collection of the national myths, legends, poetry, and history of Japan, from the earliest times down to A.D. 697, prepared under official auspices in A.D. 720, and written in the Chinese language.

NIIGATA: 新瀉. A port in Japan.

NIMBLE LADS. See *Chopsticks*.

NINGPO: 寧波 —tranquil waves. One of the five ports opened by the Nanking Treaty of 1842. Also known to the Chinese as 四明. Was occupied by the Portuguese for purposes of trade so early as 1522.

NINJIN. The Japanese term for *Ginseng (q.v.)*.

NIPON *or* NIPHON: 日本 —Sun Root. The land where the sun rises. A Japanese name for Japan, from the name of the largest island of the group. Was long held to be a Chinese term for that country; but the balance of evidence appears to be in favour of its Japanese origin. "This island, by the way, is generally called Nippon or "Nihon by foreigners, and no greater mistake can be "made, as that word in reality denotes the whole territory "of Japan. . . . . What is generally termed Nippon by "foreigners may be designated as the *main island.—*" *Adams.*

NIRVÂNA : 泥洹 *or* 湼 槃. The *summum bonum* of the Buddhists, consisting in (1) separation from life and death, *i.e.* from the circle of transmigration ; (2) absolute freedom from passion ; and (3) the highest state of spiritual liberty and bliss. Popularly speaking, "to enter into Nirvâna" corresponds with "going to heaven."

"The extinction of that sinful grasping condition of "mind and heart, which would otherwise, according to "the great mystery of Karma, be the cause of renewed "individual existence." *Rhys Davids.*

"A condition of total cessation of changes ; of perfect "rest ; of the absence of desire and illusion and sorrow ; "of the total obliteration of everything that goes to "make up the physical man." *Olcott.*

"All that words can convey is that Nirvâna is a sublime "state of conscious rest in omniscience." *Sinnett.*

Sir Edwin Arnold in his *Light of Asia* has given a new and original view of Nirvâna, partly from a conviction that "a third of mankind would never have been brought "to believe in blank abstractions, or in Nothingness, as "the issue and crown of Being." After due perception of the *Four Truths*, safe passage along the *Eightfold Path* of doctrine, and through the *Four Stages*, viz : Love of Self, False Faith, Doubt, Hatred, Lust, Love of Life, Desire for Heaven, Self Praise, Error, and Pride,—then

> As one who stands on yonder snowy horn
> Having naught o'er him but the boundless blue,
> So, these sins being slain, the man is come
> Nirvâna's verge unto.

Him the Gods envy from their lower seats;
Him the Three worlds in ruin should not shake;
All life is lived for him, all deaths are dead;
Karma will no more make

New houses. Seeing nothing, he gains all;
Foregoing self, the Universe grows "I":
If any teach *Nirvâna* is to cease,
Say unto such they lie.

If any teach *Nirvâna* is to live,
Say unto such they err; not knowing this,
Nor what light shines beyond their broken lamps,
Nor lifeless, timeless bliss.

NŌ. Japanese lyrical plays. They date from the 14th cent. A.D. and are of religious origin, being used in propitiation of Shinto gods.

NOBILITY, Five degrees of. These are 公, 侯, 伯, 子, 男, which terms are roughly rendered—duke, marquis, earl, viscount, baron. They may be perpetually hereditary; but the usual custom is that the heir always takes a title one degree lower down, until extinction, which thus must occur at most after five generations. The lineal descendant of Confucius is always a noble of the first rank.

NONYA. The daughter of a Malay mother and a European father is so called in Java, in imitation of the Spanish *noña*, whence the French *nonne* and English *nun*.

NOR *or* NUR. A Mongol word signifying *lake*, *e.g.*, Dolon-nor.

NORIMON : 乘物. A Japanese sedan or palanquin.

NOVELS. First appeared in China under the Mongol dynasty, 13th cent. A.D. They are ranged by the Chinese under four heads :—

奸 which deal with usurpation and plotting, as the *San Kuo Chih.*

淫 „ „ „ immoralities, as the *Chin P'ing Mei.*

邪 „ „ „ superstition, „ „ *Hsi Yu Chi.*

盜 „ „ „ lawless characters, as the *Shui Hu.*

NÜ-CHÊN TARTARS. See *Golden Tartars*.

NUI TI *or* NEI TI: 內地—the inner land. China as opposed to the "outside nations" 外國; or, in a more restricted sense, the interior of China as opposed to the sea-board. Hence *nui ti shui* "inland duties."

NULLAH. Correctly *nāla*. A small river, or watercourse.

NUMBA SATU. Used in the Malay peninsula as "numba one" in pidgin-English, *sc.* first-rate. A race at the Singapore meeting is called the "Numba Dua" Cup, *i.e.* Number 2 cup.

NUMERALS, THE CHINESE.

	Old form.	Common form *a.*	Short form *b.*	Lengthened form *c.*	
1.		一	〡	壹	*a.* As seen in books.
2.		二	〢	貳	*b.* Commonly used for accounts. Are said to be of Bactrian or Phœnician origin, but are known to the Chinese as 蘇州字 Soo-chow characters, or 碼字 = business characters. They are written horizontally, except when 1 and 2 or 3 come together. These are then written alternately vertical and horizontal to prevent confusion. Thus, $ 12,332.15 would be 一〢三〣二一〥, the unit place being indicated by 元.
3.		三	〣	叄	
4.		四	〤	肆	
5.		五	〥	伍	
6.		六	〦	陸	
7.		七	〧	柒	
8.		八	〨	捌	
9.		九	〩	玖	*c.* Adopted as being less liable to alteration of any kind, and used on drafts, pawn-tickets, etc., etc.
10.		十		拾	
100.		百	.1	錢	
1000.		千	.01	分	
10000.		萬	.001	釐	
100000.		億	.0001	毫	
1000000.		兆	.00001	絲	
10000000.		京 or 經	.000001	忽	
100000000.		垓	.0000001	微	
1000000000.		補	.00000001	籤	
			.000000001	沙	

OATHS. Are never administered in Chinese courts of justice in any shape or form. See *Ordeal.*

OBANG: 大判—great division. A Japanese gold coin worth 30 ounces of silver.

OBO: 鄂博. The sacred cairn, or grave-mound, of the Lamas. The line of frontier between the Khalka territory and Russian possessions is marked by such piles, and the spaces between them are called *sabu* 薩布 by the Mongols.

OCEAN RACE, THE. An annual contest—formerly, between tea-clippers sailing from Foochow round the Cape; afterwards, between steamers from Hankow and Foochow, passing through the Suez Canal—to be the first to deliver in London a cargo of the new season's teas. The chief interest of the public centred in the race between the steamers which left Hankow generally about the beginning of June.

ODES, BOOK OF THE: 詩經. One of the Five Classics, and perhaps the most valued of all by the literati of China. Is a collection of irregular lyrics in vogue among the people many centuries before the Christian era, said to have been collected and arranged, to the number of 311, by Confucius himself. Of six of these, however, only the titles remain, and the whole collection is popularly known as the Three Hundred. These are subdivided under 4 heads, namely Ballads, Greater and Lesser Panegyrics, and Sacrificial Odes. "Have you learned the Odes?" inquired the Master of his son; and on receiving an answer in the negative, immediately reminded him that unless he did so he would be unfit for the society of intellectual men. Mr. H. J. Allen has recently started a theory that they are the work of Ssŭ-ma Ch'ien (see *History, Father of*). A quotation from the *Odes* is however to be found on the Stone Drums *(q.v.)*. Translated into Latin by Lacharme, circa 1733; into English, (1) literally and (2) metrically, by Dr. Legge, 1871 and 1876. The following is a specimen:—

> The cricket chirrups in the hall,
>   The year is dying fast;
> Now let us hold high festival
>   Ere the days and months be past.
> Yet push not revels to excess
>   That our fair fame be marred;
> Lest pleasures verge to wickedness
>   Let each be on his guard.

OHAGURO. A dye used by Japanese women for blacking the teeth at marriage. It is made of iron scraps soaked in water with a little saké added, and then mixed with powdered gallnuts.

OHIO *or* OHYO: 於早. Japanese equivalent of "good morning!" but used only on meeting a person, and before 10 a. m.

OK GUE: 薆玉. A kind of fig, the seed of which is used in preparing jelly as isinglass is in Europe.

OKRAS: 毛茄. Are the miniature fruit of the *Hibiscus esculentus*, much used in various parts of the world as a vegetable and for thickening soups; especially in the southern United States, where they are known as "Gumbo." The name frequently appears in the Hongkong market list.

OM MANI PADME HUM *or* OMMANY PEMMINY: 唵嚤呢叭嘛吽—"O the jewel in the lotus! Amen;" or according to Professor Wilson, "Glory to Manipadme!" A magic formula much used in Mongolia and Tibet as a charm against evil influences, etc. The primeval six syllables, as the Lamas *(q.v.)* say. The only prayer known to Tibetans and Mongols; the first words spoken by every child, the last by every dying man.

"The wanderer murmurs them on his way, the herdsman beside his cattle, the matron at her household tasks, the monk in all stages of contemplation. They form at once a cry of battle and a shout of victory. They are to be read wherever the Lama church has spread, upon banners, upon rocks, upon trees, upon walls, upon monuments of stone, upon household utensils, upon human skulls and skeletons." *Heeley and Koeppen.*

> "Ah! Lover! Brother! Guide! Lamp of the Law!
> I take my refuge in thy name and thee!
> I take my refuge in thy Law of Good!
> I take my refuge in thy Order!—OM!
> The Dew is on the lotus!—Rise, Great Sun!
> And lift my leaf and mix me with the wave.
> OM MANI PADME HUM, the Sunrise comes!
> The Dewdrop slips into the shining Sea!"
> Arnold's *Light of Asia.*

OMETO FO *or* O-MI-T'O-FO: 阿 彌 陀 佛. Amitâbbha, i.e. boundless light; or Amida Buddha. The abbreviated form of *namah amitabbha (q.v.)*, the formula in use among Chinese Buddhists, equivalent to the *Ave* of Roman Catholics. "The very name of Buddha," says a sacred text, "if pronounced by a devout heart 1,000 or 5,000 times, "will effectually dispel all harassing thoughts, all fightings "within and fears without." This phrase is frequently prefixed in conversation to exclamatory sentences; *e.g.* 阿 彌 陀 佛 不 要 打 他 ="For God's sake don't strike him!" and is often exchanged between guest and host as the former passes into the house, in which case it answers somewhat to our *Pax vobiscum!*

OMI, Mt.: 峨 嵋. A steep mountain in the province of Ssǔch'uan, sacred to the worship of Samanta Bhâdra

(see *P'u Hsien*), and famous for a halo, known as the
"Glory of Buddha," seen from its summit. Only one
European lady, Mrs. A. Little, has so far reached
the top.

"What a number of pilgrims one meets here at certain
"seasons, and from how far they come. Aged women on
"bound feet are to be met trudging up and down these
"torturing steps." *Shanghai Mercury*, 12 July, 1892.

ONI. Devil (*Japanese*). Used as a name for a dog or cat.

OOLONG: 烏龍—black dragon. A kind of tea.

OONAM. Same as *Hunan (q.v.)*.

OOPAK. Same as *Hupei (q.v.)*.

OPIUM. From the Greek ὀπός "juice." It is the dried
juice of the unripe capsules of the *Papaver Somniferum*
or Common Poppy, and is known to the Chinese under
the following designations:—鴉片 (said to be derived
from 阿芙蓉, itself an imitation of the Arabic name
Afiyun, still used in the Straits' Settlements); 罌粟；
御米；膏；烏烟；烟土；黑土；黑貨；烏米；洋藥
etc., etc.

It is uncertain when and how opium first became
known in India; but in the *Áin-i-Alebari* (circa 1590)
the poppy is noticed as a staple crop. In 1773, Warren
Hastings, then Governor of Bengal, assumed, on behalf
of the English East India Company, a monopoly of all
opium produced in Bengal, Behar and Orissa, with certain
allowances of the drug to the French, Danes, and Dutch.

It is acknowledged beyond doubt, that long before the
English had intercourse with China, or had anything to
do with the cultivation of opium, the drug used to be
carried in quantities overland from India by way of
Burma, Yünnan, etc. In A.D. 973 the reigning Emperor

ordered the preparation of a new Herbarium, and the poppy was inserted as a cure for dysentery. Later on the Portuguese trading vessels were in the habit of importing it into Macao and Canton. The Chinese gradually coming to relish opium-smoking, which is said to have been introduced by the eunuch general and traveller, 鄭和 Chêng Ho, who died in 1431, it took its place as an article of regular trade. When Bombay passed into the hands of the British Government, opium continued to be shipped in small-sized sailing vessels, which used to take three or four months to perform the voyage to Whampoa.

There are two descriptions of the drug imported from India, under the denominations respectively of Bengal and Malwa opium.

Of Bengal opium, the growth is monopolised by the Indian Government in this way. They advance annually to the growers, who are named "Ryots," money for the cultivation of the poppy, on the distinct understanding that the produce is to be sold to the Government at a given rate. The product is then manipulated, formed into cakes and packed in chests of 40 Balls each, under Government supervision, brought down to Calcutta, and a stated quantity offered monthly by public auction at the upset price of Rs. 450 per chest, being the actual cost of production. But the competition amongst the buyers to supply the China markets is so great, that a chest generally realises about Rs. 1,250, which therefore leaves a surplus of Rs. 800 per chest for the benefit of the Indian Government exchequer.

On the other side of India, however, the Government has nothing whatever to do with the cultivation of the poppy, or with its manipulation. It is grown in native

States, principally in Malwa and Indore. The Government levies a tax of Rs. 600 per chest when brought from the interior for exportation to China, which forms all the profit or interest of the Government in the trade in Malwa opium. This is why Bengal opium always turns out of good and even quality and is never inspected by the Chinese dealers, the Government ticket which is placed on each chest being accepted as sufficient guarantee for the quality of the drug. In Malwa opium there is always an admixture of qualities whose touch varies from 50 to 75 per cent. It has to undergo a process of boiling and testing through the pipe before a bargain can be made with Chinese.

The cultivation of the poppy has of late years increased all over China, more especially in the province of Ssŭch'uan, in the north of Shensi and Honan, and in Manchuria.

The native drug is much adulterated with linseed and other stuff. Indian opium is confessedly far superior in every respect to the indigenous, and the Chinese show their appreciation of it, by paying for it double the price of the native opium. The comparative quotations are Tls. 500 for a picul of Malwa against Tls. 250 to 300 for the native product. The touch of native opium is from 50 per cent downwards.

OPIUM WAR. See *Lin*.

"Reduced to plain words, the principle for which we "fought in the China War was the right of Great Britain "to force a peculiar trade upon a foreign people." *Justin McCarthy*.

OPPOSITES. In many of their manners and customs the Chinese are diametrically opposed to Europeans. For instance, in China the left hand is the place of honour, men keep their hats on in company, use fans, mount their horses on the off side, begin dinner with fruit and end it with soup, shake their own hands when meeting friends, read from right to left down vertical columns, wear white for mourning, have huge visiting-cards, prevent criminals from having their hair cut, and regard the south as the standard point of the compass.

ORANG. The Malay word for *man*. Commonly used by foreigners in the Straits when calling to Malay coolies, etc. Hence the *orang-outang*, or "man of the woods."

ORDEAL, TRIAL BY. Is often practised in China. That is, where the statements of two parties are absolutely conflicting, either may propose the ordeal of swearing at the City Temple. There is in use a special form of oath, to be uttered aloud, before the shrine of the god, in the dim religious light which adds solemnity to the scene.

ORTHOGRAPHY. A term commonly employed by foreigners in China to denote the transliteration of Chinese characters. The orthographies for the Mandarin dialect are specially perplexing, there being as many as five or six different systems in vogue among English writers alone; and thus we have Soo-chow, Su-chow, Su-chou, and Su-cheu, all representing the two Chinese characters for the city of 蘇 州. For many years Morrison's inaccurate orthography, with no aspirates marked, supposed to represent the sounds of the Mandarin dialect as heard at Nanking, was accepted without protest, except on the part of Edkins, who tried unsuccessfully to introduce one of his own. Wade then appeared on the scene with his elementary handbooks for students of the Court Dialect, in which many of the old Nanking *k's* were turned into *ch's*, besides other changes, in accordance with the sounds heard in the city of Peking; and as students of Mandarin now invariably begin with Wade's *Tzŭ-êrh-chi (q.v.)*, it is no longer a question which is the best orthography, but which is in general use and most likely to continue so. Sir T. Wade's system may not be the best, and it certainly is not perfect, no difference being made, for instance, in the vowel sounds of 忙 or 狼 and 廣 or 謊, though the distinction between them is as clearly defined as that between the *a* and *o* in the French words *manger* and *plonger*. The chief objection to it is that the great majority of Mandarins use the Nanking sounds; on the other hand, a slightly modified Pekingese is intelligible to all. As to names of places, it would be impossible to make any beneficial change. "Kiu-kiang" must be always thus spelt, and not altered to the Pekingese "Chiu-chiang;" and so with other well-known proper names. Meanwhile, in view of the great scientific disadvantages of Wade's orthography, the Oriental Congress of 1897 appointed a Commission of Chinese scholars to consider the position and endeavour to construct a new orthography on lines acceptable to all. This scheme was carried out and the result presented to the Oriental Congress of 1899, but with no practical result.

OSAKA: 大坂. A port in Japan.

OUIGOURS *or* UIGOURS: 回紇 *or* 黑回. Descendants of the Hsiung-nu or Huns, first heard of under the Northern Wei dynasty, A.D. 389, when they were known as 高車 "high carts" from the vehicles they used. Under the T'ang dynasty they were called 回紇, and were the ruling race in the regions now known as the Khanates of Khiva and Bokhara, being the first of the tribes of

Central Asia to have a script of their own which was based upon the Estrangelo Syriac of the Nestorians. These characters are now called by the Chinese 畏 語 兒 字. The latest date at which the Ouigours sent tribute was 1296, under the Mongol dynasty, about which period the term seems to have come to mean Mussulmans, the modern 回回. It is the origin of our word "Ogre."

PADDY: 粟. Rice in the husk; from the Malayan *Pādi*. Also used of rice as it grows in the *paddy-fields*.

PADDY-BIRD: 白鷺. The white egret *(Egretta modesta)*. So called because frequently seen wading in paddy-fields.

PAGODA: 寶塔—precious *t'a* or pile. Formerly known as 浮圖 *or* 浮屠 =Buddha. The Indian *toran*. A circular or octagonal building, always of an odd number of storeys, originally raised over relics of Buddha, bones of Buddhist saints etc., but now built chiefly in connection with Fêng-shui *(q.v.)*. At Lo-yang, under the Chin dynasty (A.D. 350), there were forty-two pagodas, from three to nine storeys high, richly painted and formed after Indian models. The word has been derived from the Portuguese *pagão* = Latin *paganus*; also from the Portuguese pronunciation of the Indian *dagoba (q.v.)*, in addition to which we commend to our readers a common term in use among the Chinese themselves, viz: 白骨塔—white bones tower, pronounced *poh-kuh-t'a*. See *Stûpa*.

"I feel satisfied that we may take it as now established "that the Chinese pagoda was copied from the Topes of "the Indus valley and Afghanistan." *W. Simpson.*

PAGODA. A small gold coin, used in Madras.

PAGODA ANCHORAGE: 羅星塔 *or* 馬尾. The anchorage for foreign ships at the port of Foochow, from which city it is about ten miles distant. Scene of the destruction of the Chinese fleet by the French under Admiral Courbet, 23rd August, 1884. Pagoda Anchorage and Island are both so called from the existence of a small pagoda on the latter. The Chinese have named the island after a star—γ in Capricorn.

PAILOW: 牌樓. An ornamental gateway or arch, put up in memory of some deceased person of transcendent loyalty, filial piety, chastity, and similar virtues.

PAKHOI: 北海—north sea. A port on the extreme southern coast of the Kuang-tung province, opened to trade by the Chefoo Agreement of 1876.

PAKKA. A Hindi word meaning (1) ripe, cooked, and (2) genuine, proper. The application of this word in Anglo-Indian and Anglo-Chinese parlance is practically unlimited. It is generally understood in the sense of "real." Thus, a pony may be a *pakka* pony, and a man may be a *pakka* fool. (*Cutcha* is "raw" or "crude," and is largely used in India in antithesis to *pakka*; not in use in China).

PALAMPORES: 棉皮胎. The chintz coverlets used by the Chinese. From the town of that name in the province of Guzerat, where these counterpanes are manufactured.

PALANQUIN. A term applied in the Straits' Settlements to four-wheeled close carriages. In India it means a litter.

PALMISTRY. Has been practised for centuries by the Chinese. The *T'u shu* (see *Encyclopaedias*) deals fully with the subject and gives about 80 illustrations of hands, with all the lines marked and explained. As with us, good and bad fortunes can be foretold from inspections of the hands. The Chinese however carry the science to its logical conclusion, and give a section, with illustrations, treating of the lines on the sole of the foot.

P'AN-KU *or* PWAN-KOO. Popularly known as the Chinese

Adam. Is a legendary "Great Architect of the Universe." With his death the work of creation began. His breath became the wind; his voice, the thunder; his left eye, the sun; his right eye, the moon; his blood flowed into rivers; his hair grew into trees and plants; his flesh became the soil; his sweat descended as rain; while the parasites which infested his body were the origin of the human race.

PANSHEN ERDENI: 班禪額爾德尼—"The Precious Teacher." The spiritual ruler of Tibet; the Dalai Lama *(q.v.)* being entrusted with the management of secular affairs. The two are often spoken of together as the Tibetan "popes."

PANTHAYS. Mahommedan Chinese who, after a brutal massacre of 14,000 of their fellow-religionists at Yün-nan Fu in 1856, revolted against the yoke of China, and made an attempt to establish a separate kingdom in the province of Yün-nan, with their capital at Ta-li Fu. Ambassadors were sent to England in 1872, but failed to interest the British Government in their behalf. On the 15th January, 1873, the brave commander Tu Wên-hsiu 杜文秀, having first swallowed poison, surrendered to the Chinese, and the rebellion was shortly afterwards crushed with immense slaughter of the insurgents. The word *Panthay*, or *Pan-si*, is the name by which the Burmese at Bhamo designate Mahommedans, and has no connection, as sometimes stated, with 本地, the term itself being quite unknown to the Chinese.

PAO TAH *or* PAU TAH. A pagoda *(q.v.)*.

PAPER: 紙. Was manufactured in China in the first century. A kind of paper, called 赫蹏 *ho-ti* or 薄蹏 *po-ti*, seems to have been known in China before the Christian era.

The invention of paper however is generally credited to the eunuch-scholar Ts'ai Lun, who died A.D. 114. He is said to have manufactured it out of tow, old linen, fishing-nets, etc. Paper is now chiefly made (1) from bamboo, by soaking the woody fibre and then rubbing it to pulp in a mortar, after which it is taken up in moulds; (2) from the bark of the *Broussonetia papyrifera*, this kind being a tough article used for windows instead of glass; and (3) from rice straw, being coloured on one side by hand and used for religious and ceremonial purposes. Paper which bears any traces of writing should not be thrown down on the floor to be trodden upon, nor used for any unworthy purpose, not even to wrap things in, but should be reverentially burnt. Small crematoria for this purpose are often built by philanthropic persons in the streets of towns and elsewhere.

Japanese hand-made papers are divided into two classes. The so-called "hansi," or half paper, is loaded with about 20 per cent of rice starch; the "minogami" consists entirely of fibre. Jackets and trousers made of strong hand-made paper were supplied to the Japanese soldiers during the late war with China.

Korean hand-made papers are of a yellowish colour, with a silk-like gloss, and of extraordinary strength. In purity they are behind the better grades of Chinese papers.

PAPER-BOAT: 客船—passenger boat. A large roomy boat used on the rivers in the neighbourhood of Swatow for the conveyance of passengers and of cargoes of paper—whence the foreign term has been derived.

PAPER MONEY: 鈔. It is supposed that five centuries and more before Christ the Chinese used pieces of stamped line as a circulating medium. About 240 B.C. strips of leather were used in the same way. In 806 A.D. "flying money," which has been identified with a paper currency, was introduced. From 1154 A.D. paper money became quite common, and is still in general use all over China, notes being issued in some places for amounts less even than a shilling.

PAPICO: 白 屁 股—white stern. A small junk, of the fishing-boat class, seen at Ningpo and in the Chusan archipelago. Has a white stern; hence the Chinese name, of which *papico* is an imitation.

PARANG. A large Malay knife for cutting wood; a snikkersnee. "... whereupon the Mandor *(q.v.)* drew his "*parang* and chased him round the monkey-house, but "Mr. Murton got away."—*Hongkong Daily Press* (from *Straits' Times*), 22 September, 1877.

PARIAH. (1) From the Tamil *paraiyan* a drummer. (2) A corruption of the Indian word *parāya* "strange." Pariah dogs, *i.e.*, dogs with no owners, are not uncommon in large Chinese towns.

The Pariahs of India are men without caste, who notwithstanding keep up a kind of caste among themselves, being quite as jealous of their impurity as Brahmans are of their purity.

PARSEE *or* PARSI. Descendants of the Persians, of which Parsi is the old form, who left their native country and settled in India, to avoid Mahommedan persecution. They are Zoroastrians or Fire Worshippers. Bombay Parsees are established in business at several of the Treaty Ports, notably Canton, Amoy, Shanghai, and Foochow, dealing chiefly in opium. Their complexions having caused them to be confounded by the Chinese with Moormen *(q.v.)*, they are known by the same name, "Whiteheads" 白 頭. See *Tower of Silence*.

PA-T'U-LU. See *Baturu*.

PAWN SHOPS. Are common all over China, and are not infrequently owned by Mandarins. They may be known, sometimes by their greater height than the surrounding buildings, always by a huge character (either 當 *or* 質) exhibited in some conspicuous place. The interest charged is 3 per cent *per month*, the pledge to be redeemed within sixteen months. About half the value of the article is generally given. Unlicensed pawnshops, 押, receive pledges for three months, on more liberal terms, both as regards the amount of the loan and the interest charged.

PEACH-ORCHARD CONFEDERATION: 桃園之義. A solemn covenant, sworn to in a peach-orchard, between Liu Pei, Chang Fei, and Kuan Ti *(q.v.)*, that they would fight side by side and live and die together.

PEACOCK'S FEATHERS. A badge of merit conferred by the Emperor. The highest grade, or 花翎 "flowery feather," is actually from the peacock's tail and has either one, two, or three eyes, according to the merit of the wearer. The other kind, or 藍翎—blue feather, or plume, is from the raven's tail; but both are equally known to foreigners under the above name. Introduced only since the beginning of the present dynasty.

PEACOCK, TO. Slang term for "to call on ladies," as implying a more elegant costume than usual. Brought to China from India where it is much used; see *John Neville*, vol. i., 246.

PEAR-GARDEN, PUPILS OF THE: 梨園子弟. The first two characters form the name of the site of the Dramatic College founded by the Emperor Hsüan Tsung of the T'ang dynasty. The whole is a popular name for "actors."

PEARL-OYSTER: 貝. Used in ancient times as money, like cowries. The Chinese character was a picture, under its old form, of the open shell.

PEARL RIVER: 珠江. Name of the river at Canton, said to be so called from the island known to foreigners as Dutch Folly *(q.v.).*

PECUL *or* PICUL: 擔 *tan or* 石 *shih.* The Chinese hundred-weight = 133⅓ lbs. avoirdupois. From the Malay "pikul," a load or burden. Coolies are classed, according to their weight-carrying capabilities, as one-, two-, and even three-picul men.

PEI-TAI-HO: 北戴河. Railway station 152 miles from Tientsin, towards Shan-hai-kuan.

P'EI WÊN YÜN FU: 佩文韻府. A Concordance, or collection of phrases in the classical, historical, poetical, and philosophical literatures of China, arranged under the Rhymes in groups of 2, 3, and 4 characters to each. It was published in 1711 by order and under the superintendence of the Emperor K'ang Hsi, and its 110 thick volumes form one of the most remarkable literary works of any country or of any age.

PEKING: 北京—northern capital. Literary name 燕 *yen.* The Mongol conqueror Kublai Khan *(q.v.)* first established his court here. Has been the capital of the empire since the reign of Yung Lo, the third emperor of the Ming dynasty, who may be regarded as the founder of the modern city, which when spoken of in an administrative sense, is known as 順天府 Shun-t'ien Fu. Is divided into the so-called Tartar and Chinese cities, each surrounded by a wall, the dimensions of the former of which surpass (except in length) those of the Great Wall itself.

PEKING GAZETTE: 京報 *or* 邸抄. The small official record, issued daily throughout the year (every other day during the annual New Year's festival) at Peking, and containing the Court movements, lists of promotions, *selected* memorials from high officials, Imperial Rescripts, Edicts, and so on; but no news of any kind. Is known to have existed as far back as the T'ang dynasty, A.D. 618—907.

PEKOE: 白毫 —white hair. A kind of tea, so called because the leaves are picked very young, with the down or "hair" on them. From the Cantonese pronunciation of the above two characters.

PENAL CODE, THE: 律例. This work contains (1) the immutable statute laws of the Chinese Empire under the present Manchu dynasty, derived in great part from the previous code of the Ming dynasty; and (2) such modifications, extensions, and restrictions of these fundamental laws as time and circumstances make necessary. A revised edition is published every five years. Has been translated into English by Sir G. Staunton.

Sect. 292:—All persons playing with the fist, with a stick, or with any weapon, or other means whatsoever, in such a manner as obviously to be liable by so doing to kill, and thus killing or wounding some individual, shall suffer the punishment provided by the law in any ordinary case of killing or wounding in an affray (viz: death by strangulation or punishment in proportion to the injuries inflicted).

All persons who kill or wound others purely by accident, shall be permitted to redeem themselves from the punishment, by the payment in each case of a fine to the family of the person deceased or wounded.

By a case of pure accident is understood a case of which no sufficient warning could have been given, either directly, by the perceptions of sight and hearing, or indirectly, by the inferences drawn from judgment and reflection; as for instance, when lawfully pursuing or shooting wild animals; when for some purpose throwing a brick or a tile, and in either case unexpectedly killing any person; when after ascending high places, slipping and falling down, so as to chance to hurt a comrade or bystander; when sailing in a ship or other vessel, and driven involuntarily by the winds; when riding on a horse or in a carriage, being unable, upon the animals taking fright, to stop, or to govern them; or lastly, when several persons jointly attempt to raise a great weight, the strength of one of them failing, so that the weight falls on, and kills or injures his fellow-labourers:—in all these cases there could have been no previous thought or intention of doing an injury, and therefore the law permits such persons to redeem themselves from the punishments, by a fine to be paid to the family of the deceased or wounded person. (See *Punishments*).

PENANG, PULO: 檳榔嶼—Betel-nut Island. A British settlement in the Straits of Malacca, founded 1786 and originally known as Prince of Wales' Island.

PENANG LAWYER. A large heavy walking-stick with a big knob, sold at Penang and in the Straits generally. Said to be so called because: (1) the strength of lawyers lies in their *nobs*; (2) because formerly there was little or no law in Penang, and people were forced to "take it into their own hands." Really *layor*, a native name for the kind of cane of which it is made.

PÊN TS'AO. See *Pun ts'ao*.

PEON. One who serves on foot. A Singapore native constable.

PEPO-HWAN: 平埔番—barbarians of the plain. "The "name Pepo-hwan is applied to all the civilised aborigines "living near the mountains in the southern part of the "island (of Formosa). The one name includes a number "of ancient tribes which were formerly distinct and spoke "separate dialects. At the present time, however, Chinese "is the language used by all."—*T. L. Bullock.* See *Formosa*.

PERAK. "Silver;" a name derived from the large amount of silvery-looking tin which is found there. Pronounced *Payrah*.

PERSIMMON: 柿子. The date plum found in great quantities in China, often called the "China fig." The Peking variety is Bunge's *Diospyros Schi-tse*; the persimmon of South China and of Japan is the *Diospyros Kaki.*

PESANG. The Malay word for *banana*, in common use among foreigners in the Straits.

PETITIONS: 禀帖. Should be written in very small characters, as a mark of the petitioner's respect; and should be handed in in duplicate, one on red paper for the perusal of the official addressed and to be kept on record, the other on white paper, to be returned with the reply written in bold characters at the end and stamped with the seal of office. Petitions from the people to Mandarins should have nine columns of characters on every page; from subordinates to their superior officers, only five. The following mnemonic line is well known to all scribes and clerks employed in Chinese Yamêns:—五禀六摺 四照會; "five for a petition, six for an enclosure, four for a dispatch." Petitions are not dated, there being regular days of the month for presentation; viz, those in which 3 or 8 occurs. An extra fee will, however, secure presentation on other days.

PETTICOAT-STRING ROAD: 裙帶路. A common Chinese name for Hongkong, especially in use among the Hakkas *(q.v.)*. The Cantonese proverb says,

好女不到裙帶路
好兒不下佛山渡

"Decent girls don't go to Hongkong, nor do respectable "youths travel by the Fatshan boats;"—the sailors on the passenger-boats between Canton and Fatshan being a very disreputable set. The name was originally 君大路 Great Queen Street(?), and was corrupted by the native population to its present form.

PHILIPPINES, THE. See *Luzon.*

PHŒNIX: 鳳凰. A fabulous bird, which according to the Chinese appears only at golden epochs, and has not been seen since the days of Confucius. It is said to be the essence of water (purity in the abstract). It feeds only upon seeds of the bamboo, and drinks only from the sweetest springs. Its plumage contains the five colours and its song the five notes.

PHONETICS, THE. That portion of a Chinese character *(q.v.)* which guides the reader to its *sound*, though he may never have seen the character before. E.g.— 登 *têng*, to ascend, is the phonetic of 燈 *têng*, a lamp, which is formed by the addition of 火 fire. Such a portion of a character, when it has no phonetic value, is called the *primitive.* The analysis of Callery gave 1,040 phonetics and primitives, under one or other of which all Chinese characters could be arranged; but unfortunately exceptions and deviations are so numerous as to render this system of only comparative value.

PHOONGYE. See *Talapoin.*

PHRAONG CHOW. See *Chow fah.*

PICTURE CHOPS. See *Chop.*

PIDGIN. Business of any kind, from which word the term *pidgin* is said to be derived, through the Chinese imitation of our word, *i.e.*, business, bizzin, pishin, pidgin. By others, from the latter half of the Portuguese *occupação*. Also, from the Hebrew word meaning ransom or redemption, from a ritual observance still found among pious Jews; viz., *pidjann* or the redemption of the first-born from the priesthood, to which they have been held to be specially devoted ever since the act of grace by which the first-born of Israel were spared. This word passed into the common language, and Jewish merchants in Poland may even now be heard to ask about the "pidgen," *i.e.* business; and as Polish Jews emigrated in large numbers to England it is believed that they may have carried this slang term with them. A further etymology has been suggested in the Sanskrit *piche*, to pursue.

Commonly used as an affix—amah-pidgin, coolie-pidgin, etc. Any servant called upon to perform another's work will reply "no belong my pidgin."

"A second man had to be flogged, and a different "officer had to flog him. This second officer's physique "was not by any means equal to that of the first, and "the blows came down with far less force. He was "consequently voted not up to his pidgin."—Hongkong *Daily Press*, 4 Oct. 1877.

PIDGIN-CHINESE. The Chinese spoken by foreigners who have not the gift of tongues, and persist in arranging

their sentences according to the idiom of their native land.
See *Coolie-Chinese.*

PIDGIN-ENGLISH: 澳門話 *or* Macao talk. The *lingua
franca* of China, used by foreigners of all nationalities
who do not talk Chinese in speaking to native servants,
shop-keepers, chair-coolies, sailors, etc. Also frequently
spoken to each other by Chinamen of different parts of
the Empire, whose dialects are mutually unfamiliar and
who do not understand their own common medium,
Mandarin. The following is a specimen, by an anonymous
author, of a celebrated English poem translated into this
strange jargon.

EXCELSIOR!

That nightey time begin chop-chop,
One young man walkey—no can stop.
Maskee snow! maskee ice!
He carry flag wid chop so nice—
　　　　　Topside-galow!

He too muchey sorry, one piecey eye
Looksee sharp—so—all same my.
Him talkey largey, talkey strong.
Too muchey curio—all same gong—
　　　　　Topside-galow!

Inside that house he look-see light,
And every room got fire all right,
He look-see plenty ice more high,
Inside he mouth he plenty cry—
　　　　　Topside-galow!

Olo man talkey "no can walk!
"By'mby rain come—welly dark,
"Have got water, welly wide."
"Maskee! My wantchey go topside."
　　　　　Topside-galow!

"Man-man!" one girley talkey he;
"What for you go topside look-see?"
And one time more he plenty cry,
But all time walkey plenty high.
　　　　　Topside-galow!

"Take care that spoil'um tree, young man.
"Take care that ice! He want man-man!"
That coolie chin-chin he good night,
He talkey "My can go all right."
　　　　　Topside-galow!

Joss-pidgin man he soon begin,
Morning-time that Joss chin-chin;
He no man see—he plenty fear,
Cos some man talkey—he can hear!
　　　　　Topside galow!

That young man die, one large dog see,
Too muchey bobbery findey he;
He hand belong colo—all same ice,
Have got that flag, with chop so nice.
　　　　　Topside-galow!

Moral

You too muchey laugh! What for sing?
I think-so you no savey what thing!
Supposey you no b'long clever inside,
More better *you* go walk topside!
　　　　　Topside-galow!

There is also—

> My name belong Norval; topside that Grampian hill
> My father catchee chow-chow pay he sheep—*etc.*

The following is a good prose specimen of pidgin-English as actually spoken in China. It is supposed to be from the pen of a Nai-ma, or Chinese wet-nurse, disappointed that the colours were not trooped as usual on the Queen's birthday.

QUEEN'S BIRTHDAY.

Sir,—Long time my have stop Hongkong side, any year Queen's bursday have got that soldier man play-pidgin City Hall overside. My chin-chin you tluly talkee my what for this year no got—no have got largee lain! How fashion? Some flen talkee my that soldier man b'long alla same olo man—two time one day he no can—some man talkee that soldier man taipan he more likee walkee that horse go topside sleep! Spose b'long tlue talkee my so fashion no likee. Too spensee my have catchee that seelick jacket, that bangle, that diamond ling, allo that thing. Tluly too muchee trub—long time stop that side waitee, no man talkee my no got.

Spose soldier man b'long so fashion no can take care people that smallo pidgin, more better my chop-chop go Macao—that side have got plenty number one soldier man—no got fear.

My too muchee no likee that foolo pidgin just now Hongkong any tim have got. Chin-chin.

Naai Ma.

Hongkong, 27th May, 1878.

PIDGIN-JAPANESE. A species of hybrid, ungrammatical Japanese, spoken by foreigners who do not learn the language accurately; *e.g. Omi taksan pompom bobbery, watarksi pumguts:* "If you continue to make so much "noise in hammering those nails into that wall, I shall be "reluctantly compelled to correct you by the administra-"tion of severe corporal chastisement." Here *pompom bobbery*=the noise made by hammering nails into a wall.

PIGEON. Incorrect form of *Pidgin*. Pigeon-English *(sic)* is defined by Dr. Brewer as "a conglomeration of English "and Portuguese words, wrapped in a Chinese idiom, in "which the European dealers 'pigeon' or try to over-"reach the merchants of the Flowery Empire."

PIGGI. Pidgin-Japanese equivalent for *wailo* "go away!"

PIGTAIL. See *Cue.*

"PILLAR" DOLLAR: 本洋. The Spanish Carolus dollar is so called from the design on the reverse—the two pillars of Hercules,[1] joined by a scroll inscribed with the legend *Ne plus ultra* "nothing beyond," and supporting the arms and crown of Spain. Known to the Chinese, in common with many other foreign coins, as 鬼頭 "devil's head" money, from the royal head on the obverse. Dollars of Carolus IV. are called 四工 "the four *kung*," the old way of writing IV., viz. IIII., being mistaken by the Chinese for their own character 工 *labour* four times repeated.

PILLOW-WORD *or* Makura-Kotoba. A conventional epithet of 5 syllables, introduced ready-made (cf. *phrases faites*) into Japanese poems, usually at the beginning of a line, and so forming as it were a pillow on which the poem rests.

P'ING-YANG: 平壤. A place in Korea, north of the

---

1 The two rocks at the entrance to the Mediterranean Sea were known to the ancients by this name.

capital, and scene of a great victory by the Japanese over the Chinese on 15 September, 1894.

PIONEER of COMMERCE. The late T. T. Cooper has been frequently so called, from his book "Travels of a P. of C. in Pig-tail and Petticoats."

PIVOT-WORD. A word or part of a word used by Japanese poets in two senses, *i.e.* in one sense with what precedes and in another sense with what follows. It is the "sandwich" boat of poetry, rowing in both the first and second divisions, and so belonging absolutely to neither.

PLANCHETTE: 扶乩. Has been well known in China for centuries, and is chiefly practised by priests as a means of extorting money from the credulous. A forked stick, having a short tooth-like piece projecting at right angles from the point of bifurcation, is grasped by two men standing back to back. By simultaneous movement of the operators the "tooth" is made to describe circles on a table covered with sand and placed before the shrine of some god, until inspiration comes, and characters are traced legibly on the sand, forming an appropriate response to any question that may have been put.

PLANTAIN: 巴蕉. A tropical plant of the genus *Musa*, and order *Musaceæ*, which bears a highly nutritious fruit, nearly akin to the banana.

> I long my careless limbs to lay
> Under the plantain's shade.
> *Waller.*

"The banana tree *(Musa sapientum)* differs from the "plantain in having its stalks marked with dark purple "stripes and spots, and the fruit is shorter and rounder. "Some botanists, however, consider them as only one "species."—Loudon, *Encycl. of Gardening*.

PLUM CASH. Pidgin-English imitation of "prime cost."

POCKET SONS. Sons purchased for adoption by childless Chinese. Similarly, "pocket mother" is generally used of women who buy girls for prostitution.

POETRY, CHINESE: 詩. For ancient poetry, see the *Odes*. In modern versification, all measures from four to eleven characters in a line are to be found, and poems varying in length from a couplet to several hundred lines; but what may be called orthodox poetry, dating from the beginning of the T'ang dynasty (618 A.D.), is subject to the following conditions. Measures of either five or seven characters to the line, both forms dating from the 2nd cent. B.C., may be employed, and there should not be more than sixteen lines; at the great public examinations the poems handed in by the candidates may not exceed 12 lines in length. There must be rhyme, *i.e.* according to the rhymes found in the *Odes*, though many of these no longer rhyme to the ear. When five characters are used all the even lines rhyme; but if seven, then the first line rhymes too, the rhyming character being always in the "even" tone. The other tonal arrangements, the choice of any one of which is optional, are shown in the annexed tables, the lines to be read downwards from right to left as in Chinese.

仄	平	平	仄	平	仄	仄	平
仄	平	平	仄	平	仄	仄	平
仄	平	仄	平	仄	平	仄	平
平	仄	仄	平	仄	平	平	仄
平	仄	平	仄	平	仄	平	仄

平	仄	仄	平	平	仄	仄	平
平	仄	仄	平	平	仄	仄	平
仄	平	平	仄	仄	平	平	仄
仄	平	平	仄	仄	平	平	仄
仄	平	仄	平	仄	平	仄	仄
平	仄	仄	平	平	仄	仄	平
平	仄	平	仄	平	仄	平	平

仄	平	平	仄	仄	平	平	仄
仄	平	平	仄	仄	平	平	仄
平	仄	仄	平	平	仄	仄	平
平	仄	仄	平	平	仄	仄	平
仄	平	仄	平	仄	平	仄	仄
仄	平	平	仄	仄	平	平	仄
平	仄	平	仄	平	仄	平	平

A common and useful formula among versifiers is
三五不論，二四六分明.

It may be added that every such Chinese poem should contain if possible some historical or mythological allusion, and deal with the elucidation of a single thought.

The output of Chinese poets during their long ages of civilisation has been enormous, and contrary to generally received notions, women have been large contributors. The Wade Library at Cambridge contains among many other such works the "Poetry of the T'ang Dynasty," comprising no less than 48,900 poems, some of them being of considerable length. The Emperor Ch'ien Lung alone published 33,950 poems, mostly short ones, not to mention a large number which were never printed.

POETRY, JAPANESE. Is distinguished by complete absence of rhyme, and consists chiefly of short lyrics written in alternate phrases of 5 and 7 syllables to each. It is largely indebted to the sister muse in China. See *Tanka*, *Naga-uta*, *Haikai*, and *Kioka*.

POLYGAMY, in the strict sense of the term, is unknown in China. A man can legally have but one wife, who shares in all his honours, present or posthumous. But if a wife is without issue, the husband is justified in taking a concubine; and many rich Chinese do so even without that justification. The family status, however, of a concubine is a very different thing from that of the wife.

The *Yü-chiao-li* makes its hero marry both the heroines; but this is the license of a novelist. See *Marriage*.

POMELO *or* POMMELO. See *Pummelo*.

PONGEE: 本機—own loom. A kind of silk, similar to the Tussore silk of India. The above two characters, pronounced *pun chee*, are commonly seen on pieces of all kinds of silk, preceded by the name of the house which guarantees that the silk in question was made on its "own looms." Hence our term, now confined to one particular sort. 本織 *home woven* or *homespun* is sometimes written, but the other phrase is more usual. We cannot endorse the following:—"The name of the wheel upon "which the cocoon thread is reeled is (繃車) Pang-chih; "in Cantonese Pung-ch'e. This is most likely the origin "of the word Pongee, in French *Pongée*."—*A. Fauvel*: *China Review*, vol. vi., p. 103.

POO HIEN. See *P'u Hsien*.

POO-SA *or* P'U-SA: 菩薩. From the first and third syllables of Bodhisatva *(q.v.)*. Commonly used in China for all kinds of gods and idols. The eyes of large idols are sometimes made to move, like those of the Virgin in Catholic churches, by a very ingenious device. A white mouse is secreted in a small box inside the head, and by a simple mechanism the eyes move every time the little creature runs across its prison.

POOTOO: 普陀 or 普圖 or 普渡 or 菩陀. A sacred island in the Chusan archipelago, between Shanghai and Ningpo, where Kwan-yin *(q.v.)* is said to have resided for nine years. Inhabited by Buddhist priests, who do not permit any living thing to be killed upon the island. Neither are women allowed to live there, nor in fact any one unconnected with the priesthood.

POO-TUNG: 浦東—east of the Poo. The eastern bank of the Huang-p'u river at a point opposite the British Settlement of Shanghai.

POPE, Taoist. See *Master of Heaven.*

POPE, Tibetan. See *Panshen Erdeni.*

POPULATION. See *Census.*

PORCELAIN TOWER, THE: 報恩寺. The celebrated nine-storeyed octagonal pagoda at Nanking, destroyed by the T'ai-p'ing *(q.v.)* rebels. So called because it was faced over with variously coloured porcelain bricks, highly glazed. It was about 200 feet in height, and the circumference of the lower storey was 120 feet, each face being about 15 feet in breadth. There were 190 steps leading to the top. Bells hung from every corner of the roof of each storey, and part of the roofing is said to have been inlaid with gold. Built A.D. 1411, on the site of former structures.

PORT ARTHUR: 旅順口. Also known as Port Li, in honour of Li Hung-chang. A Chinese naval port established near Chin-chou T'ing in Shingking, and strongly fortified. Captured by the Japanese under General Oyama, 21 November 1894. Leased to Russia 1898.

PORT HAMILTON: 叵文島. A small island off the Korean coast, occupied and fortified by England in 1885, as a possible base of operations against Russia. Evacuated 27 February, 1887.

POSTAL SYSTEM. It has always been possible to send a letter with comparative safety from one end of China to the other. In all large towns there are postal hongs which undertake the job for a small fee, half payable in advance, the remainder on delivery. Steamer communication dealt a severe blow to this business, and now China is organising a Government Postal Service. Public letter-writers for the convenience of the uneducated are to be seen sitting at tables in the streets. A corner burnt off an envelope intimates that the communication inside is urgent. Sometimes two and even three corners are burnt. A feather sticking out of the letter has the same signification.

POUCHONG: 包種—folded sort. A kind of tea, so called from the method of packing it. [Cantonese.]

POW: 跑—to run; to gallop. A native word in use amongst the foreign racing communities of China.

"The course, especially at the Foochow-road corner, "is in a miserable condition, and "powing" is only possible "for the quarter-mile distance."—*Foochow Herald.*

Also used as a substantive; *i.e.*, "Come and have a *pow*;" and sometimes of a match between two ponies.

PO-YAH *or* PO-RAH *(Bhoo-ra).* The Burman term for pagoda *(q.v.).* The great Shwé Dǎgōng Pŏyāh, or Golden Dagong Pagoda at Rangoon, is 372 feet high, with a circumference of 600 feet. The gilt *htee* or umbrella at the summit cost about £30,000 in gold and jewels alone.

PRAHU *or* PRAU. A Malay sea-going vessel, as opposed to a sampan.

PRAYA. A quay or esplanade. From the Portuguese *praia*, a shore or beach.

PRAYING-WHEEL: 胡龍洞—Mongolian dragon cave. A machine into which written prayers are thrown in great numbers and then worked round by the hand. The efficacy of these churned prayers is the same as if each were repeated, with the additional advantage of speed.

"Hundreds of Tibetan priests idling away their lives "turning prayer-cylinders, and reciting the everlasting "Hung-mani Peh-man Hung (see *Om mani padme hum*). "The prayer cylinders are called Koh-loh, and some of "them are turned by water-wheels."—*Shanghai Courier*, 7th Nov., 1877.

PRECIOUS ONES, THE THREE: 三寶. The Buddhist Trinity of Buddha, Dharma, and Samgha, or Buddha, the Law, and the Priesthood, 佛, 法, 僧. Sanskrit *Triratna*.

"The philosophical atheistic schools now place *Dharma* "in the first rank as the first person in their trinity "and explain it as the unconditioned underived entity, "combining in itself the spiritual and material principles "of the universe. From Dharma proceeded *Buddha* by "emanation, as the creative energy, and produced in "conjunction with Dharma the third constituent of the "trinity, viz. *Samgha*, which is the comprehensive summa "of all actual life or existence. The common people, "however, know little or nothing of this esoteric view of "a trinity; they speak of and worship a triad of images "which they regard as three different divinities, totally

"ignoring their unity and the fact that the 'three precious
"ones' they worship are but logical abstractions,—a mere
"philosophical myth."—*Eitel.*

The *Three Precious Things* of Taoism *(q.v.)* are (1)
Gentle Kindness, (2) Economy, and (3) Humility.

PREFECT. See *Chih-fu.*

PRESENTS: 禮 儀. Are of two kinds:—(1) 乾 禮 *dry*
presents, *i.e.*, money and other valuables, given as bribes
to Mandarins or as *douceurs* from subordinates to their
superior officers; in the latter case, five times every year,
三 節 兩 壽—"on the three festivals and two birthdays,"
the birthdays being those of the Mandarin and his wife.
(2) 水 禮 *fresh* presents, such as fruit, cakes, and other
eatables. The latter generally consist of eight sorts, and,
where practicable, of *two* of each sort. A list should
accompany them for the recipient to mark off with a
○ such as he wishes to accept. It is not etiquette to
take too many, or too few, or an odd number of sorts.
A gratuity for the sender's servants should then be
placed in a red envelope marked with 代 茶 "Instead
of tea" at the top, the amount being stated in small
characters at the bottom. This sum is divided among
all the sender's servants, and is held to represent what
should have been expended in treating those who brought
the presents. An ordinary Chinese visiting-card must
also be sent with the above-mentioned envelope, bearing
the following words:—謹 領 * * 餘 珍 璧 謝; *i.e.*,
"So-and-so has reverently received * *: the rest of the
"pearls declined with thanks." If none are accepted, in
which case no gratuity is given, the formula is changed
to—心 領 璧 謝, or "Received in spirit, the presents
are declined."

PRESTER JOHN. The ruler of a tribe in Central Asia who was converted to Christianity by the Nestorian missionaries. Said to have been overcome by Genghis Khan in A.D. 1202, and his skull set in silver as a trophy. Mentioned by Marco Polo, ch. xcii., as "Il Preste Giovanni." Our name, sometimes written *Presbyter John*, is a corruption of the Mongol term "Prestar Khan," by which title he was commonly known. Gibbon calls him "a Khan of the Keraites." According to the most recent authorities, this once mythical personage now seems to be thoroughly identified with Yeh-lü Ta-shih, founder of the Western Liao dynasty or realm of Karakitai, who, after his conquest of Eastern and Western Turkestan, became known by the title of Gur-khan, and had his capital at Bala Segun. Mr. Parker however has thought fit to identify him with Chao Yüan-hao (whom he wrongly calls Yüan-min, mistaking 昊 for 旻), the founder of the 夏 Hsia State. "His second name was 嵬理 Wei-li, which looks very like William." *China Review*, XIV, p. 342.

PRICKLY HEAT. A severe form of the skin-disease known as *lichen tropicus*, which begins to show itself as soon as the thermometer rises much above 80° Fahr. The appearance of *prickly heat* is said to indicate free action of the skin, and consequently a good state of health. Warm water baths, with a few handfuls of bran thrown in, are sometimes found to allay the irritation; but unquestionably the best remedy is a lotion of 15 or 20 grains of sulphate of zinc to 4 oz. of water, applied night and morning to the parts inflamed. "Sponging with "toilet vinegar and water, or dusting with ordinary toilet "powder, will probably be found more beneficial than "anything else."—*Diseases of Anglo-Indians*, by R. Mair.

The *Lancet* gives the following remedy, declared by Dr. J. R. Somerville late of Foochow to be very efficacious:—

Sublimed Sulphur 80 per cent.

Magnesia. . . . . 15 „

Oxide of zinc . . 5 „

"The skin is first to be bathed with warm water and "a little soap; some of the powder is then placed in a "saucer, and a squeezed sponge pressed on the powder. "A portion of the powder will adhere to the sponge; this "is to be rubbed carefully in all the patches of prickly "heat, and the process is to be repeated morning and "evening."

PRINCE OF KUNG, THE: 恭 親 王. Sixth son of the Emperor Tao Kuang, uncle of the present Emperor, and for many years Regent and President of the Tsung-li Yamên *(q.v.)*. Died 30th May, 1898.

PRINTING. Has been extensively practised by the Chinese since the middle of the 11th cent. A.D.; and even as early as the sixth century the idea of taking impressions from wooden blocks seems to have arisen, though it was not widely applied to the production of books until about A.D. 930 when the Classics were so printed for the first time. Movable types are said to have been invented by an alchemist of the 11th cent. named Pi Shêng, and under the Ming dynasty these were made of copper or lead; but they have never gained the favour accorded to block-printing, by which most of the great literary works of the Chinese have been achieved. The newspapers of modern times are all printed from movable types, from 6,000 to 7,000 separate characters being required. These are arranged under the 214 Radicals, and sub-arranged according to the number of strokes in the non-radical portion.

"PROMOTION": 陞官圖. A favourite game with the Chinese, played upon a board representing an official career from the lowest to the highest grade; the element of chance is represented by the fall of four dice, and the object of each player is to secure promotion over the others. Is a useful and agreeable means of acquiring familiarity with the value of Chinese official ranks.

PROTESTANT MISSIONARIES. In 1799 the English Baptist Mission sent out the Rev. J. Marshman, who published at Serampore, 1807, "The Works of Confucius, containing the original text, with a translation." Then followed the Rev. Robert Morrison of the London Mission, 1807, author of the first Chinese-English and English-Chinese Dictionary, and also of a translation of the Bible; the Rev. W. Milne of the same, 1813, translator of the Sacred Edict; and the Rev. W. H. Medhurst of the same, 1817, lexicographer, translator of the "Shoo King," etc. Among other eminent Missionaries are the Rev. E. C. Bridgman, American Board's Mission, 1830; the Rev. J. Legge, London Mission, 1840; Miss Lydia Fay, Am. P. E. Mission, 1850; the Rt. Rev. Bishop Moule, Church Miss. Soc., 1858; the Rev. J. Edkins, London Mission, 1861; and Miss A. M. Fielde, Am. Bapt. Mission, 1866.

The Protestant faith is known to the Chinese as 耶穌教 the Jesus Teaching (see *Roman Catholic Missionaries*).

PROVERBS: 諺語. Are so numerous in Chinese as to be quite a feature of the language. Many of the most original have found their way into Japanese literature and have often been quoted as the product of Japan. The following are a few specimens:—

If you bow at all, bow low.

A man thinks he knows, but a woman knows better.

No medicine is as good as a middling doctor.

A bottle-nosed man *may* be a teetotaller, but no one will believe it.

An idol-maker does not worship the gods: he knows what stuff they are made of.

Half an orange tastes as sweet as a whole one.

Free-sitters at the play always grumble most.

Our own compositions, but other men's wives.

Gold is tested by fire, man by gold.

PSALMANAZAR, GEORGE. A literary impostor who lived in the 17th cent. and published a fabulous history of the Island of Formosa, together with a complete and rather complex language entirely made up by himself. Becoming a prey to religious fears, he put an end to his impostures and retired into private life.

P‘U HSIEN: 普 賢. Samanta Bhâdra, a famous Bôdhisatva, worshipped in China as the god of action, and popularly depicted as riding on an elephant which symbolises care, caution, gentleness, and dignity. His seat of worship is at Mt. Omi in Ssŭch‘uan.

PUCKA *or* PUKKA. See *Pakka*.

PUCKEROW, TO. Slang term, common in India and China, signifying to appropriate other people's property. Corruption of the Hindi verb *pakro* to catch hold.

PUGGREE. A sash worn round the hat, generally with its ends falling over the back of the neck, to prevent sunstroke. It is a Hindi word meaning *turban*; correctly written *pagri*.

PULO. The Malay word for *island*; *e.g.*, Pulo Nias, Pulo Penang, and Pulo Percha, which is the Malay name for Sumatra, whence our word *guttapercha*, or the *gutta* of Sumatra. It is not uncommon, however, to find this word considered as part of the name; *e.g.*, "the island of Pulo Condor." *Chambers' Encyclopædia*.

PUMMELO: 柚子 or *Citrus decumana*, L. A species of "shaddock," so called because introduced into the West Indies by a Captain Shaddock. Also known as the *pampelmoose*, and sometimes spoken of as the Forbidden Fruit. Is mentioned in the *Shoo King*: 厥包柚頭 "the bundles contained small oranges and pummeloes." Etymology unknown.

PUNCH and JUDY: 傀儡. A popular amusement in China, said to have originated from a strategic ruse adopted by the Emperor Kao Tsu, B.C. 206, in which a number of movable puppets were exhibited upon the wall of a city and thus aided the besieged monarch in effecting his escape.

PUNCH-HAUS (Dutch). First applied by the natives, and afterwards by the foreign residents, to hotels at Singapore.

PUNGHULU. The headman of a Malay village.

PUNGTARAI SEEDS: 大海子. The fruit of a tree found in Cambodia, and eaten as a delicacy by the Chinese.

PUNISHMENTS. Those recognised by the Chinese *Penal Code (q.v.)* are (1) flogging on the thighs with a flat piece of bamboo; (2) exposure in a heavy wooden collar, called a cangue; (3) banishment for a given time or permanently to a given distance; and (4) death by strangulation, decapitation, or the so-called "lingering death." See *Ling Che*.

PUNJUM. Inferior silk made from the outside layer of the cocoon. From the Indian name for a kind of raw silk.

PUNKAH. A Hindi word (pankha) meaning "a fan." Introduced into China by Europeans, and now known to the Chinese as 風扇 "wind fan," but rarely seen even in the wealthiest native establishments, where servants with large feather fans still continue to perform this function at their master's dinner-table. For the afternoon nap, small slave-girls are often employed in a similar way.

"*Punkah* says that in its own country it is pulled by a "string, and is used to *ventilate* a room."— *The Pioneer.*

"The Pankha, or large common fan, is a leaf of the "*Corypha umbraculifera*, with the petiole cut to the length "of about five feet, pared round the edges and painted "to look pretty. It is waved by the servant standing "behind a chair."—*R. F. Burton.*

PUN-TS'AO: 本草綱目. The Chinese *Materia Medica*, sometimes called *The Herbal*, an extensive work in many volumes on botany, natural history, etc. It is the work of Li Shih-chên, who completed his task in 1578 after 26 years' labour. No less than 1892 species are dealt with, arranged under 62 classes in 16 divisions, and 8160 prescriptions are given in connection with the various entries.

PUNTI: 本地—of the soil. Native as opposed to foreign; the Chinese of the Kuang-tung province as distinguished from immigrant Chinese (see *Hakkas*) from other provinces. Local, as applied to dialects, etc.; *e.g.,* "with the *Punti* and Mandarin pronunciations."

PURGATORY. See *Chamber of Horrors* and *Devils.*

PUSAN. See *Fusan.*

PUTCHUCK: 木香. The root of a species of thistle found in Cashmere. Used by the Chinese as a medicine and also in the preparation of incense. Putchuck is the term in use at Calcutta.

PWANKU. See *P'an Ku*

PYJAMAS. Large baggy trousers made of flannel, silk, or cotton, and worn at night with a jacket called a "sleep-shirt" by residents all over the East. From the Hindi *pāe* leg and *jāmā* clothing. Also known in Indian as "pyjands."

PYLONG: 惡人—a bad man. A pirate, or any desperado. From the Amoy pronunciation of the above characters—*phai lang* or *p'ai lang*.

Another, but less likely, etymology is 扒龍 *pa lung*, a kind of boat used by river pirates.

QUA as a suffix. See *Howqua*.

QUANGFOUTCHEE. See *Confucius*.

QUASSA. See *Kwasha*.

QUEEN OF HEAVEN: 天后. The guardian divinity of sailors, formerly a young lady named 林 Lin, of the Fuhkien province. Temples and small joss-houses in honour of this goddess may be seen at short intervals along all the lines of water communication throughout the empire.

QUELPAERT or QUELPART: 濟州, old name 耽羅. A large island to the south of the Korean peninsula.

QUELUNG. See *Kelung*.

QUEMOY: 金門—golden gate. A small island to the E. of the island of Amoy.

QUI HYES. Bengal Englishmen are so called, from the term "qui hye!" (correctly "koi hai!") used in calling servants.

QUINSAI. See *Kinsay*.

QUINTAL. The Spanish hundred-weight, as used in the Philippine Islands.

QUOC-NGU. A system of transcription of Annamite in Roman letters, devised by the French missionaries.

RADICAL *or* DETERMINATIVE. That part of a Chinese

character which often gives a clue to its *meaning*, has been thus named by foreigners. It is under these radicals, or keys, that most native dictionaries have been arranged; all characters having the same radical being put together, and then sub-divided according to the number of strokes in the remaining part or phonetic *(q.v.)*. Originally 540, the radicals were subsequently reduced to 214, the number in K'ang Hsi's *(q.v.)* lexicon. For example, 登 *têng* is "to ascend;" put the radical 火 *huo* "fire" by its side, thus 燈, and the meaning is "lamp," the sound and tone *(q.v.)* remaining unchanged. Substitute 目 *mu* "eye" for "fire," thus 瞪, and we have *têng* "to stare at;" but though the sound is still unchanged, the tone is altered from 1st to 4th, a difference which an ordinarily cultivated ear detects at once.

RADZA-WINS. The historical works of the Burmans.

RAGS. The slang term in China for piece goods. "There is no silk at Hankow; only tea and *rags*."

RAJA. A Sanskrit word meaning *King*.

RAMS, CITY OF: 羊城. Canton. Five Immortals are said to have entered this city during the Chou dynasty, riding on five rams, and each holding an ear of grain. When they dismounted, the rams were changed into stone, and may be seen to this day on an altar in the Five Genii shrine. Hence Canton is sometimes called the City of the Genii, and also the City of Grain.

RATTAN. The common cane is so called. From the Malay *rotan*.

RED BOOK, THE: 縉紳錄. A Chinese civil, military, and naval list, published quarterly and bound in *red*, in which are given the names, standing, etc., of all Government servants holding actual appointments. Expectant officials are not included. Four volumes are devoted to the civil service, and two to the military. From an analysis of a recent issue of this work, we learn that, exclusive of Tartar Generals, there are in the Eighteen Provinces 1757 officials holding seals, of whom 1585 are Chinese, 117 Manchus, 23 Mongol Bannermen, and 32 Chinese Bannermen. See *China Review*, vol. vi., p. 137.

RED-CAP MAHOMMEDANS, THE : 紅帽回子. A name applied by the Chinese to the Mahommedan Tur-komans who came from Persia and other countries beyond the Caspian Sea, and were distinguished by the red fez caps they wore. See *Blue-cap Mahommedans*. 紅帽 "red caps" must not be confounded with 紅頭 "red heads," a name for certain rebels who gave considerable trouble in the Kwang-tung province during the early part of the reign of the Emperor Hsien Fêng.

RED-EYEBROWS. See *Crimson Eyebrows*.

REFORM PARTY, THE : 保國會. An association of progressive officials, who in 1898 made a strenuous effort, countenanced by the young Emperor, to reform the administration of China. They were denounced by a Censor, and some half dozen were seized and summarily executed, their leader, K'ang Yu-wei escaping on a British man-of-war.

REGISTRATION FEE. An annual and highly unpopular tax of five dollars (one dollar for "artisans and labourers"), imposed upon all British subjects residing at the Treaty Ports of China and Japan, under the Order in Council of 1865.

RESCRIPT. See *Vermilion Pencil*.

RESIDENT. The officer appointed by the Chinese Government to reside—*e.g.* in Tibet, 駐藏大臣—and look after Imperial interests.

RHYMES, THE: 韻. See *Poetry.*

RI: 里. Japanese land measure＝about $2\frac{1}{2}$ miles English.

RICE-BIRDS: 禾花雀. A species of ortolan, found in the paddy-fields of southern China, and regarded by epicures as a very delicate morsel.

RICE-CHRISTIANS. Chinese who become converts to Christianity solely with a mercenary object in view.

RICE-PAPER: 蓪 紙. The so-called "paper" used by the Chinese for pictures and artificial flowers. It is the cellular tissue of the plant called *Aralia papyrifera*, the stems of which resemble a mass of pith covered by a very thin epidermis, and are from one to two inches in diameter and several inches in length. The Chinese workmen apply the blade of a sharp straight knife to these pith-like cylinders, and, turning them around dexterously, pare them from the circumference to the centre, making a rolled layer of equal thickness throughout. This is unrolled and weights are placed upon it until it is rendered perfectly smooth and flat. Sometimes a number are joined together to increase the size of the sheets.

Also known by the fancy name 菩 提 紗 "Bôdhi Crape" or the crape of Buddha.

RIN. A thin round coin of iron or bronze, with a square hole in the middle, current in Japan. Value one-tenth of a cent.

RITES, BOOK OF: 禮 記. See *Ching.* Contains a number of rules for the performance of ceremonies and "the "guidance of individual conduct under a great variety of "conditions and circumstances."

RIYO *or* RIO: 兩—a tael. An ounce of silver (Japanese).

RIYÔBU. See *Shinto.*

ROCO. A Malayan pipe. "About the time it takes to smoke a roco"＝about 10 minutes.

ROMAN CATHOLIC MISSIONARIES. The first Arch-bishop of Peking, Jean de Montecorvino, was consecrated in 1308 and died at Peking in 1330. Among the most eminent R. C. missionaries are Matteo Ricci, *d.* 1610; Adam Schall, *d.* 1666; Ferdinand Verbiest, *d.* 1688; François Gerbillon, *d.* 1707; Joseph de Premare, *d.* 1735; Joseph de Mailla, *d.* 1748; Antoine Gaubil, *d.* 1759; Joseph Amiot, *d.* 1793, and others (see *Jesuits*).

Roman Catholicism, originally styled 耶穌會 the Jesus Association, has been known for the past two centuries as 天主教 the Heavenly-Lord Teaching. After alternate patronage and persecution, it was classed in the Sacred Edict as a "strange doctrine," but in 1899 was formally recognised by Imperial Decree, the Pope being mentioned as 教皇, and Bishops receiving equal rank with Viceroys or Governors of provinces.

ROMANISATION. A term specially reserved for the transliteration of Chinese characters in religious works, as distinct from the term Orthography *(q.v.)* which is of general application. Portions of the Bible, hymn-books, etc., have been published in "romanised," and it is held that converts learn to read these more easily than translations into ordinary Chinese characters.

RŌNIN *or* LŌNIN : 浪人—wave man. A samurai *(q.v.)* who for some offence to his superior has been dispossessed of his estate, revenue, or pay, and dismissed from service. An outcast or outlaw. [The Chinese character meaning *wave* is always used of persons in a bad sense.] The "Forty-seven Rōnin" were the retainers of a certain Daimio who had tried to slay a brother Daimio, but, failing in his attempt, was compelled to perform the *hara kiri (q.v.)*. The "forty-seven" then bound themselves by an oath to avenge their master's death, and carried out the programme by penetrating into the castle of his old enemy, where, after routing some three hundred adversaries, they discovered and slew their victim, and then proceeded to disembowel themselves upon the spot. Their graves are shewn at Tokio to this day.

In 1861, four officers of the Prince of Mito made themselves *rōnin*, and left behind them the following letter :—"We become lonins now, since the foreigner "gains more and more influence in the country, unable "tranquilly to see the ancient law violated; we become "all four lonins with the intention of compelling the "foreigner to depart."

RUNNERS: 差 役. The unpaid servants at a Chinese *Yamên.* They live upon squeezes extorted from all who are unlucky enough to get entangled in the meshes of the law; *e.g.* a warrant being issued against any one, they will report, on receipt of a bribe, that he has "absconded."

Another class of "runners" exists at Canton, namely, rowdies who smuggle ashore-opium and other goods from the river steamers on their arrival from Hongkong. As soon as the steamer comes alongside the wharf, balls of the drug, etc., etc., are thrown out by accomplices on board to these men who are waiting in readiness to receive them, and who immediately make a bolt through the crowd with their booty. The converse of this practice is not unknown—throwing dutiable goods on board a departing steamer just as she is well clear of the wharf.

SACRED CITY, THE. H'lassa or Lhassa 拉 薩, the capital of Tibet, otherwise known as Budala 布 達 拉, from the hill of that name on which stands the palace of the Dalai Lama *(q.v.).* "The Tibetans having made up their minds "to prevent us going to the Sacred City peaceably...."— *Shanghai Courier*, Nov. 1877.

SACRED EDICT: 聖 諭. Sixteen moral maxims delivered in the form of an Edict by the Emperor K'ang Hsi *(q.v.)*, and amplified into the form of moral essays under his son and successor Yung Chêng by over a hundred picked members of the Han-lin College *(q.v.)*, of whose compositions the sixteen best were selected. These were further paraphrased into simple colloquial language by Wang Yu-p'u 王 又 樸, an Assistant Salt Commissioner in Shensi. They are held to contain the very essence of Chinese ethics, and should be publicly read on the 1st and 15th of every moon in all towns and cities of the empire. The following two maxims may be taken as examples:—

No. 1. *Pay just regard to filial and fraternal duties, in order to give due importance to the relationships of life.* [These relationships are five:—(1) between sovereign and subject, (2) husband and wife, (3) father and child, (4) elder and younger brothers, (5) friends.]

No. 7. *Get rid of strange doctrines, in order to exalt the orthodox teaching.* [Among the "strange doctrines" mentioned in the accompanying paraphrase are Taoism, Buddhism, and Christianity. The orthodox teaching is of course Confucianism.]

SAGE, THE. A term commonly applied to Confucius.

SAGE, THE MODERN. K'ang Yu-wei, the Reformer, has been so called. See *Reform Party*.

SAIBANSHO: 裁 判 所—place of decision. A Japanese District Magistrate.

SAIHAI. A Japanese field-marshal's bâton.

SAKÉ *or* SAKI: 酒. (1) A fermented liquor made from

rice, and largely consumed in Japan. It contains from 11 to 17 per cent of alcohol. The *masamuné* brand is considered to be one of the most choice. (2) A wine made from white grapes.

Some of the inhabitants of Takasaki in Joshiu met together in order to see who could succeed in drinking the most *saké*. Those who could drink but one sho (about two imperial quarts) were considered to have "very poor and unhappy brains" and were not permitted to enter the ranks of the competitors. Several drank from two to three sho, but the one who bore away the prize, namely a roll of silk, was he who succeeded in putting down five sho in the short space of thirty minutes.

SAL TREE: 娑 羅 or 天 師 栗. The tree beneath which Buddha passed into Nirvana *(q.v.)*, for which, in China, the *Æsculus Chinensis* is substituted.—*Hongkong Daily Press.*

SALAAM. An Arabic term meaning "Peace be with you!" The Indian servant brings his master's "salaam" to a visitor precisely as a Chinese servant says "can see."

SALT COMMISSIONER: 鹽 運 司. The art of extracting salt from sea-water is referred by the Chinese to a Minister, named 夙 沙 氏 Su Sha Shih, who lived in prehistoric times. Salt is a Government monopoly in China, and the Commissioner is a high official charged with the collection of the revenue accruing therefrom, together with the strict repression of smuggling, which is however carried on to a very great extent.

China is divided for purposes of salt administration into seven main circuits, each of which has its own source of production. The officials controlling the administration are as a rule independent of the local authorities. These circuits or divisions are: (1) Ch'ang-lu 長 蘆, which supplies the metropolitan province and the North generally; (2) Ho-tung 河東, which supplies Shensi and part of Honan; (3) Liang-huai 兩准, which supplies Anhui, part of Kiangsu, Kiangsi and Hu-kuang; (4) Liang-cheh 兩浙, which supplies Chehkiang and the greater part of Kiangsu; (5) Fuhkien, which supplies that province and parts of the adjoining provinces; (6) Kuang-tung, which supplies the two Kuang and parts of Kiangsi and Yünnan; and (7) Ssŭch'uan, which supplies all the rest of Western China. The boundaries of each of these circuits are carefully defined, and salt produced in one circuit is not allowed to be sold or transported into another,—not, at least, under ordinary circumstances.

The system of administration is nearly the same in each of the circuits. The salt is produced in certain specified places by evaporation and boiling, from sea-water round the coast, and from brine found in wells and marshes in Ssŭch'uan and Shansi. There is no restriction on the amount or mode of production, but all the salt manufactured must be sold at a fixed rate to government officials, who establish depôts near the place of production. Its distribution is undertaken by the salt merchants, who are a body of men holding licenses or warrants 引 yin from the Salt Commissioner, if there is one, or the Viceroy or Governor who superintends that particular circuit. The quantity of salt which ought annually to pass into consumption in each circuit is roughly estimated, and enough warrants are issued to cover that amount, so that each warrant is supposed to be used every year. The warrants are perpetual, that is to say, a warrant once issued may be used over and over again, may be handed down from father to son, or may be transferred to a nominee for value. The possession of one or two salt warrants thus becomes in some places a valuable asset.

Having purchased and paid for his salt, the merchant is entitled to convey it to any part of the circuit where he thinks there is the best demand for it. But he is not at liberty to sell it direct to the consumer. As he bought it at a price fixed by the officials, so he must sell it through an agent of the Salt Administration, which also fixes the selling price. The merchant having chosen the place where he wishes his salt to be disposed of, must enter it at a sort of bonded warehouse which is established in every town of importance under the charge of a *wei-yüan* from the Salt Commissioner's yamên. The salt is stored there under the control of the *wei-yüan*, to await its turn for sale. For this purpose the merchants' names are entered in a book in order of application, and the salt is strictly disposed of in the same order. The warrants are handed in at the same time and are retained by the *wei-yüan* till the salt they cover is all cleared, upon which they are handed back and the merchant is at liberty to try another venture.

Four classes of persons are permitted to deal in salt without the otherwise necessary license, namely, those over 59, or under 16, blind people or cripples, and old women without visible means of subsistence. This enables them to accept a somewhat lower rate than the ordinary shopkeeper.

SALUTES, CHINESE. For the highest officials, three guns are given as the visitor passes through the entrance to the yamên, followed, after an almost inappreciable interval, by three more as the great gates close behind him. The salute is repeated at his departure. Lower officials receive only three guns each way.

SAMADHI. A Buddhist term, signifying a power that enables its possessor to exercise an active control over all his faculties and keep them in perfect restraint.

SAMANTA BHÂDRA. See *P'u Hsien*.

SAMISEN: 三絃—three strings. The Japanese guitar, introduced from the Loochoo Islands in the 17th cent.

SAMLEI: 鰣魚—season fish *(Alosa reevesii)*. A fish of fine flavour but full of pitch-fork bones. The character 鰣 is explained by the Chinese to signify the periodical appearance of this fish, which enters the rivers in May and returns to the sea in September. Is caught in great quantities in the Yang-tsze. An inferior kind is common at Canton, where it is known as 三黎 or 三鯬—not "三犂 three plow-shares" as Dr. Williams says—and it is from the Cantonese pronunciation of these characters that our word is taken.

SAMOVAR. A Russian tea-urn, much used in Mongolia and Siberia for keeping hot large quantities of the favourite beverage.

SAMPA. The Chinese sound of the characters 三杌 *three oars*=hong-boat *(q.v.)*. Also applied to a long shallow canoe, propelled by paddles and used for smuggling opium.

SAMPAN. A Chinese boat of any kind, short of a junk, may be so called. From the Malay *sampan*, a small boat. It is written in Chinese 三板 or "three planks;" but also 杉板, 舢舨, etc.

SAMSENG: 三生—three lives. A term commonly applied in Singapore to certain roughs or bullies who hang about processions and sacrificial feasts, and are always ready for any mischief. They are spoken of in the *China Mail* of 6th April 1877 as "fighting men." The "three lives" refers originally to the slaughter on various occasions of a duck, a fowl, and a pig; but now these rowdies are called "three-life men" from the recklessness with which they expose themselves to danger.

SAMSHOO: 三 燒—thrice fired. A general name among foreigners for Chinese fermented liquors of all kinds, but specially applied to the ardent spirit known as 燒 酒 —spirit that will burn, from its having passed thrice through the process of distillation. See *Grape* and *Wine*.

SAMSHUI: 三 水. A Treaty Port on the West River in the province of Kuangtung.

SAMURAI: 士. A general name for all Japanese entitled to wear two swords. Now called *shizoku (q.v.)*.

SAN KUO CHIH: 三 國 志. History of the Three Kingdoms or rival States, 蜀 *Shu*, 魏 *Wei*, and 吳 *Wu*, into which the empire was split up at the conclusion of the Han dynasty. Upon this History has been founded a famous historical romance, which describes at great length the various events of a whole century of strife and bloodshed, and is a prime favourite with the Chinese people.

SAN TZŬ CHING. See *Trimetrical Classic*.

SANCIAN. See *Xavier*.

SANGI: 參 議. Japanese "Secretary of State," there being one over each of the following departments:—(1) Finance, (2) Foreign Relations, (3) Home Administration, (4) War, (5) Justice, and (6) Opening up new territory.

SANG-KO-LIN-SIN'S FOLLY. The mud wall built during the war of 1860—61 to keep off the Allied Forces from the city of Tientsin by the celebrated Mongol general of that name 僧 格 林 心, who was familiarly known to the British sailor of the same period as "Sam Collinson."

SAPAN-WOOD: 蘇 木. A wood brought from Siam, Manila, and elsewhere, and used by the Chinese as a dye.

SAPÈQUE. The French equivalent of the word *cash* *(q.v.)* as used in China. From *sapek*, a coin found in Tongking and Cochin-China, and equal to about half a pfennig ($^1/_{600}$ Thaler), or about one-sixth of a South German kreutzer.

SARONG. Part of the national costume of the Malays, consisting of an oblong cloth from 2 to 4 feet in width and about 2 yards in length. The ends are sewn together, and it is then worn by both sexes as a kind of kilt, tightened round the waist by certain peculiar twists. It is invariably of a check pattern, generally in gay colours. Is either of silk or cotton, or a mixture of the two. Of cotton sarongs, the most valued come from Celebes, and are known as *Kain Sarong Bugis.* Java produces the painted cotton so much admired by the Malays. They are called *Kaiü Batak.* Of silk sarongs, some of the finest are the *Kain Mastoli* of Singapore, and the *Kain Sungkit* (silk and gold thread) of Penang and Borneo.

SATBON. Soap; from the Portuguese *sabão.* This term is heard among the Chinese in Fuhkien; and in some parts of India *sábon* is the only word used.

SATSU. Same as Kin-*satz.*

SAVVY *or* SABE. From the Portuguese *saber* to know. "My savvy"="I understand" or "I know." "That boy got plenty savvy"="That boy is no fool." See *Pidgin English.*

SAYONARA. Goodbye! [Japanese.] Used by foreigners in Japan much as *chin-chin* is in China. One event on the programme of the Yokohama Races is the "Sayonara Stakes."

SCRATCH-BACK. A small imitation, in either ivory or

bone, of the human hand with the tips of the fingers slightly bent inwards. This is attached to a slender black stick, and used by the Chinese for scratching themselves, being popularly known as a 不求人 or "won't trouble you," as with its aid even the most inaccessible parts of the back are easily reached. Also known in books as 搔具 the "scratch implement."

SCREENS: 屏門. Movable wooden screens at the entrances to Chinese houses are used to prevent the ingress of evil spirits, who are supposed to be able to advance only in straight lines.

SEAL CHARACTER: 篆字. Certain elaborate forms of Chinese writing which prevailed from about B.C. 800 to about A.D. 200, and are known to foreigners as the Greater and Lesser Seal character. The Chinese employ both these styles on their *seals*, public and private; hence our term (see *Shuo Wên*). The former was invented by a Historiographer known as 史籀 Shih Chou, and the latter, a simplified form of the other, by 程邈 Ch'êng Miao, who followed this up by the invention of the 隸 *li* script, which is again simpler and more easily written than the Lesser Seal. It was from the *li* script that the modern "clerk" style was developed about A.D. 200.

SEALS, MANDARIN. Every Chinese official of any standing has had a seal of office since the establishment of the Sung dynasty, A.D. 960. The Imperial signet is called 玉璽 and is made of jade. That of the First Emperor *(q.v.)* bore the following legend: 受命於天旣壽永昌 "Dei gratiâ; may the reign be long and glorious." The seals of the highest provincial officials are oblong and made of silver, and the impression is stamped in a mauve colour, in the preparation of which no oil is used. These are often torn by the people from proclamations and such documents, being held to be good for sore places, ulcers, etc. Officials such as the Salt Commissioner and Taot'ai have also oblong seals made of copper, all of which are called 關防; but they use vermilion moistened with oil. Below them come the Prefects and Magistrates with square seals 印, also red; below them again are the petty police magistrates with wooden seals 鈐記; and last of all the *ti-paos*, also with wooden seals called 戳子. A mandarin's seal of office is invariably placed in his wife's keeping, as very serious consequences, entailing even dismissal from office, might result from its accidental loss. All dispatches, title-deeds, and such public documents, must bear a seal, or they are not accepted as authentic. During national mourning the colour of the impressions of all seals is changed to blue.

Every official seal is made with four small feet projecting from the four corners of its face. Of these, the maker breaks off one when he hands the seal over to the Board. Before forwarding to the Viceroy of the province, another foot is removed by the Board. A third is similarly disposed of by the Viceroy, and the last by the official for whose use it is intended. This is to prevent its employment by any other than the person authorised.

SEAO HAO: 銷號. A tax levied upon all junks trading on the coast of the province of Kuang-tung, as a compromise for their being excused from going to the provincial city to pay their duties.

SEA-SLUGS. See *Bicho-da-mar*.

SECRET SOCIETIES. Are common all over China. The principal one is described under Triad Society *(q.v.)*; besides which may be mentioned the teetotal Vegetarians

在禮 of the north, in which even smoking is prohibited, the Ko-lao *(q.v.)*, the Boxers, and the Golden Orchid 金蘭 *(q.v.)* or anti-matrimonial society of the south, consisting of girls who have sworn not to marry, and even of women who have left their husbands and returned to their parents. All these are equally under the ban of the law.

SECUNNEE. Helmsman. From the Persian *sukkānī*, through the Arabic *sukkān* a helm.

SECURITY CHOPS: 保單. Documents guaranteeing indemnity from loss, usually demanded by foreign merchants when engaging Chinese compradores or other servants holding positions of trust. The guarantor who signs such a document is responsible only if the principal himself has been first sued and is unable to pay. If two or more security-men sign a chop, *each is responsible only for his own share*, and not for the whole amount. To make three men each responsible for say Tls. 3,000, the security-chop should be for Tls. 9,000; or else each man should be made to sign a separate chop for Tls. 3,000. Great caution is also necessary in the wording of these documents.

SEEDEE *or* SIDI BOYS. A name often applied on board ships in the China Seas to negro sailors in general, but really a complimentary term for African Mahommedans, its meaning being "my lord." Hence the *Cid* of Spanish history.

SEEN-SANG *or* HSIEN-SHÊNG: 先生—elder born. Foreigners call their "teachers" of Chinese by this title, which as an affix to a name is equivalent to our prefix *Mr*.

SEN: 錢. The modern Japanese term for a cent. A *Ten-po sen* is a sen coined in the year 天保 Ten-po; a *Bun-kiu sen* is of the year 文久 Bun-kiu.

SENDŌ: 舩頭. The captain of a vessel (Japanese). Generally used for sailors and boatmen.

SENG-K'OI: 薪客—newly-arrived strangers. The Chinese in Java call themselves, and are generally known, by this name.

SENYO. The son of a Malay mother and European father is so called in Java, in imitation of the Spanish *señor*. Cf. *Nonya*.

SEOUL *or* SOUL. The capital of Korea. Official names 韓陽 or 漢城, the latter from its situation on the 漢 river, and 京畿道 Kingkitao or Royal Domain.

SEPOY. An Indian soldier, dressed and drilled in European style. It is a corrupted form of the Persian word *sĭpahī* "a soldier." Absurdly explained as "three-legged," the third leg being the musket as held when standing at ease.

SERANG. A Persian word (correctly written *sarhang*) signifying "commander," "overseer," "boatswain," and used on the coast of China for the head or foreman of a crew of Malay sailors, through whom all negotiations with the crew are conducted. Also sometimes applied to Malay boarding-house keepers and others, in the sense of the American "boss."

SERES. A nation mentioned by Strabo as having first supplied silk to the ancients, and generally identified with the Chinese. The word may be compared with the Tibetan *ser* and Turki *sari* meaning "yellow."

"It seems sufficiently clear that the *Seres* mentioned by Horace, and other Latin writers, were not the Chinese."
Sir John Davis.

"The 秦 Tsins of modern Chinese are to be identified "with the Sêres of the Greeks and Romans.... The "Sêres are first found in history as a tribe of nomads

"who settled along the upper waters of the 渭 Wei about
"the ninth century before Christ. . . . They soon contrived
"to expel the decadent Kings of 周 Djow. . . . This force
"of character culminated in King 政 Ching, who bearing
"down all opposition was able to confer on himself the
"title of First Supreme Emperor of Tsin or Sêr, B.C.
"221. . . . With the death of his incapable son, the Second
"Emperor, the fabric so laboriously raised fell to the ground;
"and Sêr for the future became a mere geographical
"expression."   *T. W. Kingsmill.*

SERICANA. An old name for China. See last entry.

> But in his way lights on the barren plains
> Of Sericana, where Chinese drive
> With sails and wind their cany waggons light.
> *Paradise Lost* iii, 437.

"Barren plains" is somewhat a libel on the fertile acres
of China proper; neither would any one who had ever
seen a heavy Chinese wheel-barrow under sail be likely
to call it a "cany waggon light."

SEVEN ACCUSATIONS, THE: 七大恨 *or* 七大憾.
The seven causes of hatred against the Mings, published
in the third year of the Manchu chieftain 天命 (1618)
in vindication of the war waged against that dynasty,
which resulted in its final overthrow and the establishment of the Manchu power. They comprise charges of
frontier disturbances, violation of territory, breaches of
faith, etc., etc., and will be found in the first chapter of
the 東華錄.

SEW-TSAI *or* SIU-TS'AI. See *Hsiu-ts'ai.*

SHAKU: 尺. The Japanese foot of 10 inches = 11³/₄ inches
English.

SHÂKYAMUNI: 釋迦牟尼. From *Shâkya* (one who is)
mighty in charity, and *muni* (one who dwells in) seclusion

and silence. The favourite name among the Chinese for the great founder of Buddhism. See *Buddha*.

SHAMAN: 沙門. A Buddhist monk. Also used of Brahmans and other ascetics.

SHAMEEN: 沙面—sand flat. Formerly a mere mudbank in the river close to the city of Canton, but leased from the Chinese after the capture of that place in 1857, and formed into an artificial island with an embankment of granite all round; the expense of this ($325,000) being borne by the British and French Governments in the proportion of four to one, according to which ratio the whole area was subsequently divided between the two countries. The one-fifth which forms the French Settlement, long without buildings of any kind, is 2,850 feet in length by 959 feet greatest breadth.

Shameen was originally the great rendez-vous of flower-boats *(q.v.)*, and the adjacent quarter of the city was chiefly occupied by houses of ill fame;—a fact which probably did not escape the notice of the Chinese authorities when the island was conceded to the "outer barbarians." Hence the bad sense in which the words *shameen* are still used in the colloquial of Canton and its neigbourhood. Compare *Kou-lan hu-t'ung*.

SHAN-HAI-KUAN: 山海關. An important town on the borders of Chihli and Shingking, near the point where the Great Wall reaches the sea, and now on the line of rail which is to connect Tientsin with Newchwang.

SHANGHAI: 上海—upper sea; as distinguished from the 下洋 or "lower ocean." So called since A.D. 1079. Old names 滬 'Hu [瀆] fishing-stake [estuary], and 申 [江] the Shên [river] from the name of a man 春申君 who is said to have made the Huang-p'u. Shanghai was in existence under the Hsia dynasty, say fifteen centuries B.C. It was made a magistracy by Kublai in A.D. 1279, and was one of the five ports opened by the Nanking Treaty of 1842. Often called the "Model Settlement" *(q.v.)*, in allusion to its efficient municipal administration.

SHANGHAI'S SHAME. A title which has been applied to the Woosung Bar *(q.v.)*.

SHANG-TE *or* SHANG TI: 上 帝. The Supreme Ruler; God. This is clearly the meaning of the term in many passages in the Classics (see *Term Question*).

Also the spirits of deceased Emperors, "empereurs d'en haut" as M. Chavannes calls them. Also, according to Chu Hsi, as stated by Père Le Gall, S. J., "la vertu active du ciel matériel."

The Portuguese orthography is Xang-Ti; to which we are indebted for the following gem taken from a child's Pictorial Alphabet :—

"X is Xang-ti, a god in China believed ;

"But he's mere wood and stone, so they're sadly "deceived."

SHANS, THE. A widely-spread race, occupying the southern and western portions of Yünnan and the frontier land beyond, and known to the Chinese as 老 撾. The Shans of the border-land between Yünnan and Burmah style themselves 擺 夷. "Shan" is said to be a corruption of 暹 羅 *Sien-lo*.

SHANSI: 山 西 —west of the hills. One of the Eighteen Provinces. Said to be the original home of the Chinese people. Capital city T'ai-yüan Fu 太 原 府. Old name 晉 *Chin*.

SHANTUNG: 山 東 —east of the hills. One of the Eighteen

Provinces. Capital city Chi-(*or* Tsi-)nan Fu 濟南府.
Old name 魯 *Lu*.

SHARE (pronounced *sharry*). A Japanese term equivalent
to the French *esprit*.

SHÂSTRAS: 論. Discourses, or the philosophical section
of Buddhist literature.

SHÊ-LI *or* SHAY-LEE: 舍利. The Chinese transliteration
of the Sanskrit *s'arira*, relics, or parts of the body of a
saint, gathered together after cremation and preserved in
Buddhist temples, generally beneath a handsome marble
dagoba *(q.v.)*.

SHEEDZAI: 崽仔. Cantonese term for a "boy" *(q.v.)*
or valet.

SHENSI: 陝西—west of the passes. One of the Eighteen
Provinces. The first syllable is written *shen* to distinguish
it from Shansi, though in Mandarin the two sounds are
identical except in tone *(q.v.)*. Capital city Hsi-an Fu
(or Si-ngan Fu) 西安府. Old name 秦 *Ch'in*.

SHIBAIYA. Japanese theatres; *lit.* "turf places," so called
because the first performances were held on grass-plots.

SHIMBUN: 新文. Japanese newspapers are so called;
e.g.—Choya Shimbun.

SHIMONOSEKI, TREATY OF. Negotiated between Li
Hung-chang and the Japanese authorities after the defeat
of China by Japan in 1895. By its terms, the island of
Formosa, the Pescadores, and the Liaotung peninsula,
were ceded to Japan, and an indemnity of Tls. 200,000,000
was exacted. Russia, Germany, and France combined to
prevent the cession of the peninsula.

SHIN: 神—gods; idols. According to Mr. Kingsmill, "Shin
"represented philologically the Asuri of the older Indian
"pantheon." See *Term Question*.

SHING: 升. A Chinese measure equal to about one pint English.

The Japanese *sho* (same character) is equal to nearly two imperial quarts. See *Saké*.

SHING-KING: 盛京. The name of the capital city of the Manchurian province of Fêng-t'ien, but often used for the province itself. See *Moukden*.

SHINSHIU. Same as *Monto (q.v.)*.

SHINTŌ. See *Sintoo*.

SHIZOKU: 士族. A Japanese clan. All who bear the same surname. The vassals of the old feudal system of Japan. "The *shizoku*, who used to be supported with rice "without cultivating the land, and dressed without working "a loom, and who drank the valuable sweat and ate the "flesh of the common labourer, have been deposed from "their station by the changes of time. Their pensions have "been decreased through gradual alterations, and have "at length been converted into Government bonds..... "The *shizoku's* families number more than 500,000..... "Nine-tenths of the Government employés consist of "*shizoku*....."—*Choya Shimbun*, Sept. 1877.

Formerly known as *samurai*.

SHÔ. A Japanese musical instrument consisting of 17 pipes let into a wind-chest.

SHOE FLOWER: 扶桑. The *Hibiscus Rosa-sinensis*, L. is so called, because a kind of blacking is made from its petals.

SHOES (OF SILVER): 元寶. The common name among foreigners for the Chinese silver ingot which bears some resemblance to a native shoe. May be of any weight from 1 oz., and even less, to 50 and sometimes 100 oz.; and is always stamped by the assayer and banker in evidence of purity. Tiny *shoes* are made for sale to Europeans as charms for the watch-chain. See *Sycee*.

SHŌGUN *or* SHIOGOON: 將軍. Commander-in-chief. Same as *Tycoon (q.v.)*, and known to the Chinese as 武王 Military Ruler. The last Shōgun resigned power in 1868, and retired into private life under the name of Ichido. See *Mikado*.

SHOO KING: 書經—the Book of History. This work embraces a period extending from the middle of the 24th century B.C. to B.C. 721. It is said to have been edited by Confucius himself from then existing documents which came into his hands. See *Ching*.

SHŌ-RŌ-DO: 鐘樓. A drum tower (Japanese).

SHO-SAKAN: 小屬. The old term for Japanese Government clerks of the 2nd grade; now changed to *Ni-to-zoku* (二等屬).

SHOW *or* SHOU: 壽—old age. The character commonly seen, under its seal *(q.v.)* form, thus (壽) on Chinese saucers, vases, doors, windows, fans, shoes, and any available object. Compare *Fu*. Old age and offspring are to a Chinaman the highest of earthly blessings, ranking far above power, fame, or even wealth.

SHRIMP BOATS: 蝦狗艇. Fast-sailing boats with two masts, now chiefly used by Hongkong pilots, but formerly employed by Chinese engaged in the kidnapping trade round Macao. Sometimes called *ha-t'êng* 蝦艇.

SHROFF: 銀師 *or* 看銀先生—silver expert; a corruption of the Arabic *sarráf* "banker," common in every Indian town. Chinese employed at banks and large mercantile establishments to check all dollars which pass through the hands of the firm, and eliminate the bad ones. These men pretend to distinguish three classes of good dollars, of first, second, and third qualities; but this "mystery" of the art has been exposed over and over again by their rejection of certain dollars as first class which had been paid out as such perhaps on the previous day. Shroffing schools are common in Canton, where teachers of the art keep bad dollars for the purpose of exercising their pupils; and several works on the subject have been published there, with numerous illustrations of dollars and various other foreign coins, the methods of scooping out silver and filling up with copper or lead, comparisons between genuine and counterfeit dollars, the difference between native and foreign milling, etc. etc. The best of these is the 新增銀論.—See "The Shroff's Mystery," *China Review*, vol. III, p. 1; and *Pillar Dollar*.

"Shroffing" is now applied metaphorically to persons. A Shanghai preacher once said in the pulpit, "God will shroff you, as you shroff dollars."

SHU: 銖. A Japanese coin equal to one-fourth of a *bu*. No longer in circulation.

SHUN CHIH: 順治—favourable sway. The style of reign adopted by the first actual Emperor of the present dynasty, A.D. 1644—1662.

SHUN-NING FU: 順寧府. A Treaty Port in the province of Yünnan, on the road to Bhamo.

SHUN-PAO *or* SHÊN-PAO: 申報—Shanghai announcements; 申江 being a name for the Shanghai district. A Chinese newspaper published in Shanghai, at first under the editorship of Mr. E. Major. The title-character 報 used at one time to be fancifully written, in the style called 帖寫, with a stroke too much, presumably because some

17

celebrated calligraphist took it into his head to form it in that way. Only the other day we saw 㠯 for 以, and 仌 for 人, there being in each case an authority for such variation.

SHUO WÊN: 說文. The celebrated dictionary of the Lesser Seal *(q.v.)* character, published A.D. 100 by 許慎 Hsü Shên. It is a collection of all the Chinese characters then in existence, amounting to about 10,000, analysed by the author into their original picture elements, with a view of showing the hieroglyphic origin of the Chinese language. It was the first lexicon arranged according to radicals *(q.v.)*, for which purpose 540 were called into use. For a *Key* to this work, by means of which characters may readily be found, see *China Review*, V, p. 304.

The following table shews some of the few characters wherein any resemblance may be traced to the objects meant to be expressed:—

Shuo Wên.		*Modern.*		
日	—	日	*jih,*	the sun.
屮	—	山	*shan,*	hills.
廿	—	口	*k'ou,*	mouth.
𩾌	—	鳥	*niao,*	bird.
目	—	目	*mu,*	eye.
𠂇	—	左	*tso,*	left hand.
𠃌	—	右	*yu,*	right hand.
木	—	木	*mu,*	tree.

Unfortunately we are soon at the end of these comparatively simple hieroglyphs and have to fall back upon more far-fetched specimens, such as—

貝	—	月	*yüeh,*	moon.
車	—	車	*ch'ê,*	cart.
水	—	水	*shui,*	water.
炎	—	火	*huo,*	fire.
半	—	牛	*niu,*	ox.
井	—	井	*ching,*	a well.
臣	—	臣	*ch'ên,*	a Minister.
几	—	人	*jên,*	man.
犮	—	犬	*ch'üan,*	a dog.

The explanations given by the author of the *Shuo Wên* of many of these characters are worth noting; for instance, where he shews in 木 *a tree* that the upper curve denotes the branches, the lower curve the roots; that 牛 is like an ox's head because it has a curve which would do for the horns; that the dot in the middle of 井 *a well* is the cover; and that 臣 admirably represents the *bending body* of an officer of state in the presence of his Imperial master. So in the last instance, where he mentions that Confucius says "to look on the character for *dog* is like looking on a picture."

SHUPAN: 書辦 *or* 班. The Chinese term for the copying clerks employed at Yamêns and other public buildings. Is in use at the offices of the Imperial Maritime Customs, to express the Chinese employés whose business it is to copy Chinese documents, as opposed to the linguists *(q.v.)* who speak and write English.

SICAWEI *or* SI-KA-WEI: 徐家匯. A place near Shanghai where there is now a Roman Catholic establishment, named after the celebrated statesman and scholar 徐光啟, A.D. 1562—1633, who was formerly a supporter of the Catholic Missionaries at Peking. The last character is sometimes written 圉. The Jesuit Fathers who reside there and elsewhere in China, have recently been translating and compiling many valuable works giving accurate information on a variety of subjects connected with China, thereby recalling the glories of their illustrious predecessors of the 17th and 18th centuries.

SIEN PI. See *Hsien Pi.*

SILK. Was manufactured in China many centuries before the Christian era. Mencius *(q.v.)* said, "At fifty, no warmth without silk; at seventy, no satiety without meat." First introduced into Europe as a manufacture under Justinian in the sixth century; found its way into Sicily in the twelfth century, and was carried thence by the Saracens into Spain. Francis I. planted it at Lyons in the sixteenth century, and in 1585 it reached England from Antwerp.

Chinese silks are many of them rudely manufactured of thread, coarse and unequal, devoid of gloss, and deficient in either "tram" or "organzine," the fabrics being simply woven from the raw material as it comes reeled off the cocoons. Japan supplies a much more serviceable article, and consequently Japanese silks are now very considerably in vogue.

SILKEN CORD, THE. See *Gold, Swallowing.*

SINGAPORE. Of this name two etymologies are given, the first being the correct one. (1) *Singgha* to call at, and *poorah* a place—port of call; (2) *Singa* a lion, and *poorah* residence—abode of the Lion; so called because a prince of Palimbang (Sumatra) is said to have seen a lion at this spot and to have built a city in honour of the royal beast. *Pore* or *pur* is the Sanskrit for "town" or "city," and is a common termination in India; *e.g.* Cawnpore, the *city* of the *Khan.* The city was founded and named by Sir Stamford Raffles with the name by which the island had been known for many centuries.

SING-SONG. The pidgin-English term for Chinese theatricals, which consist chiefly of recitative.

SINK OF INIQUITY. Shanghai; see *Model Settlement.*

SINKEH: 新客—new arrivals. Immigrant Chinese are so called in the Straits. They are much looked down upon by the Babas, or Straits-born Chinese, who are very proud of their nationality as British subjects.

SINIM, THE LAND OF, or more correctly "of the Sinim." It is only a conjecture that by this term, used in Isaiah xlix. 12, is meant China; such conjecture being founded on a resemblance of the first syllable *Sin* to the name of the Chinese feudal State *Ts'in* 秦 on the north-west of the empire, the existence of which dates back as far as B.C. 847. Moreover, Ts'in appears to have been the name under which China was commonly known throughout southern Asia about that epoch.

SINOLOGUE. An advanced scholar of the Chinese language, literature, etc. From the Latin *Sinae*, called by Ptolemy the most eastern nation of the world. These people were said to dwell beyond the river Meinam (Serus), and were probably Cochin-Chinese. It has recently been objected that the word S. wears a French dress, and that to preserve uniformity, English people should say "Sinologist;" but it is highly improbable that such a change will ever be successfully introduced.

SINTOO *or* SHINTŌ: 神道. The ancient religion of Japan, i.e., worship of the Kami, or gods and spirits of all kinds. Usually spoken of by the Japanese as *Kami no michi*, the way of the gods. Was universal in Japan in the sixth century when the Buddhist propagandists arrived, and at the restoration of the Mikado in 1868 became again the state religion. There exists (1) Pure

Shintō, and (2) Riyôbu, or Twofold Shintō, which latter contains an admixture of Buddhism. This compromise was suggested in the ninth century by a clever priest who declared that the Shintō gods were but Japanese manifestations of Buddha. Later on, even Confucian doctrines were blended with Riyôbu Shintō.

The characteristics of Pure Shintō are the absence of an ethical and doctrinal code, of idol-worship, of priestcraft, and of any teachings concerning a future state. There are about 14,000 gods, the chief of which is Amaterasū, the sun, first-born of Izanagi and Izanami, the original creative principles (see *Yin* and *Yang*). Each village has its special god and *miya* or shrine. The temples contain no images etc., but only a steel mirror and a few other trifles.

SIX DOMESTIC ANIMALS. The horse, ox, sheep or goat, fowl, dog, and pig.

SLAVERY in China is now chiefly confined to the purchase of girls for use as servants in large establishments. These girls are on the whole well treated; and when they reach a marriageable age, their owners are bound by custom to see that they are suitably married and started in life on their own account.

According to the *Penal Code*, no man may sell his children without their consent; but there is no doubt that this law is not very stringently enforced.

SLEEP AND THE AWAKENING, THE: 先睡後醒. Title of an article by the late Marquis Tsêng, Minister to Great Britain, in which he strove to show that China had been dozing for centuries but would now awake and take a leading part in the world's affairs. See *Asiatic Quarterly*, January, 1887.

SLEEVE DOGS: 哈巴狗. Tiny dogs, usually of the

Peking lap-dog breed (獅子狗 *lion dog*), small enough to be carried in the wide sleeves of a Chinese gentleman's or lady's dress.

The Chinese classics are often printed in what are called *sleeve editions*, *i.e.*, in 32mo., for the use of dishonest candidates at the public examinations.

SLIPPER-BOAT: 孖舲艇 *ma-leng t'eng*. A small covered passenger-boat, very sharp-pointed at the bow, used at Canton, and somewhat resembling a Chinese slipper.

The story goes that when an application was made to the Emperor for a boat design, the Empress, who was sitting by, kicked off her slipper and bade the petitioners take that.

SMALL FEET: 小脚. Poetical name "Golden lilies" *(q.v.)*. The practice among Chinese women of cramping the feet is said by some to have originated about A.D. 970 with 窅娘 Yao Niang, concubine of the pretender 李煜 Li Yü, who was overthrown at Nanking previous to the establishment of the Sung dynasty. The lady wished to make her feet like the "new moon." Others assert that the custom was introduced by 潘妃 P'an Fei, the favourite concubine of the last monarch of the 齊 Ch'i dynasty, A.D. 501. Well-cramped feet are considered a great beauty by the Chinese; there seems to be no foundation for the generally received opinion that their object in thus laming the women was to keep them from gadding about. The Manchu or Tartar ladies have not adopted this custom, and therefore the Empresses of modern times have feet of the natural size; neither is it in force among the Hakkas or the hill tribes of China and Formosa, nor among the boating population at Canton and elsewhere. The women are curiously modest about their small feet, and can never be induced to show them bare, whereas large-footed women move about freely without shoes or stockings. The practice was forbidden in 1664 by the Emperor K'ang Hsi, but four years afterwards the prohibition was withdrawn.

An Anti-Footbinding Society was started at Canton in 1899 by K'ang Yu-wei (see *Reform Party*), under the style of 不纏足會, with a membership of 10,000, but this has probably been dropped. A similar association was recently founded in Shanghai by a number of foreign ladies, and is known as the 天足會, translated by Mr. Joseph G. Alexander as "Society of the Heavenly Foot." But 天 heaven has here nothing to do with heavenly, and simply means "natural" as opposed to "artificial," a very common usage.

SMALL KNIFE REBELS: 小刀會. A band of insurgents who in 1853 captured the city of Amoy and held it for some months. The *Small Knife Society* was said to have been a branch of the *Triad Society (q.v.)*, and was introduced into Amoy by a Singapore Chinaman in 1848. See a paper by G. Hughes in the *China Review*, vol. I., p. 244.

SMELL-DOGS. Pidgin-English for hounds which hunt by the nose.

SMELLUM WATER. Pidgin-English for *scent* of any kind.

SMOKE MOUNDS: 姻埠. Small furnaces scattered over China at 2 or 3 miles apart, and used for lighting beacon-fires on occasions of great national emergency.

SNAKE-BOAT: 扒龍 *or* 長龍—paddled, or long, dragon. A long narrow boat, of great speed, in use among smugglers and pirates in the Canton waters. Propelled by short paddles, like a canoe.

SNOWY VALLEY. A valley near Ningpo, much visited by foreigners on account of its natural beauties.

SOAP-STONE: 滑石 *or* 粉石. Steatite. So called because
it looks like soap and is so easily cut. Commonly used
by the Chinese for seals, small idols, etc.

SOHODZU *or* TZOWDZA: 車子. A Shanghai wheel-
barrow, formerly used for carrying passengers, but now
superseded by the *jinrikisha (q.v.)* as far as foreigners
are concerned.

SO-I: 簑衣—rain-clothes. The peculiar brown hairy-looking
garments, of grass or bamboo, worn by Chinese fishermen
and others in wet weather, making them "look like
hedge-hogs."

SOLA. See *Toopee.*

SON OF HEAVEN: 天子. Sometimes translated "God's
Vicegerent or Lieutenant upon Earth." The title *par
excellence* of the Emperor of China, who is supposed to
hold his commission direct from on high. "It is plain, that
"the Emperors of China, like the popes of Rome, regard
"themselves as the exponents of the will of heaven."—
Middle Kingdom. An attempt was recently made to show
that 子 is only an old nominal ending, and has nothing
to do with *son*; one writer going even as far as to say
天子 means "Little Heaven" or "Our Heaven," i.e.,
the Heaven we have to do with; but Sir E. Satow
appeared in the opposition ranks with the following
quotation from the Concordance;—天子尊無爲上
故以爲子 *the Son-of-Heaven is worthy of esteem beyond
all others; therefore Heaven makes him its son.* "Brother of
the sun and moon," and other similar titles are probably the
inventions of Europeans, in spite of the very curious passage
in the 珠事記—"The Lord of Mankind calls "the sun
his brother and the moon his sister" 人主兄日姊月,—
such terms being quite unknown to the people at large.

SONGCHING. The port of Kelchu, on the east coast of Korea in the Hamchiung province, 500 *li* north of Wonsan. It has a large trade in dried fish.

SOOCHOW CREEK: 吳淞江—Woosung river. An affluent of the Huang-p'u, dividing the British from the American Concession at Shanghai. So called by foreigners because it leads to Soochow. The Chinese say that it is the real source of the Huang-p'u *(q.v.)*.

SOUCHONG: 小種—small kind. A species of tea, of many varieties. [Cantonese.]

SOY. This word is from the Japanese *shōyu* 醬油, a kind of sauce made from fermented wheat and beans. Has been wrongly derived by some from the first syllable of Soyer, the great gastronomer of that name.

SPARK TRAGEDY. A murderous attack made 22nd August 1874 by a body of armed ruffians on the passengers and crew of the river steamer "*Spark*" plying between Canton and Macao. The "pirates" took passage from Canton in the usual way; and then seizing a favourable opportunity, killed the captain, chief officer, and purser, transferred their plunder to a junk that came alongside, and made off. The only European passenger, Mr. Mundy, escaped with frightful wounds, and subsequently published an account of the affair under the title of "Canton and the Bogue," in which he took occasion to deal with other questions equally beyond the scope of his work and the narrow limit of his experiences in China. Since that event, the hatches leading down to the quarters occupied by Chinese passengers on all the Canton river steamers are carefully padlocked soon after the vessel starts, and a quarter-master watches with a drawn sword to guard against any repetition of such an attack. Loaded rifles are also placed in the saloon for the use of European passengers.

SPELLING SYSTEM: 反切. A method of expressing the sounds of Chinese monosyllables by dividing each one into initial and final portions. *E.g.* the sound of the character 光 can be formed from the sounds of 古 *ku* and 黃 *huang* (which must of course be known) by taking the initial *k* of the first and the final *uang* of the second = *kuang*. Previous to the use of this system, which was introduced by Indian Buddhists and first employed by 孫叔然 Shun Shu-jan in the 3rd cent. A.D., the sounds of Chinese characters could only be indicated by reference to other characters of similar sound. Thus 光 would be said to = 廣, on the assumption that the latter was a known quantity.

SPIRITUALISM. Has long been practised in China, though now under the ban of the law. We read how the Emperor Wu Ti of the 2nd cent. B.C., when he lost a favourite concubine whose beauty was such that "one glance would overthrow a city, two glances a State," engaged a magician to put him in communication with her departed spirit. Darkness, as with us, seems to be indispensable at such *séances*. The attitude of the Confucianist as regards spirits has been expressed by Chu Hsi, as follows. "It is "impossible to state with absolute certainty that they do "exist, and equally impossible to maintain a contrary "opinion. As therefore definite knowledge is beyond our "reach, we may well cease to speculate further."

SPRING AND AUTUMN: 春秋. One of the *Five Classics*, consisting of the annals of the petty kingdom of Lu 魯 from 722 to 484 B.C., said to have been compiled by Confucius himself. A dry and uninteresting record, dealing chiefly with names and dates; yet it was the work by which Confucius said men would know him and condemn him; and Mencius considered it quite as important an achievement as the draining of the empire by the Great Yü. Of it he said, "Confucius completed "the *Spring and Autumn*, and rebellious ministers and "bad sons were struck with terror." From this has been evolved the famous 褒貶 "praise and blame" theory, "one word of such praise being more honourable than "an embroidered robe, and one word of such censure "sharper than an axe." In later days, however, it has rather been around the marvellous commentary, known as the *Tso Chuan (q.v.)*, that chief interest has centred.

The *Spring and Autumn* owes its name to the old custom of prefixing to each entry in the national annals the year, month, day, and *season*, in which the event recorded took place; that is to say, as a native authority puts it, "spring includes summer, and autumn winter,"—*sc.* the four seasons. The explanation that "its commendations are life-giving like autumn," is untenable. The following is a specimen of this renowned work, which, but for the famous commentary above-mentioned, would throw scant light on the history of the period referred to:—

"In the duke's sixteenth year, in spring, in the king's "first month, on the first day of the moon, there fell "hailstones in Sung. In the same month six fish-hawks "flew backwards, past the capital of Sung."

SQUEEZE. Originally, the *commission* which Chinese servants, fully in accordance with Chinese custom, charged their European masters on all ¦ articles purchased. Now extensively applied both as a verb and substantive to peculation of any kind. Cf. the Indian *dasturi*.

"Formosa has long been viewed by native officials as a "fat field for the practice of what is vulgarly known as "*squeezing*, though politely termed taxation."—*Hongkong Daily Press*, 10 Oct., 1877.

STINK-POTS: 火藥煲 *or* 雷石. Earthen jars, charged with materials of an offensive and suffocating smell, formerly much used by pirates in the China seas, and a recognised weapon in Chinese warfare. The jars, which hold about half a gallon, are filled with powder, sulphur, small nails and shot. Their tops are covered over with clay and sealed with chunam. They are then put into calico bags closed at the mouth by a stout string. Several of these are packed in a basket with a quantity of joss-stick and hoisted up to the mast-head. When about to be thrown, three or four pieces of the joss-stick are lighted and inserted in each bag; and then, when the jar is smashed by falling on the enemy's deck, the joss-stick ignites the powder and the whole thing explodes, knocking down or blinding and suffocating the bystanders. A form of stink-pot has been introduced into European warfare under the name of "asphyxiating shells."

STONE DRUMS OF THE CHOU DYNASTY: 周鼓石. Ten irregular-shaped blocks of stone discovered at Fêng-hsiang Fu in Shensi in the early part of the seventh century, which now stand inside the Confucian temple at Peking, where they were placed at the beginning of the fourteenth century. Each bears an inscription in the Greater Seal character *(q.v.)* on some subject connected either with hunting or fishing. These drums are referred to the Chou dynasty which commenced B.C. 1122; and the characters, which are now much defaced, were once filled with gold to preserve them from injury, but that

was extracted on their removal to their present site. They
are probably genuine relics of early ages.

STONE FIGURES (at Chinese tombs): 石象生. These
are connected primarily with ancient Chinese superstition
relating to invisible powers of evil and the means of
controlling them,—in fact, with fetish worship; and
secondarily with the honours paid to deceased personages
of rank in the sacrifice of domestic animals to attend
them in the world of shadows. They have been called
翁仲 *Wêng-chung*, from the personal name of one 元
Yüan, who was a famous warrior under the First Emperor
and whose statue was set up beside his grave.

STÛPA: 藪斗婆. A raised mound or tower for containing
relics—originally, the various parts (84,000 in all) of
Buddha's body. Known as *Dagop* (see *Dagoba*) in Ceylon.
The modern pagoda.

SUMPITAN. The Malay "blow-pipe" or bamboo tube
through which by a strong puff of breath the natives
discharge small arrows (sometimes poisoned) with great
force and effect. Is chiefly used for killing birds.

SUN, THE: 日. Symbol of the Male or Positive Principle
in nature. There is a story, ascribed to a writer of the
2nd cent. B.C., telling how a general of the 11th cent.
being engaged in a bloody battle and fearing that
night would interfere with his victory, raised his spear
and shook it at the declining sun, which straightway
went backwards in the sky to the extent of three
zodiacal signs.

SUNDIALS: 晷. Have been known to the Chinese for
many centuries, but it is not clear at what date they
first came into use.

SUNG DYNASTY, THE: 宋紀. A.D. 960—1280.

SUNGEI. The Malay term for a river, commonly occurring in the names of places.

SUNRISE KINGDOM. Japan *(q.v.)*.

"Neither opium-smoking nor feet-binding is known in "the Sunrise Kingdom, a fact which differentiates the "inhabitants strongly from the people of the Middle "Kingdom."—*Rev. W. E. Griffis.*

SUPERINTENDENT OF TRADE: 通 商 大 臣. A title given, since 1861, to (1) the Viceroy of Chihli, who is Superintendent of foreign trade at the noithern ports of Tientsin, Newchwang, and Chefoo; and (2) to the Viceroy of the Two Kiang, who holds the same position with regard to the remaining Treaty ports on the Yang-tsze and in the south.

SURNAMES. See *Hundred Family Names.*

SÛTRA: 經. That part of the Buddhist canon which contains the actual sayings of Shâkyamuni Buddha. Each begins with 如 是 我 聞 *this is what I have heard.* See *Tripitaka.*

SVASTIKA: 卐. A mystic emblem of great antiquity, regarded as the symbol of Buddha's heart 佛 心 印. Known among the Teutonic nations as "Thor's Hammer," and used in India in primitive times as a sign for marking cattle. Svastika is derived from *su* "well" and *as* "to be," meaning "it is well" or "so be it," and implying complete resignation under all circumstances. It is always directed towards the right; the other 卍 directed towards the left is called Sauvastika. Svastika is the first of the auspicious signs on the foot-print of Buddha; Sauvastika is the fourth. The latter, with its crampons to the left, occurs in K'ang Hsi's lexicon under radical 十 *ten* with four strokes added. It is stated to be a form of 萬 *ten thousand*, and the following verse is quoted:—

蓮 花 卍 字 總 由 天

"The lotus and the *sauvastika* must have come from heaven."

SWAN-PAN *or* SUAN-P'AN. See *Abacus*.

SWATOW: 汕頭. One of the thirteen ports opened by the Treaty of Tientsin, 1858. Originally a small fishing village, it is now a bustling town with a large export trade in sugar. All business was formerly carried on at "Double Island," where may be seen the ruins of mercantile houses, godowns, etc., and which is still inhabited by foreign pilots and their families; but in 1862 the British Consulate was opened at Kak-chio 角石 on the opposite side of the harbour to the town of Swatow. Our word is the local pronunciation of the Chinese characters.

SWORD-WRACK. An absurd name for a rowdy gang of Chinese who some years ago gave great trouble at Newchwang. The term is 刀匠兒 *sword-smith*, which was evidently misinterpreted as 刀架兒 *sword-rack*, the two Chinese expressions being identical in sound. The *w* was probably added by the "devil."

SYCEE: 細絲—fine silk. Chinese lump silver is so called, because, if pure, it may be drawn out under the application of heat into *fine silk* threads.

Another explanation says that the term originated in the five northern provinces, as follows. When the Shansi bankers melt silver into ingots, after it has been liquefied and poured into the mould, and before it has again solidified, the mould is lightly tapped, when there appear on the surface of the silver fine, silk-like, circular lines. The higher the "touch" of the metal, the more like fine silk are these circlings on the surface of the silver.

Hence ingots of full quality are classified as sycee. See *Shoe*.

A wag has remarked—

> Some ask me what the cause may be
> That Chinese silver's called *sycee*.
> 'Tis probable they call it so
> Because they *sigh* to *see* it go.

Must not be confounded with the Indian word *syce*, which means "a groom."

SZECHUEN *or* SSŪ-CH'UAN: 四 川 —four streams. The largest of the Eighteen Provinces. Capital city 成 都 府 Ch'êng-tu Fu. Old name 蜀 *Shu*.

TA! TA! 打 打 —strike! strike! A common Chinese cry in a riot or other disturbance, when violence is intended. Foreign travellers and sportsmen have not unfrequently heard this threat directed against themselves; and on the occasion of the Tientsin Massacre, it is said that the whole street in which stood the establishment of the Catholic sisters resounded with the ominous word.

TA CH'IN *or* TA TS'IN: 大 秦. A country mentioned on the Nestorian Tablet *(q.v.)* as the seat of the Luminous Teaching or Christianity, and further treated in Chinese accounts of foreign countries. It had been identified with various regions by various writers, until Professor Hirth settled the question by showing in his "China and the Roman Orient" that the term could only refer to Syria.

TA JEN: 大 人 —great man. The title of Chinese officials from Taot'ais upwards; in some cases equivalent to "His Excellency."

TABASHEER. A siliceous concretion found inside the joints of the bamboo and employed by the Chinese as a medicine.

TABIK. The Malay salutation = Salaam!

18

TABLET OF YÜ: 神禹牌 *or* 岣嶁石—the Kou-lou stone, i.e., the stone which formerly stood on the Kou-lou peak of Mount 衡 Hêng in the modern province of Hupeh. It is said that when the Great Yü 大禹 (B.C. 2278) rested from his labours of draining off the waters of the Chinese deluge (洪水), he recorded the event upon a tablet of stone and placed it upon the Kou-lou peak. Ssŭ-ma Ch'ien, the historian, passes it over in silence, but it appears to have been mentioned by a Taoist mystic in the 1st cent. A.D. The spot was visited by the great Han Yü who died in 824, and again by Chu Hsi who died in 1200, but neither of them could find the tablet. It was finally discovered on another peak in 1212 A.D., more than three thousand years afterwards. Imitations of this tablet are to be seen at Wu-ch'ang Fu opposite Hankow, and in the Yu-lin temple near Shao-hsing Fu in Chêhkiang; but the inscription on the original stone, which has long since disappeared, is believed by many to have been nothing more nor less than a gross forgery of modern times. For translations by Dr. Legge and Ch. Gardner, see *China Review*, vol. II., p. 300.

It may perhaps be worth noting that the identification of the so-called "tadpole" characters *(q.v.)* in which this famous inscription is written has not been carried out with perfect consistency. In the original there are no duplicates, yet in the modern transcription we find 嶽 twice over, and 承 once by itself and once in composition where it would be quite impossible for any except an enthusiast to detect the identity of the two. Besides this, the formation of these characters is such as to leave no doubt that they were traced with a brush, and not with the stylus employed until about two centuries B.C. Rubbings of the Tablet may be seen in Legge's *Chinese Classics*, III, Pt. I, 73; in the Journal of the North China Branch of the Royal Asiatic Society for 1868; and in No. 3, Vol. III, of *The Far East* (New Series).

TABOO, TO: 把持. A term used to express the custom, common among Chinese merchants, of combining against and refusing to trade with any unpopular firm. It is also employed in reference to names which may not be written or uttered, in which case the Chinese equivalent is 諱. The word is of Polynesian origin and is also in use among the Maoris.

TADPOLE CHARACTER: 蝌蚪字. The ancient form of Chinese characters as seen, for instance, on the Tablet of Yü *(q.v.).* So called by the Chinese from their resemblance to tadpoles swimming about in water.

TAEL: 兩—an ounce (of silver)=579.84 *grs.* From the Hindu "tola," through the Malayan word "tahil."

16 tahil = 1 kati.

100 kate =.1 pîkul.

40 pîkul= 1 kôian.

A *tael* is merely an ounce weight of pure silver; there is no such coin. It is not however a uniform weight, neither is the bullion of uniform touch or purity. Thus *Tls.* 100 of the standard weight=only *Tls.* 98 of the *k'u p'ing* or Treasury scale, while they= *Tls.* 102 of the Shanghai scale.

TAGAL *or* TAGALO. One of the dialects of the Philippine Islands, of essentially Malayan character but differing considerably from the Malay language as heard in the Straits' Settlements. Is spoken in Manila.

TAH. A Pagoda *(q.v.).* 塔 *t'ap*=tope.

TAIFOO: 大夫. The Chinese term in the north of China

for a medical man, and thus commonly used among foreigners.

TAIFOO: 大副—great assistant. The name in use among Chinese sailors employed on foreign coasting-vessels to designate the Chief Officer.

TAIKONG *or* TOKONG: 舵工—steersman. A head boatman. Used in the south of China, and equivalent to *lowdah (q.v.)* in the north.

TAI-MUNG. A small lightly-built, lorcha-rigged Chinese war-junk.

TAIPAN: 大班—great manager. The head of, or partner in, a foreign house of business. The beggars and little boys all over the south of China shout "Taipan!" "Taipan!" to any foreigner from whom they wish to extract a gratuity, so general is the belief that every foreigner in China must necessarily be engaged in trade. Formerly the title applied to all foreign Consuls.

T'AI-P'ING *or* TAE-PING: 太平—great peace. The name chosen by the so-called Long-haired Rebels 長毛賊 for the new dynasty which, but for the assistance rendered by Colonel Gordon to the Imperial side, would in all probability have been established. The rebellion that goes by this name broke out in the south of China in 1850, under the leadership of Hung Hsiu-ch'üan 洪秀全, who pretended that he had a mission from God and called himself the Heavenly Prince 天王. As it spread northwards, various large cities fell into the hands of the rebels, among others Nanking, which the Heavenly Prince at once consecrated as his capital. These, however, were gradually recovered by the exertions of the Ever Victorious Army *(q.v.)*, and the rebellion was finally crushed by the re-capture of Nanking in July 1864, a day or two before which the Heavenly Prince put an end to his life by poison.

T'AI-T'AI: 太太. The title given to the wife of any *official* who wears a button. We have heard of a missionary lady who always insisted on being thus addressed by her servants, to the no small amusement of the latter. One of the proper Chinese designations for a lady, whose husband does not happen to be an official, is 娘娘 *niang-niang*.

T'AIWAN: 臺灣—(1) extensive bay; (2) terraced bay. The island of Formosa *(q.v.)*, once known as Kelung *(q.v.)*. From its growing importance it was erected into a 19th province, but after the war of 1894—5 it was ceded to the Japanese. "The Chinese name of it, "Taiwan, or Bay of the Raised Terrace, probably refers "to the square flat-roofed block house, Fort Zelandia, "built by the Dutch when they were in possession of "the island, and which is now a mark for vessels making "the anchorage at the capital, Taiwan-fu."—*Herbert J. Allen*.

T'aiwan (now T'ainan) Fu was one of the thirteen ports opened to trade by the Treaty of Tientsin, 1858.

TAKOW: 打狗—beat the dog; a corruption of the original name 打鼓 beat the drum,—from the Chinese name for Apes' Hill, derived from the beating of the waves upon its rocks. The port of the city of T'aiwan Fu, in South Formosa. Opened to trade by the Treaty of Tientsin, 1858, but not formally occupied until 1864.

TAKU: 大沽. A small village at the mouth of the Peiho or northern river, near which were situated the celebrated forts passed by the allied forces in 1858 and taken in 1860, a severe repulse having been sustained there in

1859. The new forts now erected on the spot are armed with Krupp guns.

TA LIEN WAN: 大連灣 *or* 大例俺灣. A bay at the southern extremity of the Liaotung peninsula, leased to Russia, with Port Arthur, in 1898. See *Dalny*.

TALAPOIN. A Buddhist priest is so called in Burmah and Siam. In the presence of women or in the street, the phoongye *(priest)* always has a fan to screen his face. This fan is made from the leaf of the Tala-pat palm, with a handle shaped like an S. Hence, Buddhist priests have been termed *Talapoins*.

TAMASHĀ. An Arabic word meaning "entertainment," "show," "spectacle," etc. Often used in the general sense of "function."

TAMERLANE. See *Timour*.

TAMSUI: 淡水—fresh water; also known as 滬尾. A port at the northern end of the island of Formosa, opened to trade by the Treaty of Tientsin, 1858. Bombarded by the French in 1884. "It is an uninteresting place."— *Chronicle & Directory for China, Japan, etc.: 1877.*

T'ANG DYNASTY: 唐朝. A.D.618—907. The Elizabethan age of Chinese literature. Chinese in the south of China still call themselves "Men of T'ang." See *Tōjin*.

TANGO. A Korean coin, 6 parts copper to 4 parts lead, issued in 1883 and intended to be legal tender for 5 of the old coinage, 105 being equal to the Mexican dollar. Their value has now fallen to over 200 per dollar.

TANGRAM. A very uncommon name for the familiar Chinese puzzle in seven pieces (七巧)—five triangles, a square, and a lozenge.

TANGUT *or* TANGOUT: 西夏. An ancient kingdom, which existed from A.D. 1032 to 1227 and occupied what is now known as the province of Kansuh. It was founded by Chao Yüan-hao, who invented a written language identified by the late Professor Déveria with the unknown script on the gate at the pass beyond Peking. The name Tangut is earlier; it appears in an inscription dated 734.

TANHA. The Buddhist "will to live," or force which, under the guidance of Karma, causes the production of every new being. See *Buddha*.

TANKA : 蛋 家—egg people. The boat population of Canton; so called from the name of a tribe, and not from the shape of their boats, now known as "egg-boats." They are the descendants of an aboriginal people, driven before the advance of Chinese civilisation to live in boats upon the river, being for centuries forbidden by law to live ashore. The Emperor Yung Chêng (1730) allowed them to settle in villages in the immediate neighbourhood of the river; but they were then, and are still, excluded from competition for official honours, and are forbidden by custom to intermarry with the rest of the people.

TAO : 道—the Way, the eternal Way, as Lao Tzŭ expressly tells us, and not the way which can be walked upon (see next entry). Chuang Tzŭ says, "What there was "before the universe was Tao. Tao makes things what "they are, but is not itself a thing."

"When the subjective and objective are both without "their correlates, that is the very axis of Tao. And when "that axis passes through the centre at which all infinities "converge, positive and negative alike blend into an "infinite One."

TAOISM : 道 教. A system of philosophy founded by Lao Tzŭ *(q.v.)* some six centuries before the Christian era.

Has been styled *Rationalism* and *Naturalism* by various writers. Its leading doctrines teach man that for purposes of this life his soul was withdrawn from existence as a unit in an infinite mass of perfect vitality which circles unceasingly in space around the polar star. They further teach how, by a course of non-resistance and inaction, to bring his moral and physical natures into perfect harmony with their environment, the result being a complete victory over all obstacles to human happiness and even over death itself. Thus death, which would otherwise mean annihilation, becomes merely a re-absorption into the Central Source or First Cause. About the time of the Han dynasty *(q.v.)* pure Taoism became corrupted by an admixture of superstition in the form of alchemy and a search for the elixir of life. A severe struggle followed upon the subsequent introduction of Buddhism, but the two religions soon began to flourish peaceably side by side, and even to borrow from each other, so that at the present day many dogmas and ceremonies are preached and practised promiscuously by priests of either faith. Both are really under the ban of the law (see *Sacred Edict*), and both are professedly despised by disciples of the pure ethics of Confucius. Thus it is always necessary to distinguish between the Taoism of today and that of its founder two thousand and more years ago. In one passage, alluding to the pure Taoism of Lao Tzŭ, Chu Hsi says, "His teaching may be summed up as the "*Doctrine of Surrender to others.*" In another place, dealing with modern Taoism, he writes thus:—"Buddhism "stole the best features of Taoism, Taoism stole the worst "features of Buddhism; it is as though the one stole a "jewel from the other, and the loser re-couped the loss

"with a stone." He also said "The teaching of Lao Tzŭ
"aims only at the preservation of man's vitality."

The members of the Taoist Trinity, 三清 or Three
Pure Ones, are Lao Tzŭ, P'an Ku, and Yü Huang Shang
Ti. There is also a trinity of the Primordial Powers
三元, which are Heaven, Earth, and Man.

TAO-SZE *or* TAO-SSŬ: 道士. Taoist priest (see last
entry). The celebrated "Zadkiel," who publishes an annual
almanac in which the principal events of the coming
year are foretold, calls himself a "Tao sze" of the "Most
Ancient Order of the Svastika" *(q.v.).* Taoist priests are
generally considered by the Chinese to be able to perform
miracles and work cures (see *Mesmerism*).

TAO-T'AI: 道台. Called by foreigners the Intendant of
a Circuit (of Prefectures), into a number of which each
province is subdivided, and wherein he usually has general
control over all affairs civil and military, subject of course
to the approval of the *Fu-t'ai* or (and) *Tsung-tu (q.v.).*

TAO TÊ CHING: 道德經. A small treatise, consisting
of only 5,321 characters, which since A.D. 666 has been
generally accepted as the canon of Taoism, and has been
attributed, but on insufficient grounds, to Lao Tzŭ himself,
being in all probability a work of the second or third
century after Christ. About a twentieth part of it consists
of what were perhaps genuine utterances by Lao Tzŭ,
handed down by tradition. It has nothing whatever to
do with the Taoist religion of modern times. It is quite
unknown to the people at large, and is very widely
unread by native scholars who one and all regard it as a
spurious production of the Han dynasty. It is never once
mentioned by Confucius or Mencius, or even by Chuang
Tzŭ, the great disciple of Lao Tzŭ, whose writings are

devoted exclusively to the elucidation of Tao as taught by his Master and who flourished as late as the 4th and 3rd cent. B.C. Yet this precious work has been included in the *Sacred Books of the East*. The following are among the intelligible specimens of this otherwise obscure work :—

"To the good, I would be good. To the not-good, I "would also be good,—in order to make them good. To "the faithful, I would be faithful. To the not-faithful, I "would also be faithful,—in order to make them faithful.

"The truth is not agreeable. That which is agreeable "is not the truth. The good do not argue. Those who "argue are not good. The wise make no display of their "wisdom. Those who make such display are not wise."

Some enthusiasts have found the word *Jehovah* in the following :—

"That which when looked for eludes the sight is called "*I* 夷 the Invisible. That which when listened for eludes "the ear is called *Hi* 希 the Inaudible. That which when "felt for eludes the touch is called *Wei* 微 the Intangible. "These three cannot be thoroughly investigated. Therefore "they may be brought together under one denomination." [I-hi-wei=Jehovah.]

TARTARS *or* TATARS: 達子 *or* 達達兒 *or* 韃靼, etc., etc. Vaguely applied to the various tribes inhabiting the steppes of Central Asia, and to the Manchus, the founders of the present dynasty, that portion of Peking in which the latter reside being known as the Tartar City. "The Revolt of the Tartars" is a magnificent essay by De Quincey, describing the flight in A.D. 1771 of a whole Tartar nation from Russia to China, where, after endless sufferings on the way, the remnant of their host was received back into the fold by the Emperor Ch'ien Lung himself. These Kalmuck Tartars had been incorporated into the Russian empire in 1616, and their migration was a real one; the details, however, and especially the numbers, were supplied from the author's own imagination.

TARTAR-GENERAL: 將 軍—Commander-in-chief. The Manchu *(q.v.)* commanders of Bannermen garrisons, stationed at certain of the most important points of the Chinese Empire, are so called. Their presence is meant as a check upon the action of the civil authorities. Strictly speaking, they rank with but before the Viceroy; practically, their ranks are regarded as equal.

TA TS'IN. See *Ta Ch'in.*

TA-TSING *or* TA-CH'ING DYNASTY: 大 清 朝—the Great Pure dynasty. The name of the present or Manchu dynasty. Actually established 1644. Is considered remarkable amongst the Chinese for the mildness of its Penal Code.

TATHAGATA *or* JULAI: 如 來 佛. A name of Gautama Buddha, implying that he came in the same manner as all previous Buddhas.

TAU-KWANG *or* TAO-KUANG: 道 光—glory of right principle. The style of reign adopted by the Emperor who ruled China from 1821 to 1851.

TEA: 茶 (book name 茗). Introduced into Europe towards the close of the 16th century under the name *tcha* (which is still retained in the Portuguese language, less the initial *t—cha*) or *chaw*, the former being the Cantonese pronunciation of the Chinese term. First taken to England in the 17th century. The word *tea* is from the Amoy and Swatow readings of the character 茶, namely *tay*; and thus it was originally pronounced:—

That excellent, and by all Physitians approved, China Drink, called by the
Chineans *Tcha*, by other Nations *Tay* alias *Tee*, is sold at the Sultaness Head,
a cophee house in Sweetings Rents, by the Royal Exchange, London.

The Weekeley Newes, 31 Jan. 1606.

> Here thou, great ANNA! whom three realms obey,
> Dost sometimes counsel take—and sometimes *tea*.
>
> *Pope.*

By degrees, the word came to be used in England
of any infusion; *e.g.*, cowslip tea, linseed tea, beef
tea, and—

> Why will Delia thus retire?
> Why so languish, live away?
> Whilst the sighing crews admire,
> 'Tis too late for hartshorn *tea*.

Cowper, in his *Task*, alludes to tea as—

> .... the cups
> That cheer but not inebriate ....

and Churchill, in *The Ghost*, thus refers to the old custom
of foretelling events by tea-leaves:—

> Matrons, who toss the cup, and see
> The grounds of Fate in grounds of Tea.

The best pun on the word is contained in a line from
Virgil's eighth *Eclogue*—

> Te veniente die, te decedente canebat,

quoted in this sense by Dr. Johnson.

The growth of the China tea trade may be illustrated
as follows:—In the year 1678, the East India Company
carried to England as a speculation 4,713 *lbs*. In 1760
the amount had increased to over 2,000,000 *lbs*. In
1780, it was upwards of 20,000,000 *lbs*. In 1869, it was
203,753,000 *lbs*, more than half being taken by Great
Britain and its possessions.

TEA-BOAT. Another name for the *Hotow (q.v.)*.

TEA-CLIPPER. A fast-sailing ship, built to carry tea from
China to London, with special reference to the great

annual Ocean Race *(q.v.)*. No passengers were taken, every available space being filled with tea and all the energies of the crew concentrated upon the race, the prize for which consisted in a high premium paid upon the tea carried by the winning vessel.

TEA-GOBBERS. A slang name for tea-tasters or Chaaszes *(q.v.)*.

TEA-POY *or* TEPOY: 茶几. A small table, light and handy, convenient for tea or other drinks. From *tea* and the Latin *podium*, through the French *appui* (compare *hodie* and *aujourd'hui*), or the Spanish *apoyo* a support. The form "tepoy" is common, but of course incorrect. Cf. the Persian *tinpāe* three-footed; *sc.* a tea-poy.

"A nest of four tea-poys costs from $5 to $12."— *Treaty Ports.* [Tea-poys are always made in sets or nests of so many different sizes, the smaller fitting closely inside the larger.]

TEE-TAI *or* T'I-T'AI: 提台. A high provincial official in charge of the military administration of his province as regards native troops, the Manchu force being under the exclusive command of the Tartar General *(q.v.)*.

TELEGRAPHY. As it would be impossible to telegraph Chinese characters, the following method has been devised. Six thousand eight hundred and ninety-nine leading characters have been ranged under numbers 0001—6899, and the transmission of messages is carried on as with an ordinary cypher code. This system is said to have been the invention of a Frenchman named Viguier, of the Imperial Maritime Customs.

TEMPLES. The general name in use for all kinds of Chinese places of worship. May be roughly distinguished as follows:—

寺—Buddhist: always monasteries.

庵— do. generally nunneries.

堂— do. either monasteries or nunneries.

觀—Taoist:[1] either monasteries or nunneries.

宮—(1) Taoist: always monasteries. (2) Spiritual shrines of Emperors 萬壽宮, of Confucius 學宮, and of other deceased worthies.

廟—(1) generic term; (2) large Buddhist temples dedicated to various deities and *uninhabited by priests*, roadside shrines, etc., etc.

祠—the ancestral halls of private individuals.

Buddhist monasteries are also known as 蘭若僧迦藍林, etc., etc. All temples, of no matter what denomination, must exhibit on the altar a tablet inscribed with the words 萬萬歲爺 "Lord of ten thousand times ten thousand years," *i.e.*, the Emperor, as a proof that religious convictions are not allowed to interfere with political fidelity. Buddhist priests shave the entire head; Taoist priests do not. Red walls imply that the temple was founded by Imperial sanction. The huge figures at the gates of an ordinary Buddhist monastery are two door-keepers, one on either side; and further on, the four Heavenly Kings, who are set there to guard the place from evil demons. The first shrine contains images of the Three Precious Ones, the Buddhas past, present, and to come, otherwise known as the Buddhist Trinity *(q.v.)*; the second contains a dagoba which covers some relic of Buddha; and the last a figure of Kwan-yin, the Chinese goddess of mercy.

The Confucian Temple 文廟 is to be found in every

---

[1] Occasionally occupied by Buddhist priests, having passed into their hands by sale or by the expulsion of the Taoists.

Prefectural and District city, and in every market-town throughout the empire. Its walls are generally red, which was the official colour under the Chou dynasty. It contains commemorative tablets of Confucius and of a large number of scholars of later ages whose writings have tended towards elucidating or disseminating the teachings of the great Sage.

TEMPO: 天保—may Heaven protect. A Japanese oval bronze coin, sixteen and a fraction being equal to 1 *bu.*

TENNO: 天皇—Heavenly ruler. A title of the Mikado *(q.v.).*

TENSHI: 天子—Son of Heaven. A title of the Mikado *(q.v.).* Cf. *Son of Heaven.*

TEPO. See *Ti-pao.*

TEPOY. See *Tea-poy.*

TERM QUESTION, THE. A bitter controversy which has raged for many years past among the various sects of missionaries as to the correct rendering of "God" into Chinese. The first difficulty arose between the Jesuits *(q.v.)* on the one side and the Dominicans and Franciscans on the other, the latter objecting to the use of such terms as 天 *T'ien* "Heaven" and 上帝 *Shang-ti* "Supreme Ruler" as representing the material heavens and the spirits of deified Emperors instead of the true God. The question was referred first to the Emperor K'ang Hsi, whose decision favoured the idea that 天 was the Supreme Being; and then to the Pope, the final result being that Clement XI published in 1704 a decree to the effect that 天主 *T'ien Chu* "Lord of Heaven" was henceforth to be the Catholic term for God, and such it has remained to the present day. The Roman Catholic religion had previously been known as 耶穌會 the Jesus Association (see *Protestant Missionaries*); and Ricci, not venturing to risk a borrowed term for God, coined the expression 陡斯, the sounds of which were meant to represent the Latin *Deus*.

As regards the Protestant difficulties on this point, Dr. Morrison gave his preference to 神 *Shin*, the common name for the numerous gods and P'u-sas *(q.v.)* of the modern Chinese Pantheon, in the hope of convincing the Chinese "that their ideas of *Shin* are erroneous." In this he has been followed by many, who object to the use of *Shang-ti* on the ground that "the early sovereigns "of the Chinese worshipped the spirits of their deified "ancestors" under this term. Sir J. Bowring suggested Θ, the first letter of the Greek Θεός "God," and some Protestants have agreed to adopt the Roman Catholic *T'ien Chu*; but the learning of the missionary phalanx has now for many years been chiefly arrayed on the side of *Shang-ti*. Other terms used by the Chinese in the sense of God, Providence, the Creator, etc., are 天公, 太上, 無假, 造化者, 皇天.

To outsiders, the discussion presents at least one feature of absurdity; namely, that every newly-arrived missionary *adopts* whatever term may be in force with his own party on the mere assumption that it is the right one—an assumption too that he rarely if ever departs from in after life. In fact, to parody the words of a great teacher, mere accident has decided which of these terms is the object of his reliance; and the same causes which make him a *Shinist* in Ningpo, would have made him a *Shang-ti-ite* in Canton or Peking.

[At a prayer-meeting where missionaries of different sects were collected, the minister at whose house the gathering took place thanked God for the abundant blessing which had everywhere followed on the use of the term *Shang-ti*. His brethren—those at least of the number who used *Shin*—though prevented by decorum from rising from their knees, testified their disapproval by audible coughs.—*Edinburgh Review*, No. 300].

TERRA JAPONICA. See *Cutch*.

THEATRE. Omitting all mention of the so-called "pantomimes" of the Confucian period, the modern Chinese drama is believed to date only from the 13th cent. A.D., when Mongol Emperors were occupying the throne of China. Under the T'ang dynasty, 7th to 10th cent., a kind of operatic performance with music and song had been much in vogue, and from this the present drama may well have been developed, though the connecting links have not as yet been traced out. Chinese plays are either *civil* or *military*, in reference to the more or less polished style employed. Tragedies and farces are common to these two classes, the military plays being further characterised by greater rapidity of action. The actors are all male, no women having been allowed to appear since the time of the Emperor Ch'ien Lung *(q.v.)* whose mother was an actress. They are a tabooed class, and even their descendants down to the third generation are disqualified for an official career. Their various *rôles* are classified as follows, each actor being called upon to perform only such parts as are comprised under the class to which he particularly belongs:—

(1) *Shêng* 生.

    a. As the Emperor, or heavy father.

    b. As successful general, or rising statesman.

    c. As "walking gentleman."

(2) *Ching* 淨.

The villain of the piece. Generally some rebel chieftain or daring outlaw.

(3) *Tan* 旦.

   a. As Empress, or aged dame.

   b. As respectable middle-aged lady.

   c. As fast young lady of the period.

   d. As servant-maid.

(4) *Ch'ou* 丑.

The low-comedy man or woman.

The stage has no curtain, and no scenery. The orchestra is on the stage itself, behind the actors. There is no prompter, and no call-boy. Stage footmen wait at the sides to carry in screens etc. to represent houses, city walls and so on, or hand cups of tea to the actors when their throats become dry from vociferous singing. Dead people get up and walk off the stage; or while lying dead, contrive to alter their faces, and then get up and carry themselves off. There is no interval between one play and the next following, which probably gave rise to the erroneous belief that Chinese plays are long, the fact being that they are very short. According to the Penal Code *(q.v.)* there may be no impersonation of Emperors and Empresses of past ages, but this clause is now held to refer solely to the present dynasty.

THOUSAND CHARACTER ESSAY: 千字文. A piece of composition, containing exactly 1000 *different* words arranged in intelligible though disconnected sentences. Was put together in a single night by Chou Hsing-ssŭ 周興嗣, a distinguished scholar of the 6th century A.D., his hair turning white under the effort. Hence the essay (and even the writer) is often spoken of as 白首文 or Essay of the White Head. Is the second primer put into the hands of a Chinese schoolboy (see *Trimetrical Classic*), and is studied more for the sake of gaining a knowledge of its 1000 characters than for any useful information to be found therein. The following is a specimen:—

> Like arrows, years fly swiftly by:
> The sun shines brightly in the sky;
> The starry firmament goes round;
> The changing moon is constant found.
> The heat remains, the fuel spent—
> Be then on time to come intent.
> A dignity of mien maintain,
> As if within some sacred fane.
> Adjust your dress with equal care
> For private as for public wear;
> For all men love to crack a joke
> At ignorant and vulgar folk.

[There is also a *Thousand Character Essay* for girls. See *China Review*, vol. II., p. 182.]

THREE-CHARACTER CLASSIC. See *Trimetrical Classic*.

THREE TEACHINGS, THE, *or* THE THREE *KIAO*: 三教. A collective term for Confucianism, Buddhism, and Taoism; that is, the ethics of Confucius, and the unorthodox religions of Buddha and Lao-tzǔ *(q.v.)*.

A wit has remarked that the Chinese have in reality 四教 or four *kiao*, the fourth being 睡覺 "sleep," 覺 in this expression having precisely the same sound in Mandarin as 教.

THRONELESS KING, THE: 素王. A name first given by Chuang Tzǔ, 4th and 3rd cent. B.C., to the man who applies to all mundane affairs the great principle of Inaction. The term is now associated with Confucius, chiefly from a passage in the 列國志, Bk. 78: 水精之子繼衰周而素王 "the son of crystal shall succeed "the decayed Chows and be a throneless king." The allusion is to his moral sway.

THUG. A Hindi word, pronounced *Tug*, signifying "deceiver," and applied to assassins of a peculiar class who first gain the confidence of their victims and then take a favourable opportunity of strangling and robbing them.

TIAO: 吊. Properly speaking a string of 1000 cash=about one dollar, but varying in different places.

TIBET: 西藏, or under the Ming dynasty 烏斯國. "The name Tibet, by which since the days of Marco "Polo the country has been known in European geography, "is represented in Chinese by the characters *T'u-pêh-t'êh* "圖伯特 T'ubod, intended probably to reproduce the "sound of the appellation given to it among the Mongols." —*Mayers*.

Dr. Williams says the word is derived from *Tupo*, country of the Tu, a race which overran that part of the world in the 6th century.

TICAL. A Siamese silver coin equal to about 60 cents. The new *tical* has a triple umbrella on one side and an elephant on the other.

TIC-A-TAC. A kind of Chinese boat.

TIENTSIN: 天津, being elliptical for 天河之津 the ford of the Heavenly River. One of the thirteen ports opened by the Treaty signed there in 1858. The foreign settlement, situated on the right bank of the Peiho at the outskirts of the town, is called 紫竹林 *Tzŭ-chu-lin*, grove of red bamboos, and was described in the *Shanghai Courier* of 15 Oct. 1877 as "a very frequented spot, to "which sailors are in the habit of resorting to get drunk."

TIENTSIN MASSACRE. On the 21st June 1870, the Roman Catholic cathedral and the establishment of sisters

of mercy at Tientsin, the French Consulate and other
buildings, were pillaged and burnt by a mob composed
partly of the rowdies of the place and partly of soldiers
who happened to be temporarily quartered there. All the
priests and sisters were brutally murdered, as also the
French Consul and his chancelier, another French official
and his wife, besides several other foreigners. For this
outrage a large indemnity was exacted, the Prefect and
Magistrate were banished, and the then Superintendent
of Trade, Ch'ung-hou, was sent to France with a letter
of apology from the Emperor.

The Chinese at Tientsin had been previously irritated
beyond measure by the height to which, contrary to their
own custom, the cathedral towers had been carried; and
rumours were afloat that behind the lofty walls and dark
mysterious portals of the Catholic Foundling Hospital,
children's eyes and hearts were extracted from still
warm corpses to furnish medicines for the barbarian
pharmacopœia.

TIFFIN. The mid-day meal; luncheon. From the Persian
tafannun. There is a strange similarity between this
word and the north-country *tiffing,* which means to take
a snack at any odd hour between regular meals.

TIGERS. Chinese soldiers are sometimes so called from
the tiger's head on their shields, painted with a huge
gaping mouth and eyes, and intended to strike terror into
the hearts of their enemies. The tiger is the Chinese "King
of beasts," as shown by the markings on the forehead
which run into a very close imitation of the character
王 *wang,* a king. This character is also reproduced on
the shields above-mentioned. The soldiers are occasionally
dressed in imitation tiger-skins, with tails and all complete;

and yell as they advance to battle, in the hope that their cries will be mistaken for the tiger's roar.

TILLA. A word used in Central Asia for about ten shillings-worth of silver. ? Tael.

TIME. See *Year*, *Moon*, etc.

TIMOUR: 鐵木兒. The great Mongol conqueror, a Turk by descent, and son of a Governor of the province of Kesh. Was called Timurlenc, "Timour the lame," from a defect in his gait caused by a wound received in battle. Hence the corrupted form of his name, Tamerlane. Timur, in a Turkish dialect, means iron, which sense is preserved in the first Chinese character employed as above. Born A.D. 1333; died 1404, on his way to invade China. His tomb, known as Gur Amir, is still to be seen at Bokhara.

TINCAL: 硼沙. Borax of a more or less impure quality. [Persian.]

T'ING-CH'AI: 聽差—one who *waits* to be sent on *official business*. Messengers employed at Chinese Yamêns and at Consulates in China are so called.

TI-PAO: 地保. A headman of the people, selected by the local Mandarins, and responsible for the peace and good order of the district over which he is set. The post is considered an honourable one; it is occasionally lucrative, but very often burdensome and trying in the extreme. For instance, if a *ti-pao* fails to produce any offenders belonging to his district, he is liable to be bambooed or otherwise severely punished. All petitions and other legal instruments should bear the *ti-pao's* stamp (戳), as a guarantee of good faith. See *Seals, Mandarin*.

Besides the above officer, the people have a custom

of themselves electing a private *ti-pao*, who is called 値事 *chih shih*, manager of affairs, because small local quarrels and other little difficulties are referred to him for arbitration.

TITHING SYSTEM: 保甲. Was introduced into China by 衛鞅 Wei Yang, who drew up a Penal Code for the Ch'in State, about 361 B.C. Ten families make a *Chia* 甲, and ten Chia make a *Pao* 保 or *Li* 里. Each Chia and Pao must elect a headman to serve for one year, subject to the approval of the District Magistrate; and all the members of the tithing are mutually responsible for the good behaviour of one another.

TO: 斗. The tenth part of a *koku (q.v.)*=about half an imperial bushel. [Japanese.] See *Tow*.

TO ON: 都音. A pronunciation of Chinese used by the Japanese and representing the sounds of the language as heard at the capital under the T'ang dynasty. See *Go On*.

TOBA: 拓跋. The family name of the Emperors of the Northern Wei dynasty, founded A.D. 398 by Toba Kuei. It is explained as 土后 Earth Lord, *earth* being the chosen element of the Yellow Emperor *(q.v.)* from whom the House of Toba claimed descent.

TOBACCO: 烟. Is said by the Chinese to have been introduced from the Philippine Islands under the name of 淡巴菰 *tan-pa-ku* or 八角 *pa-koh*. It was regarded as a specific against malaria; however in 1628 its import was prohibited, and when people began to grow it, the penalty, first of banishment and then of death, was imposed. Others say it was carried from Japan into Manchuria, through Korea, some 280 years ago. Its cultivation was at first prohibited as likely to interfere with the production of food, but it soon came to be widely grown, especially in the neighbourhood of Kirin where the soil is well suited to the plant. The Manchus then brought tobacco to China.

TŌJIN: 唐人—a man of T'ang *(q.v.)*. Originally, a Chinaman; but now contemptuously used for all foreigners by Japanese.

TOKAIDO: 東海道—the road of the eastern sea. The great highway of Japan extending from Yedo to Kiyoto, along the eastern coast.

TOKIO *or* TOKIYO: 東京—eastern capital. A bastard-Chinese name for Yedo, the capital of Japan, for which it was substituted in 1869, when the Mikado took up his residence there. [Pronounced with the accent on the first syllable.] The term "eastern capital" refers to the Bakufu days, when Kiyôto and Yedo were distinguished as Saikiyô, western capital, and Tôkiyô, there being then two governments, one *de jure* at the former and one *de facto* at the latter.

TOLO PALL: 陀羅經被. A sacred ornamental pall believed by Buddhists to assist the progress and ensure the happiness of their spirits in the next world. These palls are presented by the Emperor to Manchu and Mongol princes after death, as an especial mark of favour, and are buried with the corpse. In the lamaseries of Tibet, however, there are always some on hand to be let out on hire to the public generally. From the Sanskrit word *dharani* a charm or spell.

TOM-TOM *or* TAM-TAM. A Hindi word, meaning *drum* or *tambourine*.

"These night watchmen, with their small gongs *(q.v.)* "and tom-toms, remind us very much of what we have

"read of the watchmen who by night guarded the streets
"of ancient Rome."—*Walks in the City of Canton.*

TONES: 聲. The modulations of the voice by which Chinese
words of different meaning but of the same phonetic
value are distinguished one from the other. In the
Pekingese dialect, *a corpse, time, to send,* and *business*
are all pronounced *shih*; but with the aid of the four
tones, these words are as unlike to the native ear as if
they were *shah, shih, shoh,* and *shuh*. The number of
tones varies with the dialect; some dialects possess as
many as eight or nine, but Pekingese has only four.
Even thus there are a great number of words pronounced
exactly alike both in tone and otherwise, though written
differently; and it is often only by the requirements of
the subject, that is, the context, that the hearer is enabled
to judge of the sense.

The tones have given rise to a still-unsettled controversy; many declaring that it is possible to speak Chinese
thoroughly well without any knowledge of these tones,
while others hold an exactly contrary opinion. The fallacy
here involved is obvious. A person need have no *mnemonic*
knowledge of the tones, *i.e.*, he need not *know* a word
to be of any special tone; but unless in speaking he
utters the word in its proper tone, or approximately so,
he will almost infallibly be misunderstood (see *Mao-tzŭ*).
It is a common error to believe that a musical ear is an
aid towards distinguishing and reproducing the tones of
the various dialects, for many of the best speakers are
very deficient in that respect, and *vice versâ*.

Down to the 3rd cent. B.C. it appears that the only
tones distinguished were the 平 even, 上 rising, and 入
entering. Between that date and the 4th cent. A.D. the

去 sinking tone was developed. In the 11th cent. A.D. the even tone was divided into 上 upper and 下 lower, and a little later the entering tone disappeared from Pekingese. The name of 沈約 Shên Yo, who died A.D. 513, is generally associated with the first systematic classification of the Tones.

The following mnemonic stanza is often committed to memory by Chinese who are learning the southern Mandarin dialect:—

入聲短促急收藏	去聲分明哀遠道	上聲高呼猛烈強	平聲平道莫低昂

TOPAZ. A name applied during the 17th and 18th cent. to half-caste Portuguese, then to soldiers of this class, and finally to menials on board ship, such as bath-room attendants and others.

TOPE: 塔婆. See *Stûpa*.

TOPEE, SOLA. A pith helmet, worn as a precaution against sunstroke. From the Hindi *sholā*, a pithy reed, and *topee* a hat. Occasionally wrongly written *solar*, because supposed to have some connexion with the sun. The word *top* or *topi* has been derived from the Portuguese *topo* "a hat," and has been claimed as one of the few surviving linguistic traces of Portuguese ascendancy in India; it is probable however that the native term is the older of the two.

TOPOSZE: 舵浦司. The Assistant Magistrate or 分司

of the T'o-p'u sub-district, resident at Swatow, though his sub-district is situated to the west of that town.

TORI-I: 鳥 居—bird's dwelling. An arch or similar structure of wood or stone, erected before the gates of Sintoo *(q.v.)* temples in Japan.

TORTOISE: 龜. One of the four sacred animals of China. The origin of Chinese writing has been fancifully traced to the marks on its shell. See *Eight Diagrams*. Is an emblem of longevity.

Vulgarly known (1) as 王 八 *Wang Pa*, from a nickname given by the people of his village to Wang Chien, who after a youth spent in violence and rascality became the founder of the Earlier Shu State, dying A.D. 918. Or (2) as 忘 八 *Wang-pa*, the "creature which forgets the eight rules of right and wrong," from a superstitious belief in the unchastity of the female. Hence, *wang-pa* is a common term of abuse, equivalent to cuckold. When depicted on a wall, it stands for *commit no nuisance*, "if you do, you are a *wang-pa*," being understood. Sometimes the character 中 is used instead, as resembling in shape the animal referred to.

TORTURES. Of these a long list might be given; they exist, however, rather in name than in practice, the more severe forms being absolutely prohibited, though Chinese prisoners are *occasionally*, under great stress of circumstances, subjected to very barbarous treatment. To extort evidence from a man, the bamboo is applied; women are slapped on the cheeks with a flat piece of hard leather (皮 掌 嘴). Instruments for squeezing the fingers and ankle-bones are authorised under the *Penal Code*, but "any magistrate who wantonly or arbitrarily applies the "question by torture, shall be tried for such offence;" and where competition for place is so keen, few officials would dare risk their career in such an unsatisfactory way. Besides, few Chinese prisoners need more than the majesty of the law to frighten them into either telling the truth or swearing to a falsehood as the presiding magistrate may require. The real tortures of a Chinese prison are the filthy dens in which the unfortunate victims are confined, the stench in which they have to draw breath, the fetters and manacles by which they are secured, absolute insufficiency even of the disgusting rations doled out to them, and above all the mental agony which must ensue upon imprisonment in a country with no *Habeas corpus* to protect the lives and fortunes of its citizens.

In all cases of rendition of prisoners from the colony of Hongkong to the Chinese authorities, a guarantee is required from the latter that at the ensuing trial no tortures will be applied. "Many who know the punish-"ments inflicted by the Chinese upon their criminals think "them dreadful, but they are exceeded by those which "David inflicted upon individuals whose only crime was "fighting for their country (2 Sam. xii. 31)." Inman's *Ancient Faiths.*

TO-SSŬ-TI-'RH. The Mahommedan password in China. Equivalent of *Bismillah*, the first word of the Koran.

TOUCH: 色. A conventional term used by assayers and referring to the purity of silver.

TOURGOUTHS: 杜爾扈特. A division of the Kalmucks or Eleuth Mongols.

TOW *or* TOU *or* TU: 斗. A Chinese peck. See *To.*

TOWCHANG: 頭騌. A term from the Amoy dialect, used in the Straits' Settlements for cue or pigtail.

TOWER OF SILENCE. A Parsi burying-ground is so called. The Parsis do not commit their dead to the earth, but expose corpses upon an iron grating, to the birds of the air and to the agency of sun and dew, until all the flesh is gone and the bones fall through into a pit beneath.

TOWKAY: 頭家 —head of the house. The common term in the Swatow and Amoy districts for *master*, whether of a family or shop. The leading Chinese merchants, or employers of immigrant Chinese labour in the Straits, are called *Kay-tows (q.v.)*.

TRANSIT PASSES. In consequence of the heavy inland exactions to which both foreign imports and native produce for export had been subjected by the Chinese provincial customs' authorities, it was agreed by the Treaties of Nanking and Tientsin that foreign merchants should be allowed to commute such duties by a single payment of $2^{1}/_{2}$ per cent *ad valorem* on such goods when imported into or exported from China. *Transit passes* are the documents which accompany such foreign-owned goods, as a proof to the officials *en route* that the proper duties have been paid. The Chinese call them (1) 三聯單 *triplicate certificates*, to cover native produce for export, and (2) 稅單 *duty certificates*, to cover foreign imports going up country. The system has not been found to work satisfactorily, many foreign merchants having taken out passes for goods owned by Chinese and thus inflicted great injury upon the native Customs' revenue. In the case of imports, it may be argued that by Treaty British manufactures should be allow to penetrate China free of all prohibitive exactions, without reference to mere ownership.

TREASURER, THE PROVINCIAL. See *Fan-t'ai*.

TREATIES. British,

        with China (1) dated 1842

             „   „   (2) „   1858

             „ Japan   „   1858

             „ Korea   „   1884

             „ Siam   „   1856

TRIAD SOCIETY, THE: 三合會. A Secret Society, still existing in China, though strictly forbidden by the Government, the ceremonies of initiation into which present many curious coincidences with those of Freemasonry. The name chosen signifies the union of Heaven, Earth and Man, as symbolised in the character 王 *wang* a king or prince, the three horizontal lines of which are joined together by a third. In the reign of Hsien Fêng, the Society actually went so far as to produce a cash *(q.v.)*, now known to collectors under the name of the "Triad." On the reverse it has 合 above the hole and ⊙ below, besides two Manchu characters. The name of this sect is sometimes written 三河 *three rivers*, from the place where it is said to have originated. Also known as the Heaven and Earth Society 天地會. Dates from the reign Yung Chêng, 1723—36.

TRIMETRICAL CLASSIC: 三字經—three-character classic. The first book put into the hands of a Chinese school-boy, being a short guide to ethics, history, science, biography, etc., all in one. So called because arranged in rhyming sentences of *three* words to each. Probably composed during the Sung dynasty by Wang Ying-lin, otherwise known as Wang Po-hou, and consequently about six hundred years old. The following is a specimen:—

> The little Hsiang at nine years' old could warm his parents' bed—
> Ah, would that all of us were by like filial precepts led!
> The baby Jung when only four resigned the envied pear:
> Deference to elder brothers then should be our early care.

Imitations of the *Trimetrical Classic*, embodying the leading doctrines of Christianity, have been published by both Catholic and Protestant missionaries in China, and a similar work was also issued by the T'ai-p'ing rebels.

TRINITY, THE BUDDHIST. See *Precious Ones, The Three*. For the Taoist Trinity, see *Taoism*.

TRIPANG. Bicho-da-mar *(q.v.)*.

TRIPITAKA *or* TEPITAKA: 三 藏—three baskets, or collections. The triple canon of the Buddhist scriptures, consisting of (1) the *Sûtras* addressed to the laity, (2) the *Shâstras* addressed to the dêvas and brahmas of the celestial world, and (3) the *Vinaya* addressed to the priesthood. Containing about 1,752,800 words in all. These were orally preserved until the 1st century B.C. when they were committed to writing in Ceylon. In one verse Buddha summed up the whole of his religion:—

> To cease from all sin *(Vinaya)*;
> To get virtue *(Sûtras)*;
> To cleanse one's own heart *(Shâstras)*;
> This is the religion of the Buddhas.

TSATLEE: 七 里—seven *li*. A kind of silk, so called from the place where it is made.

TSIEN. See *Ch'ien*.

TSIN-SZE. See *Chin-shih*.

TSUBO *or* TSZBO: 坪. A Japanese land measure of 6 feet square.

TSUNG-LI YAMÊN: 總 理 衙 門—general managing bureau. The modern Chinese Foreign Office, established in January 1862, after the capture of Peking by the allied forces in 1860. It is a consulting body of high Chinese officials, and forms the channel of communication between foreign Ministers and the Throne.

TSUNG-TUH : 總督. Viceroy or Governor-General of one or more provinces, within which he has the general control of all affairs civil and military, subject only to the approval of the Throne. The Viceroy is the survival of the "noble" 諸侯 of feudal days, and almost as independent as his prototype. His seal *(q.v.)* is oblong.

T‘U SHU. See *Encyclopaedias.*

TUAN BESAR. "Great master," or head of the establishment. Used in the Straits much as *Sahib* in India. (Malay).

TUI-TZŬ : 對子. Antithetical couplets, inscribed on scrolls, and used as wall-decorations in Chinese houses. The following is a specimen, taken from the autograph original of H. E. Li Hung-chang, Viceroy of the Two Kuang :—

達　義　始　行　守　信　可　復
順　理　則　裕　平　情　乃　龢

Be clear as to your duty, and then you may begin to act; hold fast to truth, and you will be able to substantiate your words. Move in accordance with eternal principles, and you will profit thereby; practise self-control, and you will find yourself in harmony with all men.

TUKANG. A Malay prefix meaning "workman;" *e.g. tukang-ayer* the water workman, *sc.* the house-coolie.

TUNG-CHE *or* T‘UNG CHIH : 同治—united rule. The style adopted by the Emperor who reigned over China from 1862 to 1875.

T‘UNG-CHIH : 同知. A Sub-prefect *(q.v.)*, often called "second Prefect" 二府.

T‘UNG-P‘AN : 通判. A "third Prefect" 三府, or Assistant Sub-prefect.

TUNG WAH HOSPITAL, THE. A hospital at Hongkong where sick Chinese are treated upon native pathological principles and under the superintendence of their own doctors. The influence of this institution has been brought to bear in more than one instance on matters quite beyond its proper sphere of action; hence it is regarded with no favourable eye by many European residents in Hongkong, who object to the association with such an establishment of any political or commercial significance whatever. The name *Tung Wah* 東華 signifies "for *Chinese* of the Kuang-*tung* province."

T'UNG-WÊN-KUAN : 同文館. Otherwise known as the "Peking College," an establishment at the capital for the instruction of Chinese students in the languages, literatures, and sciences of the West, under the guidance of foreign masters. The pupils, whose ages have been known to vary from fifteen to fifty, receive a small monthly allowance from the Chinese Government to induce them to attend regularly the classes and lectures provided for their benefit. A similar institution on a small scale exists at Canton under the same Chinese name; otherwise known as the "Chinese Government School."

TURFAN : 吐魯番. A Subprefecture in Outer Kansuh.

TURKOMANS *or* TÜRKMEN. Inhabit that tract of desert land which extends on this side of the river Oxus, from the shore of the Caspian Sea to Balkh, and from the same river to the south as far as Herat and Astrabad. Compounded of the proper name *Türk*, and the suffix *men*, which corresponds with the English termination -*ship* or -*dom*. It is applied to the whole race, conveying the idea that these nomads style themselves pre-eminently Turks. Turkoman is a corruption of the Turkish original.

20

TUTENAGUE. A term first applied by the Portuguese to the spelter or zinc of China. Etymology unknown.

TWANKAY. A kind of tea from 屯溪 T'un-ch'i, a town in Anhui, whence our name. The widow in the burlesque of "Aladdin" is known by this designation.

TWATUTIA: 大稻埕 —great rice drying-ground. A large town about 12 miles up river from the port of Tamsui in Formosa, where all settlements are made of the tea which is exported from Tamsui to America.

TWO KIANG, THE: 兩江. Formerly denoted the two provinces of Kiangnan and Kiangsi; now stands for Kiangsi, and the two provinces of Anhui and Kiangsu into which Kiangnan has been subdivided.

TWO KUANG, THE. The two provinces of Kuangtung and Kuangsi *(q.v.)* are jointly spoken of under the above title.

TWO-TAILED PIG, THE. A Chinese nickname for the Siamese national emblem, the celebrated "white elephant." This animal is really an albino of a light mahogany colour, and is supposed to be the incarnation of some future Buddha.

TYCOON: 大君 —great Prince. Same as the Shōgun *(q.v.)* or former "temporal" Emperor of Japan, in whose hands was all the real power. Submitted to the Mikado in 1867. Wrongly written 太官 great official. The term is said to have been coined by a preceptor of the Shōgun as a fitting title under which his master might be represented in the Treaty with Commodore Perry, 1854. "The full "title of the Tycoon was 征夷大將軍 Sei-i-tai Shogun, "or Barbarian-repressing Commander-in-chief. The style "Tai Kun, Great Prince, was borrowed, in order to convey "the idea of sovereignty to foreigners, at the time of the

"conclusion of the Treaties. * * * * The title Sei-i-tai
"Shogun was first borne by Minamoto-no-Yoritomo in the
"seventh month of the year 1192 A.D."—Mitford, *Tales
of Old Japan*.

TYPHOON *or* TYFOON. A cyclone, or revolving storm
of immense force, the speed of rotation being all the
time in an inverse ratio to that of translation, and *vice
versâ*. Typhoons seem to be eddies formed by the meeting
of opposing currents of air, and blow in the northern
hemisphere from right to left, in the southern from left to
right. Has been derived from the Chinese 大 風 *tai fong*,
a great wind, the chief objection to which is that the
Chinese have special names for the typhoon and rarely
if ever speak of it vaguely as a "great wind." They say
暴 風, or 颱 風, or 颶 風, etc., etc.; and Dr. Hirth
has shown that the second of these, read 颱 風 *tai fong*,
is a local term in Formosa for the cyclone, and probably
the real source of the term. Also (2) from the Arabic
tufan, and (3) from the Greek τυφῶν, both meaning
whirlwind, which words however were in all probability
taken by the Greeks and Arabs from other sources.

> My coursers are fed with the lightning,
>   They drink of the whirlwind's stream;
> And when the red morning is brightening,
>   They bathe in the fresh sunbeam;
> I desire, and their speed makes night kindle;
>   I fear, they outstrip the *typhoon*:
> Ere the cloud placed on Atlas can dwindle,
>   We'll encircle the earth and the moon.
>   *Shelley*.

With regard to the term 颶 風 given above, it is explained
in the 越 南 志 as a 四 方 之 風, literally "four quarter
wind," the quarters being of course N. S. E. and W.
In another work we have 颶 風 以 四 面 俱 至 也, which
has the same meaning.

TYPHOON FLY: 蜻蜓. The common dragon-fly is so called; the presence of these insects flying round and round in large numbers being considered as a sign of heavy weather.

TZŬ-ÊRH-CHI: 自邇集—the "from near" collection. The name of Sir Thomas Wade's well-known work for students of the Chinese (Mandarin) language. So called from a sentence in the Doctrine of the Mean *(q.v.)* which says that the way of the superior man 辟如行遠必 自邇 may be compared with the way of one who would travel far—he must begin from what is near; the allusion being to the elementary and progressive nature of this manual.

UCHAIN. The old name for Young Hyson *(q.v.)* tea.

ULA. A Mongol word signifying *mountain*; *e.g.* Khan-ula.

ULA GRASS: 烏拉草. One of the three valuable products of Manchuria, the other two being sables and ginseng. It is used by the natives for wrapping round the feet and also for stuffing mattresses.

UMBRELLA DANCE. See *Fan Danee.*

UMBRELLAS, RED. These insignia of rank are of two kinds, (1) the large red umbrella 紅傘 and (2) the smaller red sun-shade 日照, and are both found among the paraphernalia of civilians down to the sixth grade inclusive. The remaining three grades should properly use blue umbrellas; but a Chih-hsien for instance, though only of the seventh grade, has almost invariably the brevet rank of a *T'ung-chih* of the fifth grade, and is therefore entitled to use a red umbrella. The military are arranged on a slightly different scale, all below the sixth grade being only allowed a large umbrella of ordinary make to keep off the sun.

"The court was numerous: fan-bearers on the right,
"and fan-bearers on the left, bearers of the parasol, etc."
[From a description of the Pharaohs in Evelyn Abbott's
Hist. of Antiquity.]

The complimentary, or Ten Thousand Names Umbrella
萬 名 傘 *Wan ming san*, is a large red umbrella presented
by the people to any official who may have won their
approbation of his rule. It is covered with the names of
the subscribers in gilt characters.

URH (*or* ÊRH) YA, THE: 爾 雅. Otherwise known to
foreigners as the *Literary Expositor*. A thesaurus of terms
used in the classics and everyday life of an early period,
embellished with drawings of a great number of the
objects, explained and arranged under nineteen heads.
It has been attributed to Tzŭ Hsia, a well-known disciple
of Confucius, born B.C. 507, and was incorporated in the
Confucian Canon. Chu Hsi, however, whose authority on
such points is the highest available, said 不 足 据 以 爲 古
we are not justified in regarding it as an ancient work.

USURY. Three per cent. per month is the maximum legal
interest in China, upon money lent under any conditions.
But the accumulated interest may never exceed the
principal. Thus, when interest which has been received
equals the principal still due, the lender should claim
such principal, and, if he wishes to continue the loan,
make a fresh start. Otherwise, the borrower may claim
every item of interest paid subsequent to that date as an
instalment towards clearing off the principal.

When money is lent for a period of years, the interest
is generally calculated as if there were only ten months to
the year. This is called 長 年 官 利; according to which,
one per cent. per month would be ten per cent. per annum.

VEDAS GOLD. A kind of damask interwoven with gold thread, and about 2 feet 2 inches in width.

VEGETARIANS: 在 禮. A sect, the members of which abstain from meat, wine, and tobacco. They are violently anti-Christian, and carried out the shocking massacre of missionaries at Kucheng, near Foochow, in 1895.

VEILS: 面 帕. Were worn in public by Chinese women until the reign of the first Emperor of the Sui dynasty, A.D. 605—618, who abolished them and substituted a kind of turban. Veils have always been worn by brides from the very earliest ages.

VERMILION PENCIL: 硃筆. A Minute or Rescript, endorsed in *red* ink, nominally by the Emperor himself, on all documents submitted to the Sacred Glance. The following specimens are copies from the Treaties of Nanking and Tientsin, respectively: 著 照 所 以 議 行 and 俱 著 照 所 會 議, signifying the Imperial consent to the two instruments in question. It is worthy of note that the sign-manual of the old Emperors of Delhi was written with red ink.

VICEROY. See *Tsung-tu*.

VIHĀRA. A Buddhist monastery.

VINAYA: 律—law. One of the divisions of the Buddhist canon (see *Tripitaka*), containing the rules for ecclesiastical discipline and so on.

VINEGAR, TO CHOW-CHOW. Pidgin-English equivalent of *to be jealous*. This phrase is merely a literal translation of the Chinese metaphorical expression 喫 醋, the origin of which will be found in *Chinese Sketches*, p. 68.

In the deed of gift by which a Chinese child is transferred from its parents to another person, will be generally seen an item of so many dollars or taels payable by the transferee as "ginger and vinegar money." This phrase is used by synecdoche for the whole expenses of bringing up the child; and is derived from the fact that every Chinese mother is presented, immediately after parturition, with a draught of ginger and vinegar, the former of which is supposed to prevent her catching cold, and the latter to increase the needful supply of milk.

VISAYA *or* BISAYA. The aboriginal dialect of the southern Philippines. See *Tagal.*

VISITS, OFFICIAL. Superiors notify their subordinates of an intended visit, so that the latter may be ready to receive them. Subordinates simply go and await their turn to be admitted. It is not etiquette for equals to notify each other beforehand of their visits; hence a delay at the gate while the host is putting on his ceremonial dress. These rules do not apply to foreign officials who are regarded as "guests." A convenient method of calling on an official much inferior in rank is 過 門 拜 to stop at his door, send in a card, and pass on. Foreign officials may also avail themselves of this plan for "saving the face" of an officer on whom they could not well call in the ordinary way. See *Etiquette.*

WAGAKUSHA. A term for Japanese scholars especially devoted to the native learning and religion of Japan, as opposed to the Kangakusha *(q.v.).*

WAILO *or* WHILO. Pidgin-English for "Go away!" From the Cantonese sounds of 去 咯 be off!

WAI-SING *or* WEI-SING LOTTERY: 闈 姓—examination names. A kind of sweepstakes, once a very popular form of gambling among the Cantonese, on the result of the public examination for the second degree; the holder of a successful candidate's name being the winner of a greater or less sum according to position on the published list. Being now strictly prohibited in Canton, the lottery is still organised in Macao, whence tickets are smuggled in large numbers to brokers in the former city for distribution. Winning tickets are not paid unless their price has previously reached Macao.

WAI-YUN *or* WEI-YÜAN: 委員 —deputed officer. An officer of any rank deputed to perform certain duties.

WAMPEE *or* WHAMPEE: 黄皮 —yellow skin. A fruit found in Southern China.

WǍNLI *or* WÊNLI: 文理. Style; composition. Read *mǎn-li* in the south. Missionaries speak of Bibles translated into the book-language, as written in "wên-li," to distinguish them from translations into the colloquial.

WAN-SHOU SHAN: 萬壽山 —hill of an old age of 10,000 years. The hill near which the palace of Yüan-ming-yüan *(q.v.)* once stood, *Wan-shou* being a figurative expression for the Imperial birthday. The Emperor is commonly spoken of as 萬歲爺 "Lord of 10,000 years," *i.e.*, of all the ages; while "Lord of 1,000 years" is a title given to the Heir Apparent.

WANG: 王. A prince.

WANG-HAI-LOU: 望海樓 —Sea-view Pavilion. A fanciful name, very commonly given by the Chinese to any ornamental building which commands a view over sea, lake, river, or other piece of water.

WARAJIS: 草鞋. Japanese straw sandals.

WAR TAX. See *Likin*.

WATER CLOCK. See *Clepsydra*.

WAYONG. The Malay word for "theatre." Used in the Straits much as *sing-song* in China.

WEAPONS. See *Arms*.

WEI-CH'I: 圍 碁—surrounding checkers. A complicated Chinese game played with a checker-board and counters, and said to have been invented by the Emperor Yao, two thousand years B.C. An analysis of the elements of *wei-ch'i* appeared in the *Temple Bar* magazine for January 1877.

WEI-HAI-WEI: 威 海 衛. A strongly fortified place at the point of the Shantung promontory. Surrendered to the Japanese by Admiral Ting, who forthwith committed suicide, 7th Feb. 1895, and finally leased by China to England in April 1898.

WEIGHTS AND MEASURES.

Weight.

16 兩 *taels* = 1 斤 catty *(q.v.).*
100 斤 *catties* = 1 擔 picul *(q.v.).*
120 斤 „ = 1 石 stone.

Long Measure.

10 分 *fên* = 1 寸 *ts'un* (inch).
10 寸 *ts'un* = 1 尺 *ch'ih* (foot = 14.1 English inches or 0.3581 mètres). [1]
10 尺 *ch'ih* = 1 丈 *chang.*

Money.

10 忽 *hu* = 1 絲 *ssŭ.*
10 絲 *ssŭ* = 1 毫 *hao.*
10 毫 *hao* = 1 釐 *li* (see *likin*).
10 釐 *li* = 1 分 *fên* (candareen).
10 分 *fên* = 1 錢 *ch'ien* (mace).
10 錢 *ch'ien* = 1 兩 *liang* (tael).

---

1 As fixed by Treaty. The Chinese foot measure varies in different places and in different trades. The tailor's foot is the longest, the metropolitan foot about 9/10 of an inch less, and the Canton foot between the two.

Capacity.

10 合 *ho* = 1 升 *shêng* (pint).

10 升 *shêng* = 1 斗 *tou* (peck).

10 斗 *tou* = 1 石 *shih*.

Land Measure.

4 角 *chio* = 1 畝 *mou* = 26.73 sq. poles.

100 畝 *mou* = 1 頃 *ch'ing* = 16.7 acres.

WÊNCHOW: 温州—warm region. A port on the coast of Chehkiang, opened to trade by the Chefoo Agreement of 1876.

WÊN SHU: 文殊. The Indian Manjusri, a famous Bôdhisatva, worshipped in China as the God of Wisdom, and popularly depicted as riding on a lion, the symbol of bravery.

WHAMPOA: 黄埔—yellow reach. Strictly speaking the port of Canton, from which it is about 12 miles distant. That foreign steamers proceed farther up the river than this point is a privilege accorded by the Chinese authorities in the interests of trade, and might be taken away at a moment's notice by the Superintendent of Maritime Customs. [Rule IX., Special Local Regulations.] Sailing vessels still continue to discharge cargo here.

WHANGHEES: 竹竿. Canes of all kinds.

WHEEL KING *or* Chakravarti. A King who rules the world, and causes the wheel of doctrine everywhere to revolve. The Sanskrit word is from *chakra* wheel, the symbol of activity.

WHITE ANTS: 白蟻. The popular, but incorrect, name [1] for *termites*, a genus of insect distinct from the ant, though the two are somewhat similar in their habits.

---

1 It is a curious fact that the Chinese name for this insect is also *white ant*.

Attracted by lights, they fly into houses after nightfall, and shed their wings all over the place. By putting a plate of water near the lamp, they may be caught in large numbers. The chief mischief they do is, in the larva stage, by eating up all the wood that falls in their way, getting into houses and gradually consuming the largest beams and rafters until at length the building falls with a crash. They will not, however, touch camphor wood; neither do they like the light of day; but all clothes' boxes, pianos, etc., should be raised on bricks covered with lime to prevent them crawling up, and should be carefully examined from time to time. "An American "flag-staff, the pride of an Oregon forest, was soon after its "erection honeycombed and prostrated by that omnivorous "destroyer. It is commonly believed that wherever a "poison is found growing, an antidotal plant will be found "not far off. This is paralleled by noxious insects—the "white ant for example has an enemy in a small black "ant to which it affords support. A singular battle was "observed the other day, between two columns of these "insects, if that can be called a battle where all the "injury that was inflicted was suffered by one side. The "black ants seized and carried off the white ones, if not "without remonstrance on the part of the latter, at any "rate without resistance. Tobacco is virulent poison to the "white ant. A colony lately invaded a box of cheroots, "which on being opened showed that the cigars had "proved fatal to them instantaneously, as none of them "had let go their hold of the tobacco."—*Dr. Macgowan.*

WHITE COCK. Is carried with coffins on the way to interment, "under the belief that this bird alone can guide the ghost to its destination." *Williams.*

"The Chinese cannot explain the origin of this custom."
Doolittle.

At the oath-taking previous to initiation into the Triad Society *(q.v.)*, a white cock is killed. Its death is symbolical of the death of the candidate to the influences of the outside world, previous to his re-birth as a just and upright man and a brother. The cock is chosen because of its *vigilance*, and its white colour is emblematical of purity of heart.

WHITE ELEPHANT. See *Two-tailed Pig*.

WHITE LILY SECT: 白蓮教. Name of a well-known Chinese secret society, the exact origin of which is not known. A White Lily society was formed in the 2nd cent. A.D. by a Taoist patriarch named Liu I-min, and 18 members used to assemble at a temple in modern Kiangsi for purposes of meditation. But this seems to have no connection with the later sect, of which we first hear in 1308 when its existence was prohibited, its shrines destroyed, and its votaries forced to return to ordinary life. The father of the famous Han Lin-êrh, who died in 1367, was executed for his adherence to the fraternity, the members of which are believed to possess a knowledge of the black art.

WHITE PIGEON: 白鴿. A kind of lottery, the simplest form of which is organised as follows. Out of twenty given characters, the players each choose ten, as inscribed upon a ticket for which they pay 5 cash. Then the banker chooses ten; and to any one whose ticket contains five of these, he pays 6 cash; if six, 76 cash; if seven, 750 cash; if eight, Tls. 2.50; if nine, Tls. 5; if ten, Tls. 10. The game is said to be so called because gamblers who lived inside the city of Canton were in the habit, when visiting by night the gambling-houses outside the city, of taking with them white pigeons which they flew from time to time to let their families know the result.

WIGOUR. See *Ouigour*.

WILLOW PATTERN. The origin of this design is not known. It has been explained as portraying the secret love of a young lady for her father's secretary, discovery, flight, pursuit of relentless parent, and finally transformation of the lovers into two turtle-doves. The name is further said to have been adopted because the flight took place at the time when the willow sheds its leaves. Unfortunately, the turtle-dove is not regarded by the Chinese as an emblem of fidelity in love.

WILLS: 遺書—in the European sense of the term, that is to say documents controlling the devolution of a dead man's property, are quite unknown in China. Theoretically, all property belongs, not to an individual, but to the family of which he is a member, and at his death goes by law to his male children in equal shares, or failing them, to collaterals in a certain definite and well-known order. Final instructions are often delivered either verbally or in writing, but these refer generally to minor details and would not avail to vary the normal devolution unless acquiesced in by the interested survivors.

WINE: 酒. A conventional name for the ardent spirit distilled from the yeasty liquor in which boiled rice has fermented under pressure for many days. See *Samshoo* and *Grape*.

WONSAN. See *Gensan*.

WORLD-HONOURED, THE: 世尊. Buddha *(q.v.)*.

WRITING, ART OF. See *Characters* and *Shuo Wên*.

WRITTEN PAPER, RESPECT FOR. See *Paper*.

WU-CHOU FU: 梧州府. A Treaty Port on the West River in Kuangtung.

WUHU: 蕪湖—weedy lake. A port on the river Yang-tsze, in the province of An-hui, opened to trade by the Chefoo Agreement of 1876.

WUNK: 黃犬—yellow dog. A term commonly applied by foreigners to the ordinary Chinese dog. From the Ningpo pronunciation, *wou^n kyi*, of the above two characters.

WU-SHIH-SHAN: 烏石山—black rock hill. A hill within the city of Foochow, about 300 feet in height, upon which stands a residence of the British Consul.

The "Wu-shih-shan Case" was an action brought in 1879 by the directors of a temple on this hill against the Rev. J. Wolfe to define the rights of the parties to certain land occupied by the defendant. It was then decided that if rent is owing, a Chinese landlord can take back his premises. If no rent is owing, he cannot let them to any one else; but he can always resume possession, if he wants the premises for his own use, by giving reasonable notice.

WU-SUNG *or* WOOSUNG: 吳淞. A town at the mouth of the Hwang-poo river, the approach to Shanghai. Above it is situated the celebrated "Woosung Bar," which is said to be silting up fast and gradually closing the mouth of the river, and has long formed a serious obstacle to the movements of large steamers. The Chinese Government steadily refuse to dredge this bar, alleging that it would be an evil policy thus to deprive Shanghai of its "Heaven-sent Barrier" *(q.v.)*—one of its natural and most effectual means of defence. The bar is sometimes called "Shanghai's Shame."

XANADU. A corruption of *Shang-tu* 上都 "imperial

capital," the summer residence of Kublai Khan, about 180 miles north of Peking.

> In Xanadu did Kubla Khan
> A stately pleasure dome decree :
> Where Alph, the sacred river, ran,
> By caverns measureless to man,
> Down to a sunless sea.
> *Coleridge.*

The river here mentioned has generally been regarded as an invention of the poet. Mr. W. H. Wilkinson however speaks of a great cave at Fang-shan, beyond Peking, "that runs no one knows how far underground, for a subterranean river stops the way."

XAVIER, St. FRANÇOIS. The first Roman Catholic missionary to China. He never set foot on the mainland, but died at 上 川 山 Sancian Island or St. John's near Macao, 1552, aged 46. The native maps indicate the existence of his tomb on this island by the words 聖 人 墓 "Saint's grave," though he was actually buried at Goa.

YACONIN *or* YAKUNIN: 役人. Any official employé of the Japanese Government.

YADOYA. A Japanese inn.

YAKOOB BEG: 阿古柏. The celebrated Mussulman conqueror and Ameer of Kashgaria, which country he held in subjection for 12 years, until he either died or was assassinated at Korla in the early part of May 1877, after which Kashgaria was reconquered by the Chinese. Born 1820. See *Athalik Ghazi.*

YAK'S-TAIL. The tail of the Tibetan ox 犛牛; used as a fly-flapper. See *Chowry.*

YALU: 鴨綠. A river in the north of Korea, at the mouth of which the Japanese gained a great naval victory over the Chinese, 17th Sept. 1894. At the same time the Japanese vessels were so severely injured that they could not follow in pursuit.

YAMATO: 大和 (formerly 大倭). The name of the province in which was situated the old capital of Japan. Now used for the whole empire of Japan.

YAMBU: 元寶. Corruption of *yüan-pao*, a large shoe of sycee. Thus pronounced in Central Asia.

YAMUN *or* YAMÊN: 衙門. The official and private residence of any Mandarin who holds a seal. Offices of petty mandarins who have no seals are 公所 *Kung so*, public places. The isolated wall before the entrance gate (影壁 *shadow* wall) is placed there as a bar to all noxious influences, which are supposed to travel only in straight lines (see *Fêng-shui*); and the huge animal painted on the inside so as to attract the attention of the mandarin every time he leaves his Yamên, is the *t'an* 貪, the accursed beast *avarice*, against which he is thus duly warned. Sometimes an enormous red sun is depicted on the "shadow wall." It is typical of the pure and bright principle *yang* 陽 (see *Yin and Yang*); and daily suggests to the inmates of the place the desirability of making their administration pure likewise.

YANG-KING-PANG: 洋涇浜. A creek at Shanghai between the British and French Concessions.

YANG-KWEI-TSZE: 洋鬼子—foreign devil. See *Kwei-tsze*.

YANG-TSZE KIANG: 楊 (*or* 楊) 子江—river of Yang-tsze, 楊子 being the old name of a district. Has been erroneously translated "Son of the Ocean," from the first character being wrongly written 洋, and is often spoken of (*Illustrated London News*, 8th Dec., 1878) as the "Yang-tsze-kiang river." Is also familiarly known to the Chinese as the Long River 長江, and as 江 *the*

River. The Chinese consider the 岷江, which enters the Yang-tsze near Hsü-chou Fu in Ssŭch'uan, as the main stream, and not the Chin-sha river. See *River of Golden Sand*.

The Valley of the Yang-tsze, including the richest provinces of Central China and now regarded as the legitimate sphere of British influence, was in 1891 the scene of serious anti-foreign riots, two British subjects being killed and many houses and churches being destroyed at various important centres.

YAO *and* SHUN : 堯 舜. Two monarchs of antiquity, held up by the Chinese as models of piety and virtue. Yao came to the throne B.C. 2356 and reigned until 2280, when he abdicated in favour of Shun whom he took from the plough-tail, to the exclusion of his own profligate son, solely on account of Shun's reputation for filial piety and brotherly affection. According to Mr. Kingsmill, *Yao* is the Ouranos and Varuna of Greek and Indian mythologies.

YASHIKI. A Daimio's feudal mansion.

YAYSOO. See *Yeh-soo*.

YEAR. See *Moon*.

The Chinese day is divided into 12 hours of 120 minutes each. The months are *lunar*, and are spoken of as "moons" *(q.v.)*. Twelve of them go to the year, except every third year which has thirteen, an intercalary *(q.v.)* month being inserted to make up the difference with the solar year. Some months have 29, others 30 days. There are four seasons, which begin and end on certain days; and the year is subdivided into 24 solar terms, of which the more important are :—

1. 立 春 —the beginning of spring. Falls about the

5th February, and is kept as a festival in honour of agriculture, an ox being led in procession through the towns and villages. On the day before, the Prefect is carried in state to perform certain acts of worship, and every mandarin, high or low, is bound to yield the way. Consequently, the higher officials never leave their yamêns on that day.

2. 清明—clear and bright. Falls about the 5th April, and is the day on which the Chinese visit their ancestral burying-places.

3. 夏至—summer solstice. Falls about the 21st June, and is devoted by the mandarins to acts of congratulation at the spiritual shrine of the Emperor. See *Temples*.

4. 霜降—frost descends. Falls about the 23rd October, and is generally spent by the military in reviews and martial exercises.

5. 冬至—winter solstice. Falls about the 22nd December. Ceremonies as at the summer solstice.

6. 大寒—great cold. Falls about the 21st January. On this day it is lawful for all who choose to commit to the ground their still unburied relatives, the ordinary course being to select some propitious date.

The chief Chinese festivals are the New Year, when all business is at a temporary standstill, the Feast of Lanterns *(q.v.)*, and the Dragon-boat festival *(q.v.)*.

YEDDO *or* YEDO: 江戶—river's door. Formerly written *Jeddo*, according to the Dutch orthography. Same as *Tokio (q.v.)*.

YEH, GOVERNOR: 葉明琛. The infamous Viceroy of the two Kuang provinces, who was captured at the bombardment of Canton in December 1858 by the Allied Forces, and banished to Calcutta where he shortly afterwards died. [See *Arrow*.] He is said to have beheaded as many as 70,000 of the T'ai-p'ing rebels who fell into his hands. His father was a petty druggist at Hankow and of a very religious turn of mind.

YEH-SOO : 耶 穌—Jesus. Thus written in K'ang Hsi's lexicon, and explained as 西 國 言 救 世 生 也 "said by western nations to have been born to save mankind." The name of a once well-known steamer, the *Yesso*, was thus written in Chinese upon the paddle-boxes, until the attention of the owners was called to the impropriety of such a term. See *Protestant* and *Roman C. Missionaries*.

YEIGWA MONOGATARI = A tale of glory. The first history in the Japanese language. It covers about two centuries, ending with A.D. 1088.

YÉLANG : 唉 哈. A common term in Canton for an auction. Probably from the Portuguese *leilão*, through the Malayan *lélang* which means auction, as seen more markedly in the Swatow variation 嘮 嘓 *loy-lang*, actually pronunced *lélang* in Amoy.

YELLOW CAPS, THE REVOLT OF THE : 黃 巾 賊· A rebellion which broke out A.D. 184 towards the close of the Han dynasty, and resulted in the final division of the empire into the Three Kingdoms. So called from the yellow caps or turbans worn by the insurgents. The actual rebellion was subdued by Liu Pei and his brother-members of the Peach-Orchard Confederation *(q.v.)*.

YELLOW EMPEROR. See *Hwang Ti(a)*.

YELLOW FLAGS. See *Black Flags*.

YELLOW GIRDLE. See *Girdle*.

YELLOW JACKET. See *Ma-kwa*.

YELLOW RIVER. See *Hoang-ho*.

YELLOW SEA. The sea which washes the eastern coast

of China is so called, from the yellow colour of its water, "saturated with the loam of 1,500 miles away" brought down by the river Yangtsze.

YEN: 園. Japanese term for a dollar.

YESSO *or* YEZO. The northern island of the Japanese empire.

YIH KING. See *Changes, Book of*.

YIN AND YANG: 陰陽. North and south banks of a river; light and shade; male and female; natural and supernatural, etc. The primeval forces from the interaction of which all things have been evolved. Expressed thus ☯ by the Chinese, the dark half being the *yin* or female principle; the light the *yang* or male. "The simplest form "of matter would be the dot..... From the dot then "all things took their rise; the germ in the centre of the "egg from which the world had sprung. But the dot was "not sufficient to express the spreading universe he saw "on every side..... How could it be made appear? The "answer followed, by the secret of existence: limitation..... "The circle was the natural symbol (suggested perhaps "by the horizon), beginning and ending in itself simply, "and equally confining all within it; the circle round the "dot expressed sufficiently the first great thought and "gave him tools to work with..... and the new thought "struck him that if the central germ must spread, ere "it could do so it must lose its unity: without division "there could be no life. He altered his symbol: instead "of the central spot he now drew two."—*Alabaster*. See *Doctrine of the Ch'i*.

YO-CHOU: 岳州. A Treaty Port in Hunan.

YÔJANA. A measure of distance, said to be either four or eight *goshalas*, a goshala being the distance at which the bellowing of a bull can be heard, or nearly two miles.

Such space as man may stride with lungs once filled,
Whereof a gow is forty, four times that
A yôjana.

> Arnold's *Light of Asia.*

YOKOHAMA : 橫濱. A port in Japan.

YONI :? 龍門. See *Linga.*

YOROSHII : 宜. Can do; good; O. K. etc. Much used by foreigners in Japan.

YOSHIWARA : formerly 葭 原 rush-ground, from the number of rushes growing there, now 吉 原 the abode of joy. A large enclosure at Tokio, consisting of 2 square *chō* of land, where may be seen

> Famæ non nimium bonæ puellæ
> Quales in mediâ sedent Suburâ.

It is similar to the πορνεῖα of the Greeks, established by Solon, and was first opened in A.D. 1626 with the consent of the Government, the idea being to remove a necessary evil so far as possible from the public eye. The Yoshiwara is also known as 不夜城 the Nightless City, and contains about 3,000 women. See *Hadaka-odori* and *Jon-nuké.*

YOURT. A Mongol tent or encampment.

YÜ, THE GREAT : 大禹. A semi-mythological hero and Emperor who flourished twenty-three centuries before Christ, and drained the empire from a great flood, which has been identified by some with the Biblical Deluge. See *Tablet of Yü.*

YÜAN DYNASTY : 元 朝—original dynasty. Founded by the Mongol conqueror Kublai Khan *(q.v.)* A.D. 1280; ended 1368.

YÜAN-MING-YÜAN : 圓明園—round bright garden. Formerly the summer residence of the Emperors of China, lying about 9 miles from Peking. Destroyed by the Allied Forces in 1860, out of revenge for the ill-treatment of a number of European prisoners captured by the Chinese. We need make no apology for introducing here the following clever verses, written by Mr. E. C. Baber in imitation of W. S. Gilbert's celebrated ballad "Brave Alum Bey."[1] Flat and unintelligible to a new arrival, these lines are, to an older resident in the Far East, full of exquisitely turned burlesque; and they constitute, moreover, an apt illustration of Anglo-Oriental terms in general.

> In Yuen-ming-yuen, all gaily arrayed
> In malachite kirtles and slippers of jade,
> 'Neath the wide-spreading tea-tree, fair damsels are seen
> All singing to Joss on the soft candareen.
>
> But fairer by far was the small-footed maid
> Who sat by my side in the sandal-wood shade,
> A-sipping the vintage of sparkling Lychee,
> And warbling the songs of the poet Maskee.
>
> Oh fair are the flowers in her tresses that glow,
> The sweet-scented cumshaw, the blue pummelow,
> And dearest I thought her of maids in Pekin,
> As from the pagoda she bade me chin-chin.
>
> One eve, in the twilight, to sing she began,
> As I touched the light notes of a jewelled sampan,
> While her own jetty finger-nails, taper and long,
> Swept softly the chords of a tremulous gong.
>
> She sang how "a princess of fair Pechelee
> "Was carried away by the cruel Sycee,
> "And married by force to that tyrant accurst,
> "That Portuguese caitiff, Pyjamah the First.
>
> "Tho' her eyes were more bright than the yaconin's glow,
> "And whiter than bucksheesh her bosom of snow,
> "Yet alas for the maid! she is captive, and now
> "Lies caged in thy fortress, detested Macao.

---

1   "Each morning he went to his garden to cull
>   "A branch of zenana or sprig of bul-bul,
>   "And offered the bouquet, in exquisite bloom,
>   "To Bucksheesh, the daughter of Rahat Lakoum."

"But she muffled her face in her sohotzu's fold,
"And the gaoler she bribed with a tao-t'ai of gold,
"And away she is fled from the traitor's hareem,
"Tho' the punkahs may flash, and the compradores gleam."

Thus she ceased;—and a bumper of opium we took,
And we smoked the ginseng from a coral chibouque,
And we daintily supped upon birds' nests and snails,
And catties, and maces, and piculs, and taels.

Then we slew a joss-pigeon in honour of Fo,
And in praise of Fêng-shui we made a kotow;
And soon the most beautiful girl in Pekin
Fell asleep in the arms of her own mandarin.

YULOH, TO. To scull a boat with an oar at the stern. From the Shanghai pronunciation of 搖 *yao* to work 魯 *lu* an oar. Hence the Shanghai sampan or passenger-boat is often called a *yuloh*.

YUNG CHÊNG: 雍正—concord and rectitude. The style of reign adopted by the third Emperor of the present dynasty, 1723—1736.

YÜNNAN: 雲南—south of the clouds. One of the Eighteen Provinces, only recently recovered from the Panthays *(q.v.)*. Capital city Yünnan Fu 雲南府. Old name 滇 *Tien*. Fogs hang like a permanent dividing-line upon the verge of the Ssŭch'uan highlands; and these misty clouds give the name to the southern province beyond,—Yünnan.

YÜNNAN OUTRAGE, THE. The murder of Mr. Margary at Manwyne, a small town on the extreme south-west frontier of China. Mr. Margary had been deputed to meet an expedition sent by the Government of India to explore a new trade-route into China viâ Burmah, and had already made a splendidly successful journey from Hankow on the Yang-tsze right across to Burmah, where he actually joined the expedition; but volunteering to proceed ahead in order to ascertain the truth of some unfavourable rumours, he was set upon and murdered in

February 1875. The instigators and perpetrators of this deed escaped detection.

ZAYTON *or* ZAITUN *or* TAITUN. Col. Yule makes this city the modern Chinchew Fu 泉 州 府 near Amoy, and suggests that from it is derived our word *satin* (which has also been derived from 絲 緞 *ssŭ tuan* silks and satins): but Mr. G. Phillips maintains that it should rather be identified with Chang-chou Fu 漳 州 府.

ZEALANDIA, FORT. A stronghold on the S. E. coast of Formosa, 2$\frac{1}{2}$ miles from the capital city, formerly known as T'aiwan Fu. Was built by the Dutch in 1630, before their final expulsion by Koxinga *(q.v.)*. See *Dutch Forts*.

ZEHOL. See *Jehol*.

ZEN. The miniature Japanese dining-table, supplied to each person at meals.

ZENDAVESTA. The Sacred Book of Zoroastrianism or the ancient religion of the Parsees. From *zend* or *zand* Commentary and *avesta* the Law,—the Law and the Commentary.

ZENGHIS. See *Genghis*.

ZICAWEI. See *Sicawei*.